TRT
Turkish Radio-Television Corporation

Stranger in Own Home

Stories of Audience

Participating in the Short Story Competition 2006

TSR
VOICE OF TURKEY

TRT
TÜRKİYE RADYO ve TELEVİZYON KURUMU

STRANGER IN OWN HOME, TRT Publications, 2008
First Edition, 2008

Produced by:
TRT Voice of Turkey Radio

Coordinated by:
Pınar Şenel

Translated by:
Üstün Bilgen Reinart
Ahmet Antmen

Edited by:
Aslı S.Gündoğar

Nikbinlik Translation Office
www.nikbinliktercume.com

Format:
Gülümser Yalçınkaya

Cover Design:
Ayhan Bilasa

Edition:
Published in Ofset Facilities,
General Secretariat of TRT
Printing and Publishing Directorate

ISBN: 978-975-7655-83-1

TRT
Department of Foreign Broadcast Voice of Turkey Radio
06109 Or-An Ankara/Türkiye
Tel: (+90.312) 490 98 20 – 490 98 06 – 490 98 08
Fax: (+90.312) 490 98 45
http://www.trt.net.tr
e-mail: tsr.oyku@trt.net.tr

I greet all of you warmly from the Voice of Turkey Radio, which has allowed our voices to be heard across the world for seventy years - since 1937 when continuous broadcasts started.

The Voice of Turkey Radio, which operates within the structure of the Turkish Radio and Television Organization, the public broadcaster of our country, addresses Turkish citizens across the world with its broadcasts in Turkish, and gives information about Turkey to the whole world, with its broadcasts in foreign languages. Today, thanks to our radio that broadcasts in 29 languages including English, French, German, Spanish, Italian, Bosnian, Bulgarian Romanian, Macedonian, Greek, Serbian, Albanian, Hungarian, Russian, in the languages of the Kirghiz, Uzbek, Turkmen, Tatar, Cossack and Georgians, and in Urdu, Russian, Chinese, Arabic, Persian and in Azeri Turkish, and that are accessible not only on shortwave radio but also on the Internet, the world public has a chance to know our country a little better.

The Voice of Turkey Radio that has provided a second family to our citizens who have migrated to other countries since 1960, when the first agreements on migrant labour were signed. The Voice of Turkey Radio helps keep the ties with the Motherland, with news from the Motherland, and with cultural programs that reflect our common values. The Turkish Radio and Television Organization continues to be the most reliable source on the correct use of the Turkish language, for our citizens who are away from their country. The book you hold in your hands, which is made up of the winners of a story-writing contest, reflects this understanding.

The purpose of this contest was to provide a new opportunity to our citizens away from home, to express themselves in their mother tongue. We wanted to inspire them to literary production, and to support effective and accurate use of the Turkish language. When we evaluate the feedback we have received from our listeners and when we consider the strong participation - 118 contestants and 173 stories from 18 countries, we are deeply fulfilled to realize that we have attained our goal. I thank all of our colleagues who have contributed to this work, and everyone who has supported this contest that has allowed many young people who were born outside Turkey and are growing up in foreign countries, to know their mother tongue better.

I take this opportunity to express the hope that the Voice of Turkey Radio that aims to serve in the best way to its listeners across the world, and that celebrates its 70th anniversary in this service, will yet grow for many years, together with you, its listeners and supporters. I thank you, and once again, offer you my deepest regards and warm greetings.

İbrahim Şahin
General Director

Settled into Strangeness in Their Own Lives

Our initiative was a gentle nudge to those who want to use literature to reflect upon life's experiences. We were not expecting it to receive such attention; but the waves generated by the stone we threw into the water, from one bank of a river grew and grew to ever-larger circles.

One of our starting points in organizing a story context was to offer Turkish immigrants who were living in various countries by using a foreign language in their daily lives, an occasion to think and write in Turkish. The expressive possibilities of a story might have found and revealed a striking image, a forgotten reason and a consequence noticed too late, from the depths of the waves of daily lives. And that is what happened: in these texts, we found expressions of the immigrant experience that are not easily encountered in interviews, news and research.

For many immigrants, this was the first stirring of a desire to write a structured text. Many, who may have had wished to write stories but lacked the courage, tried their hands at writing for the first time. Some were already writing – the contest provided them with the opportunity to produce new work. Even though some of the texts remained outside the story genre, all of them represented the result of a wish to think more deeply.

Knowing that the writers were immigrants, we were expecting the majority of the stories to be inspired by the experience of migration. Actually, even though no subject matter had been suggested, half of our participants wrote on finding themselves caught between two countries and two identities. Thus, we were able to put together a collection of texts on the immigrant experience – one of our starting points. The book you are about to read reflects this.

All of the participating stories that received the writers' permission for publication were included in the Turkish version of our book. However, the selection that makes up the English and German versions is made up of the winners and those written around the theme of immigration. We consider the publication of immigration stories written by Turkish immigrants in these two major languages important because we hope that these texts, many of which are based on first-hand experience, will lead to insights into the problems of Turkish immigrants who live in Western Europe.

The stories that were considered worthy or mention or encouragement by the selection jury were not ordered according to merit. Similarly, in this book, the order in which the stories appear is not in any way related to the jury's judgment of the text's merit. We attempted to bring together stories on related themes, or stories that seemed to draw their material from similar experiences. You will note, as you read along, that our book is made up of several wholes that contain many parts. When taken all together, what emerges is almost a single, large text.

We chose to remain faithful to the writers' own descriptions of their backgrounds in the short biographies that we gave at the beginning of each story. In the case of writers whose new works were published or received a prize during the time while this collection was being prepared for publication, we did our best to include the new information.

We met on the bridge of language. We shared the feelings of those who were cold in Canada, sad in Holland, longed for home in Germany. We found people at crucial breaking points of their lives flowing in cities that are unknown to us. When we lifted our eyes, we found ourselves in those stories. We also became settled but foreign in our own lives.

Literature is meant to do that, is it not?

With love, respect and friendship for all whose labour meets with knowledge and with art for the sake of a better world.

Pınar Şenel
Producer

CONTENTS

Appendices Regarding Awards

First Prize

Türkay Yalnız / Holland

Born in Silifke, İçel in 1968. Before deciding on writing as an occupation, he graduated from university and carried out research on physiology. At the moment, while he lives in Tilburg, writes and works on "Hand in Hand for Turkish", he tries not to neglect playing with Doğa, and reading books to him.

Preface to Father's Occupation

The story that you are about to read was sent along with another piece, to the first of the competitions that we, the publication committee of the magazine titled *Hollanda'da Türkçe* ***YAZIN*** *(Turkish Writing in The Netherlands),* have organized for the third time this year to enhance a sense of appreciation for literature in our people living in this country, and to encourage them to discover their own talents in writing stories. But since we could find no information about the writer except for the pseudonym "Unknown Writer" on an envelope, and since it appeared that it was written with help from a professional, it is first one of the two texts to which we were unable to award a prize.

While he was busy working on this first story which he began to write with the encouragement of a novelist he had met, and which he entitled *Baba Mesleği -Father's Occupation-,* he also wrote down the strange dreams that woke him up at night and urged him to write, under the title Sonsuz *Hikâyeler Diyarı'ndan -From The Land of Endless Stories.* We suspect he had them revised by his novelist friend from Ankara, and he sent it to our competition, two days before the deadline. Five dark but gleaming and colourful dreams resembling each other were presented in seventeen pages including various quotes under the title Winter, Spring, Summer, Autumn and Winter again. From the excerpt the writer had placed at the end, we gathered that he believed his texts were not written in the story form. Although we as the members of the jury did not consider the texts "stories," we found them "worthy of mention," but were unable to announce this because of the reasons given above.

The texts betrayed some obvious inexperience, however the magic finishing touch of a skilled hand was evident in both works. Because of this, throughout the month of reading and evaluating the entries, and even on the night when we gave out the prizes, we kept casting glances at each other as if to ask: "Are you the one playing that trick on us?"

Until then, we had thought that we knew everyone here whose hands might hold a pencil to write anything in Turkish, let alone someone who had published three novels. Yet now we had an "Unknown Writer," who had participated in our competition with two stories consisting of twenty- four pages together. He was encouraged to read and to write fiction by a novelist from Ankara who was working on his fourth novel.

Despite all our efforts and research, we have not been able to find any clues as to the identities of either the novelist or the *"Unknown Writer,"* or the key person who might have led us to those two writers: Sufi to whom *From The Land of Endless Stories* was dedicated.

In the two years that passed since then, no one came forward upon reading the stories we published in the column of our magazine called "From an Unknown Writer" to say, "I am that Unknown Writer," or "I know the novelist who encouraged that writer!" It was as if neither of those writers had ever existed.

Just like stories and dreams. They existed, yet they did not exist...

At the last meeting of our publication committee, in the interest of solving the puzzle, we decided to send the story entitled *Father's Occupation* and the work entitled *From The Land of Endless Stories* by the unknown writer –unfortunately, we had to take out the Spring and Fall sections due to space restrictions– to the story competition launched by the Radio Voice of Turkey.

We were hoping that the prospect of a magnificent holiday in Turkey with his wife and child would incite the mystery writer to come out.

We now leave you with his first story, *Father's Occupation.*

Father's Occupation

It would never have crossed my mind that one day I would sit down to write a story. Well, actually, it would not have crossed anyone's mind that someone like me whose last visit to a library without the coaxing of anyone, with his own free will, took place only in seventh grade; who borrowed a book but who threw it aside before reading even half of it, and paid fines equal to the price of the book - and equal to his weekly allowance - after having received notice from the library that it was six months overdue; someone who doesn't even remember the title of the last children's book that he read many years ago, and who has, thanks to his friends humouring him because he was larger in size than all of them, and because he was the one who selected the class team, reduced his involvement with libraries to zero until the end of his school years, in the name of never having to pay such a "hefty" fine again, someone who could establish no relationship with any type of book, fictional or otherwise, what with games, classes, puberty, girls, exams, internship, finding a job, being in love, marriage, having a child -would ever sit down to write a story. Not only that, but also that he would enter his story in a competition...

Seeing myself holding a pen -not to fill out a form, to pay bills or to write down a phone number but to write a story that's on my mind, instead of minding my own business, instead of finding comfort in the predictable swings of a pendulum while I travel from home to work and from work back to home as I've been wont to do, takes me by surprise. Watching her husband of seven years at the guest room table, aroused and awake, buried in books as though he were on the trail of a secret instead of settling on an armchair to watch TV after dinner and a brief wrestling session with his two-year-old son, takes my wife by surprise.

I'm not even sure if I want to be the narrator of this story that I try to write after my wife has gone to bed, because I don't want her to catch me pouring my heart out fervently on the sheets before me only to suspect that I might be writing to a secret lover.

This uncertainty and surprise belong to someone who suddenly finds himself writing a section from the life of a novelist with three published novels, something that would not be attempted by the novelist himself; someone who has an ordinary life story with an ordinary introduction, familiar development and unclear ending, and does not have a story, to tell even sketchily, from which a single lesson can be drawn.

The strange thing is that although it amazes me to find myself scribbling on sheets of paper with a ball point pen, I don't experience myself as someone who writes a story for the first time as the lines proliferate. I do not know whether this is because I have been buried in story books and novels for months, or because the story I'm going to tell here is based on lived experience with a clear beginning and ending.

I could explain the reasons of my uncertainty and surprise above. What about this inexplicable carefree attitude that I have? Is the underlying cause of this the excessive encouragement I had received from the Novelist to write down his interesting story and his promise that he would personally correct the sentences that I knew I would mess up during the process of narration?

Ever since I let him know my final decision, all I think about are the details of the story, which I keep noting here and there in order not to forget. I jot down those details, not only on the sheets of paper that I take out as soon as everyone goes to bed at nights, but also on the margins of pamphlets, torn pieces of envelopes, cigarette packages, and even on the reverse side of bills at the store, as soon as the customers leave. From time to time, I get strange looks, but still, I can't stop. I keep writing things down.

Through the nights of the voyage that I've set out on to tell that story, I can't avoid writing down the strange, dark and beautiful dreams that wake me up frequently from my restless sleep in my bedroom when I don't fall asleep on the guest room couch. I tiptoe quietly into the bathroom, and perch on the toilet cover, I note down as many details as I can remember.

I encountered the person who dragged me into this solitary adventure for two, no matter that involves two people, on a train, about seven months ago. It was in a second class compartment where I rushed in at the last moment, just before the rain started to pour, looking for a seat. With an apologetic smile, he removed his briefcase from the seat to make space for me.

When I settled down on the seat beside him, and the train moved, he returned to the task that was occupying him, which had been interrupted with my arrival. He was reading from a book, and taking notes in a pad-something, I later learned, he did during every trip.

When I noticed his book was in Turkish, I decided to lay aside the concern over whether I would be disturbing him and I started to chat.

He was from Ankara, but he had been living here for a long time. He was writing novels in Turkish. He was on his way to a read excerpts from his third novel which was published last year in a "Meet the Reader" event at a public library of a small town, quite far from his home.

This was the first time I was meeting a published author, especially one who wrote in Turkish. My curiosity had overcome my usual morning lethargy. How does a person become a novelist? Can a novelist earn enough to live on, especially if he is writing in his mother tongue in a foreign country?

When he realized my excitement and curiosity and put away his book and his note pad in his briefcase with his warm smile, the first drops of rain began to slide down the windowpanes.

He had published his novels in Turkey, but thanks to a Turkish bookstore owner here, now his novels were a vailable at the Turkish section of libraries in this country. His first novel was being translated to be published and sold at all the bookstores here next year.

"I learned how to write novels, all by myself, like a blind man deprived even of the luxury of a seeing-eye dog," he said. "By reading a great deal, and by taking refuge in writing patiently whenever the wear and tear of life threatened to pull me down. Don't for a moment think that I intend to offend you, but I do know the ordinary worries of ordinary people, because I live with those worries too. What I do is to put make up on life's face. To dress it up when it might look its ugliest. To lend sparkles and ornaments on even the dullest and plainest of lives. To pour water on a stale life and slide it into the oven to freshen it up so that it will warm up and gain flavour like a hot, fresh loaf of stone cooked bread.

You make a certain face when I say "a nut made of steel", or let us say "a finger someone has cut off with its ring to throw at a lover" right? Every morning, when I think about leaving home to sell my soul for money by accepting other people's work as though they were my own, I feel that very same thing that you feel when you make that face.

We are alike, you and I. Really, both of us are condemned to a routine; I, in front of my computer screen, and you behind a counter, we are both a waiting the death that will awaken us at the end of this particular dream we call life."

It was impossible not to be affected by his words, but I was not really convinced that you could write a novel by just reading and writing. "Was there really no one who mentored you?"

He answered my question smiling like a high school student who was caught cheating by an optimistic teacher who believes that students can learn even while preparing to cheat. "I said I learned it all by myself, but my occupation is really one that was handed down to me from my father."

"What do you mean? Is your father a novelist as well?"

The rain that was falling drop by drop just a little while ago, was now beating the window panes.

"No, he never had the patience to become a novelist. Or, perhaps when he had patience, he didn't have the time or the circumstances to write, and when he had time and appropriate circumstances, he did not have the patience. Still, he couldn't live without saying the beautiful words that gathered at the tip of his tongue or without writing those words down if he liked them. I know he used to write long letters to his friends, but I don't remember him toiling at a story.

He was a man of soul. A city poet who loved his city, someone who immortalized his love in rhyming stanzas. When he saw beauty, when his feelings or his muse tempted him, he would grab pen and paper and write down the lines that came to his mind. When he finished his poem, he would seat whomever he found around except my mother, and he would recite his stanzas and expect comments and criticism.

If I happened to be the one he found at home, I used to find an excuse such as school work to run away before the criticism session started. My older brother, who was said to be the one who most resembled him physically, used to be the one subjected most frequently to those criticism sessions because he was generally on the same wavelength with my father.

As for my two younger sisters who hung around together like Siamese twins, they would heap praise on my father in hopes of receiving a hefty allowance whenever they were called to one of these poetry sessions when they were in the middle of messing around with us, or helping my mother out in the kitchen. Afterwards, they would immediately go back to messing around with us or helping my mother out in the kitchen.

My mother who had no interest in literature or in books, and who regretted the money "wasted" on newspapers, did not hide her boredom with my father's poems, which she had heard sufficiently before we were born. Knowing this, my father did not even attempt to approach her with his poems.

Friends who had heard my father's poems several times and knew his talent for oratory used to invite him to weddings so that he might impart valuable wisdom to the newly-wed couple and give them the secrets of a happy life in their new home. At these weddings, just when the guests would begin to let loose and enjoy themselves, the orchestra was asked to stop the music suddenly, and my father would be invited to the podium and handed a microphone.

Even if the wedding's hosts had not made a request to my father in advance, he would gently take out the text of his speech from his pocket, under the guests' puzzled looks -who is this guy?- and he would read the lines full of hope and good wishes, written for that special day, disregarding the guests' impatient attitude. His speeches all resembled each other because the purpose was always the same.

As his speech dragged on, the volume of the hum, already a part of the whole scene from the very beginning, would begin to increase to include grumblings here and there, as the people who still wanted to dance the night away, those sluggish ones who were never asked to dance and even the hosts who had already started chatting with their guests found it impossible to hide their boredom.

Only the bride and the groom seated at a table covered with white cloth would listen attentively and patiently to the entire speech filled with lots of advice, sipping their drinks and whispering to each other from time to time.

Ever since my father had discovered that the microphone would be offered to him at these weddings, he had made it a habit to recite his poems (epithalamiums) especially written for these ceremonies, like he did with all of his own poetic works. When he folded his text and put it back into his pocket, the bored guests would let out a sigh of relief, "thank goodness, we'll return to enjoy ourselves," but their pleasure would be interrupted when instead of handing the microphone back, my father would carry on with an epithalamium from memory.

From time to time, there were smart hosts who timed my father's appearance well. When that happened, everyone except children would listen carefully to the eloquent speech and epithalamiums of the orator, and applaud his praises of life and happiness. The bride and groom would then be so touched that my father would be asked to recite another poem suitable to the occasion. At such moments, my father would feel fulfilled and joyous, so much so that he might even attempt something outside his habits and dance.

Of course, not all friends invited him with similar intentions. Some invited him only as an ordinary guest. When that happened, my father would sit with his prepared text folded in his pocket, and an epithalamium including the names of the bride and groom on his mind, awaiting the interruption of the music, but that moment never came. Even when the whole thing stopped for cutting of the cake and the presentation of the gifts, belly dancing or round dancing would follow and as he would still sit in anticipation, the guests would begin to take leave, and we would have to return home like everybody else. On the way home, a heavy silence would reign in the car. Only my sisters who fell asleep in the car, only to wake up the next day with the help of our nudges, would be oblivious to this kind of heavy silence, in the same way that they were oblivious to the rare moments of joy that we all felt when my father's poems were greeted with enthusiasm.

The next morning, that heavy silence would be broken. For days to come, my father would talk about the wedding where he was not invited to the microphone.

He would go on and on, reproaching himself, feeling slighted, and venting his frustration of the wedding hosts on my mother. The tranquility and cheerfulness of our home life would be replaced with mayhem.

If my mother sensed in advance that my dad would not be invited to the microphone at a wedding, she would warn him: Look, if they don't invite you to the microphone, don't get mad. This friend was at the wedding of so and so, and while you recited your speech, he had not stopped chatting.'

We, the children, were witnesses of my mother's warning. Unfortunately, we also knew that such a warning was the first sign of an approaching storm, which was visible by the dark clouds on my mother's face throughout the wedding where we sat quietly, knowing that my father had already folded two white sheets filled with words and placed it in his pocket before leaving home.

Four years before my father's retirement, on a warm summer evening, while I was placing the tray of watermelon my mother had sliced in the kitchen and asked me to take outside on the table of our balcony, I heard my father say to my brother, 'Do you know what I'll do with my retirement fund?'

As my brother pretended to find an answer to his question, he continued: 'I will collect and publish all my poems in one volume, or maybe in two.'

My father departed from this world before he could collect his poems in a volume. Suddenly. During the time after that summer evening, when we frequently heard him repeat his intention of publishing his poems, neither he nor we could have imagined that he would die so suddenly, without fulfilling his dream.

My father was a man of soul. Perhaps his own literature training was limited to his high school years, just like mine, and perhaps he too had discovered the value of stories and poems after encountering the harsh face of life.

He was a man of dreams, but not unrealistic enough to quit his job at the municipal government in hopes of an income from five hundred copies of poetry books that might not even sell.

Sometimes I ask myself: 'Would he have done it if it were not for us?' But knowing his impatience, and his inherited assumption that a regular job as a civil servant represented security in a world where a regular income was necessary, I conclude that he would not have...

Today, I am the one who has those sheets of poems, most of which are not even typewritten, but are manuscripts of tidy handwriting held together with a ribbon, that he used to keep so carefully. I'm hoping to publish those poems as a volume, together with the letters and texts left at my brothers' when I have enough means to do so. I hope that my father's soul may thus rest in peace.

I'm also considering using some of his stanzas as epigrams (with his own pseudonym) for the beginning of the chapters in some of the novels that I'll write in future. Of course when the time comes..."

I was so absorbed with listening to him, that I don't remember at all when the rain stopped and the bright blue of the sky emerged.

"Did you ever write about your father?"

His answer to this question was what drew me to read feverishly, and to get lost in books instead of settling in an armchair before the TV to watch a film until I would fall asleep from fatigue, each evening.

"How about if you were to write about him?" he asked. "Novels might be challenging, but almost everyone who puts a little effort into the task can write a story. Besides, I heard from a writer friend that next year, the Turks here will organize story competitions, just like the Moroccans."

He had not even asked me what I did for a living. Yet, he thought I was capable of writing a story!

When I told him that I would be getting off the train soon, he wrote down his telephone number on a sheet of paper that he tore off a small pad, and asked me to call him when my mind was made up.

"Skill is required not for the telling of one's own story," he said, as he handed me the piece of paper, "but especially for the telling of the untold, and sometimes imaginary stories of others, as if they were actually lived and as if they were one's own."

As I headed to the store where I worked, he would return to his book and his note-pad, and continue his voyage to the town where he was expected for a reading.

That day, when I walked out of the train station, I realized for the first time that I was looking with new eyes at the cold, wet heap of bicycles, waiting silently and patiently for their owners on the square to the left, and the skeletal remains of the corpses of a few abandoned bicycles left behind by city vultures at their usual abode of railings on the iron bridge across the river further down.

What he predicted turned out to be true. A literary magazine named *Hollanda'da Türkçe* ***YAZIN,*** which I began to notice at the newsstand and buy about three weeks after our meeting, announced a writing contest in its January edition. I was surprised at its long life of two and a half years of publishing. There were to be no restrictions on subject, length or numbers of entries. The only condition was that the stories be written in Turkish. The deadline was March 21.

Filled with excitement, I telephoned him during the lunch break, just as I had done after reading his first novel with admiration, which I had found in the Books in Turkish section of the public library where I had become a member again, after many years.

He shared my excitement with the same warmth that he had expressed during our first meeting on the train, and at my previous phone call.

He said he would have no objection to my telling his story, without giving his name, and certainly no objection to my entering the story into a contest, after completing it. He even offered to look it over to make some corrections.

He had completed research, and was about to start writing his fourth novel. While writing, he preferred emails or faxes to telephone calls as tools of communication. At that time, I had no Internet at home, and I did not like communicating by fax. We decided to communicate by old fashioned mail.

His response to the first manuscript section that I sent to him expressed his surprise and pleasure at discovering how strong my memory was... Of course, the pages which I had filled with black ball point pen scribblings were returned with overflowing corrections and marks in red.

When he returned the second draft I had sent him, he included in the envelop a writing guide, which he said was an extra copy that he owned. "This is a source as important as the dictionary," he had written in the note he had attached to the guide. "The more you use this, the more helpful you'll find it..."

After that, I went through a period when I became so aware of my faults of language that I couldn't even see the story I was writing. During that period, I sent him a letter -without including the fourth draft- in which I said that I would not be able to complete the story.

He wrote back, telling me that he was not surprised at my decision. He added that he often faced a writer's block himself, and he knew that the only solution lay in writing; writing patiently. He ended his letter with this sentence: "How can there ever be a story written perfectly when there is no life that's lived perfectly?"

When he sent back my eleventh draft with his corrections, he had attached a yellow piece of post-it with this note on it: "Good. From now on, I leave you to it. Of course you'll come up with a title as well."

I sat down before the computer, to type out the whole manuscript in its final form, without touching a single comma. Just when I reached the stage when I thought there was nothing more to add, it occurred to me to add the note below, without his knowledge. And then, lacking confidence in my own writing, I sent the story back to him, and asked him to please correct the twelfth draft as well.

He did not turn me down!

The mailman just delivered the corrected manuscript and I typed it out. I also added a great title on top of the first page. I should now get it out of the printer and add a pseudonym.

What should it be? What should it be?

Note to the Reader:

I tried to tell the story of the writer, to the best of my ability. Please don't go assuming that the long sentences are mine, and don't encourage me to write on my own like the writer himself does, because if you could only see the first version of my story, you would be surprised that I even undertook such a project. You might say, "He is a writer, is he not?" Then let him write his own story just as he writes the stories of others. You would find it very strange that someone like me -who cannot even be considered a good reader, let alone a good writer- ever attempted to write a story and enter it in a competition.

I also am one of those who think that everyone should know their limits. Don't be fooled by the fact that I was taken in by the writer's game. I have the same misgivings that you might have.

Alright, a couple of more words, and I'm wrapping up this "Note to the Reader."

One: Do not believe every story you hear or read.

Two: Surely, this story has still some faults-despite all those corrections. However, as the writer once said to me, "How can there ever be a story written perfectly when there is no life that's lived perfectly?"

March, 2004

Second Prize

Şakir Doğan / Germany

He was born in Belbarak village of Hacıbektaş, Nevşehir in 1968. His first story was published by *Demokrat Türkiye (Democratic Turkey)* magazine when he was fourteen years old. He collected some of his poems in the book titled *Karıncaların İntiharı (Suicide of Ants,* 1997, Kora Publishing). His stories were published by *Adam Öykü, Kitap-lık, Eşik Cini* magazines. His novel titled *Yaratıcım ve Ben (My Creator and I)* was published in 2006 by Kora Publishing. He has been living in Berlin since 1980. He is married and has a son.

Begonia

to my mother and the Gladziwa family

The ground floor flat was composed of four rooms. It had five large windows across the street. Curtains weren't drawn and window shutters weren't closed until late at night in the darkness of winter, and even until morning on some days. Not drawing curtains and not closing window shutters at night were the forerunners of Christmas. Some boulevards, avenues and streets of the city were decorated with high voltage bulbs. Windows were especially resplendent. As if competing with each other, everybody bedecked their windows with Christmas trees, pictures of Santa Claus, and stars made of variegated bright papers. They also fixed variegated small bulbs onto edges of windows.

In our street, Ms. Else was the one who most beautifully bedecked windows. She acted simply and didn't lumber up like some others. She elaborately considered where to put each single object. She gently covered branches of some flowers on window frames with white cotton. It seemed like a scene where Santa Claus was leaving snow-covered forest with Reindeers riding the coaster. And there were children waiting for gifts...

Berlin was again resplendent; there were only two days before the Christmas. While walking in front of the ground floor flat, I stopped next to the chestnut tree on the pavement. I lighted up a cigarette. I was fiddling around just like waiting for somebody, but in fact I focused on the window. Tulle curtains got dirty, glasses got dusty, and the room was illuminated by a dead light. My heart was torn out. And I said myself that "If Ms. Else were here now, everything would be different."

We had recently moved to the apartment building and had no relation with neighbors. Residents of apartment building laid on entertainment in the court each year for the Christmas. They also dropped an invitation card in our postbox that year. None of our family members went to the entertainment, and curtains of windows overlooking the court were drawn rigidly. We heard voices, laughs, and noises of the people outside. Momentarily, the door-bell was rung. My father passed by the door and entered the kitchen. My six-year old brother opened the door. My mother could do nothing other than smiling the comer. She didn't know German well, so I helped her.

The comer was an almost fifty-year old woman who was slimline and who had short, blonde hair. Her blue eyes were sparkling. She was smiling.

"Won't you come outside?"

"No, my family doesn't want to come."

"Then," said her "you must come with me." Her voice is plausible.

I obtained permission from my father, and went out with her happily. As soon as I entered the court, everybody glanced at me curiously. I got excited, and tried to smile at people glancing at me.

Elsa Gladziwa introduced me to her husband Günter and her son Wolfgang. A boy and a maid were standing next to Wolfgang. "They are my grand children," said Ms. Elsa who touched their hair. She showed the dog lying on the ground lazily. It was massy and had long ears. "And this is Jozef," said her. Jozef raised its head and yawned as if it had understood that she was talking about it. Wolfgang was sitting in a bent double manner on the two-wheeled chair. His head and body declined leftward a little bit, and his arms were almost immovable. I failed to hide my grief. I asked what had happened. His sickness was osteoporosis. Ms. Else sadly told me that her son was declining daily and slowly.

It was impossible to decide what to tell and how to behave in such a condition. I also became entangled for a while. Then, I smiled and looked at her son who was almost thirty years old. He also smiled at me heartily.

"What would you like to drink?" said Ms. Else. And then she took a brief look at me.

"How old are you?"

"Sixteen."

"Then I don't need to address you formally. What do you like to drink?"

That night, I got acquainted with Ms. Else, our next-door neighbor. She asked questions and dealt at length about my mother. After returning to home, I talked about Pantomime and my speech with Ms. Else. I would have never forgotten her and the Gladziwa family after that night.

While I was going to school every morning, they took Wolfgang away to his business place. He was still an officer in municipality, his old business place. He was working by means of an electronic device fixed to his arms. Ms. Else doted on him. She dressed her son with a suit every morning. His shirts were ironed and immaculate. She always chose the necktie most suitable to his clothing. And Wolfgang's perfume... It engrossed whole attention of some women passing across the street. They couldn't believe that such a nice perfume was coming from a disabled man. They continued walking curiously as if looking for the real owner of that perfume.

Ms. Else brought small gifts to us at Easter and Christmas. She either knocked our door or left chocolate in front of it at least once in a month. My younger brother was the one who got pleased most with that. My father didn't take chocolate. She also considered my mother and presented her flowerpots as gift. Fairly pretty flowerpots... She took a glance at flowers while passing by the window. My mother took excellent care of them, but flowers faded in utmost two weeks. Ms. Else really saddened when she saw faded flowers. When I encountered with her, she asked me "Why does your mother let flowers fade?" My mother also loved flowers very much. She caressed their leaves and even talked with them. For some reason or other, flowers of Ms. Else faded. My mother smiled ashamedly whenever she came across with Ms. Else.

When I said that "Your flowers faded because my mother talks with them in Turkish," she smiled pleasantly.

It was a Saturday morning in springtime. Somebody rang the bell. I got hardly surprised when I saw Ms. Else. She was the one who most often knocked at our door. She had a flowerpot and a chocolate palette in her hand. She smilingly presented them. She said "Car is waiting for me, so I must go," and moved away so rapidly that I couldn't even thank her for gifts. The hotter the weather was, the more cheerful they became. Either at Friday nights or in Saturday mornings, they departed from the apartment building and they spent their weekends in their summerhouse; and they brought damson plum, apple, pear, strawberry in accordance with seasonal conditions.

It was a begonia with large flowers. Its pale red flowers were almost pink. The plant had lots of buds. She wrote characteristic of flower and how to take care of it on a paper. I translated that into Turkish and told to my mother one by one. My mother abided what was written. Despite this, all flowers faded and buds were shed, however begonia was still alive.

Jozef passed away. Its death was regretfully notified to us by Ms. Else. Her grand children still couldn't believe in its death. In their view it was impossible to set the same value on another dog. They had taken it when it was too young. They liked him as if it had been an individual of Gladziwa family. But, said she, it had died. She told these in the corridor at one sweep.

I left my family and moved to another street. I visited them at least once in a week. When I went to visit them, my mother told me what she had seen and heard. "Her grand children left home. I stared them through the window while they were going. They had grown up in less than no time." One of them was twenty and the other one was eighteen years old. Ms. Else had felt so sad and had cried because of their departure. She had said that "Our house become very still after their departure. We are only three people in such a large house. We got used to absence of Jozef; but their departure really depressed us. They have their own rooms, yet they would certainly leave us one day. They promised to visit us frequently." Then she had asked about me. She asked how I was and whether I could support myself... "Your sibling told these to me one by one," said my mother. She was very sad because she saw through window that Ms. Else was slimming down day by day.

It was early March. I was in my mother's house. When I got into the house, I came across with an amazing silence. My sibling was at university. My father hadn't come to home for one week. My mother didn't know where he was and she got neither worried nor curious about him. She was still and dispirited. "Don't you eat something?" asked she. She was watering flowers and she was unhappy. I told that I had snacked at office and didn't want to eat anything. I was also affected by that amazing silence. I forbore asking what had happened and waited for my mother to answer.

"Don't you eat something?"

"No mum, I don't."

When my mother was exactly sure that I didn't eat anything, she said "Our neighbor passed away. May she rest in peace." Her voice was plangent. And she cried silently a little later. Her tears were dropping from her lashes to her face slowly.

I knew that my mother had never lied. But I didn't want to believe in that Ms. Else had passed away. I imagined her while smiling sparklingly. Our kind neighbor passed away in her seventies.

"What a kind neighbor she was, she further doted on her son."

My mother felt really depressed about her sick neighbor and considered him. But I wasn't sure whether she thought him or her own future. Leaving my mother in an exhausted and sad condition, I returned to my house.

"And now his father is taking care of his son. He hardly pushes two-wheeled chair. He stops, takes a breath and pushes it again. Ambulance was called twice recently. I wondered whether this was for the father or his son. I couldn't learn this. Sometimes his grand children visit them. The daughter bore a child. The son is a car addict and has a massy dog. Its name is Yesof. Even if they don't come frequently, his grand children visit them from time to time. Her husband Günter is the one who got most depressed by the death of Else..." said my mother. And when she couldn't find any other thing to tell, she started caressing the begonia. Sometimes she looked through window and got lost in thought. She didn't even notice that I went.

Tulle curtains got dirty, glasses got dusty, and the room was illuminated by a dead light. My heart was torn out. And I said myself that "If Ms. Else were here now, everything would be different." The father and his son were sitting side by side at one end of the oval table for six people. Their necks declined. Head of one declined rightward. And head of the other declined leftward together with his shoulder, he seemed as if he fell to the table. One of them was on chair, and the other was on two-wheeled chair. They were absolutely silent. Their dishes were in front of them. They looked at television at times. The first channel was broadcasting The Eighth O'clock News. Father covered the spool near dish by his hand. He raised his right arm slowly up to the intersection point with his body. His arm shook. He put his arm down gently, he plunged his spool into dish rather slowly. He fixed it in dish for a while. He flushed his elbow to the table, he bended his ankle and took spool in his mouth. Without taking his eyes off from television, he chewed slowly and for a long time. He drank a little water. Then, he started feeding Wolfgang, his son, with the same movements. I got extremely distressed. Waiting on the sidewalk and watching them cut me to the heart any more. I also gave up visiting my mother and walked across the street slowly. I couldn't bear listening distresses, complaints, fears, pains of her. My father had moved to his lover's house. My brother had never slept at home for a while. He stayed with his lover every night. "Please, have a talk with him," said my mother. And why didn't I visit her frequently? She was also distressed because of this.

"I couldn't sleep a wink in this empty house. I awakened in fear at midnights. That night your brother stayed at home. So, I got very happy. I was sleeping in silence. All of a sudden, I awakened by hearing a siren. I got on my two-wheeled chair and fixed my dead legs on it. I swiftly drove the wheeled-chair, and lifted up window shutters. There were two ambulances waiting in the street. Their lamps were flashing. I awakened your brother. I opened the door. There were some people standing in the corridor. I recognized that they were grandchildren of Else. Two men in dark clothes carried away someone within body bag. It was exactly Mr. Günter. I said that, poor man could bear absence of his wife only for one year. Then Wolfgang got out, his neck declined as if it would be broken into two. An attendant of first aid service was pushing his wheeled-chair. You had to see his face. He was full of grief and he was absolutely exhausted. When he saw my two-wheeled chair, he tried to fling all his energy into raising his head. We caught each other's eye. His gaze was sorrowful. I had my eyes full with tears. If only, I said. The son had passed away instead of the father."

My mother stopped talking. She cried silently again. While caressing the begonia in front of her, she was looking at the street.

"My story will also end just as Wolfgang's. I will also go the rest home in the end. Oh God, please rescue me from such an end."

"Mom, you aren't like Wolfgang. You can stand on your own feet."

"No, my dear son, I can't. While trying to take something from the ground on the previous day, I fell down from the wheeled-chair. I was alone. Telephone was far away from me. I tried to creep up to the phone. I failed to carry my heavy body. Even if I had carried my body, the telephone had been put on a very high place. It was impossible for me to reach there. I was helpless. I didn't know what to do. I was afraid of soiling my underclothes. I was woeful and begged the God to grant me death. I couldn't do anything other than waiting for your brother who would possibly visit me for a while in the evening. Nevertheless, I shouted for help as far as I could do. There was nobody in the street. Even if somebody passed through the street, could he/she hear my voice? Window was closed. I looked for a rigid object to break windowpane. There was nothing which I could reach. I was waiting hopelessly; all at once the door was opened. I started crying sobbingly when I saw your brother. He couldn't restraint himself, and he started crying, too. He came to the house as if he had felt that I fell down. When he had been together with his friends, he had felt bored and anxious, and hence he came to the house. Nevertheless, while crying I begged the God to grant me death."

While I couldn't look her in the eye, I said that "Please mom, don't say anything more. We are and will be with you forever."

We had discussed with my brother and decided to put our mother in rest house. My mother probably felt this. While turning her head towards me swiftly, her arm banged to the flower all of a sudden. Begonia fell down. Ceramic flowerpot was broken and its soil scattered to the carpet. My mother looked at the plant which she caused to fall abstractedly and at length.

Third Prize

Buket Düzgen / Austria

She was born in 1970 in Çanakkale. She was graduated from the Guidance and Psychological Counseling Department of Ankara University in 1993. She got married in the same year and moved to Italy because of her husband's job. She has been living in Vienna since 2004, and working as a volunteer at a program that aims to improve the adaptation of Turkish children by strengthening their social skills.

The Thaw

With hesitant steps, I was approaching the house which didn't have any visitors for a while. Did every return to the house where I was born have to be so painful? There was no one who didn't want me there; but no one awaited me eagerly, either.

I wonder if he ever missed me. I never found out.

It is impossible to expect much from someone who is unable to express his feelings.

All I expected was a warm smile, after the "hello" uttered when I entered the house. Each time I looked at him, this is what I thought: "Owning something does not mean that that thing belongs to you; belonging is established when you have ties of feeling." He had probably never felt he belonged with the family he had. He was my father.

With these confused thoughts in my head, I rang the doorbell of our house, which I had left at the age of 18, for study purposes. These days, it took a while before the door was opened. My father could lift his weary body off the armchair in the corner of the living room, only slowly. He finally opened the door. He welcomed me with his usual distant attitude. I could only reply his greeting. Not taking the occasional telephone conversations into account, we had not seen each other for two years. At first glance, the distance between us could cause stress, but in time, one gets used to something that's chronically painful.

I had a small handbag with me. I brought it in. After a short silence, he asked: "How was your trip?"

In fact, I knew that he would ask this question. During the fifteen years since my departure from home, neither the timing nor the mechanical tone of this question had changed. I had developed the habit of answering this routine question, in a routine manner. As usual, we had done our homework.

"Good. But you know that traveling tires me out."

"Then you had better rest for a while." he answered.

He always wanted me to rest because it would rescue him from a challenging situation. Any face-to-face relationship was challenging for him. Seemingly, there was no problem. My father had considered me. But after his suggestion, there was no point in staying with him. We would both silently withdraw to our rooms. Once again, the relationship between us would fail.

In the house where my mother and my father had established two separate lives, I entered my mother's room, which made me feel unbearably sad ever since she died. It was three years now. I can't get used to her absence. It's as if everything in the house still holds traces of my mother's hands. The lavender sachets she put in drawers are all dried up now, but their scent fills her room. I realize even more clearly now, that while she was alive, there was vitality in this house. The photographs that I had sent my parents from distant lands are in frames, smiling back at me. Her favorite was the one where I was holding two ice-cream cones, and where I had scribbled: "I'm licking the second one for you."

It used to be so easy to make my way into my mother's heart. All her life, she tried to create small joys to make up for the closeness she had expected but not found with my father. Every spring, she used to plant pansies in pots on the balcony. When I heard her talking to them, I used to sense that she was trying to forget her loneliness. I wonder if it's because they know that they are not going to experience great joys that makes some people look for small joys... My passion of look beyond the visible has caused me much trouble, but you can't change a person's nature, can you?

My mother had wept for hours, saying "I can't do without you," when we found out that I had won the entrance exams of a university in another city far away from Ankara. Her sadness had broken my heart, but with the arrogance of puberty, I had promised myself that I would never be like her. Even if I loved my children very much, I would not be one of those servile mothers. I would be a career woman, and would stand on my own two feet. How great words they are. It was almost our destiny to be the rebellious daughters of mothers who were martyrs. We thought it would be a big accomplishment to be different from our mothers.

My return to home during vacations would be sufficient to inject vitality into my mother. She used to wait for me out on the balcony. Even before entering the house, I used to feel how her heart would beat. "My daughter," said she while embracing me, and smelled my hair.

When you are loved so unconditionally by one parent, you direct all your efforts for winning affection of your father who hardly demonstrates his affections. Of course, I wasn't aware of that when I was young. Now I remember that when I was eight-years-old, I had bought lemon flower cologne for my father as a gift on a religious holiday. Those days, we always had a bottle reserved for guests. I wanted my father to have his own bottle.

"Happy holidays," I said and gave him the cologne I had bought for him excitedly.

He said, "Thanks. Can't you afford to buy brand name perfumes?"

It was the first disappointment of my childhood which I locked up inside a bottle of lemon flower cologne, and never spoke about it to anyone.

When I saved my allowances to buy him a brand name perfume, I supposed that I could please him. I was wrong. "Do you think I have a bad smell?" he had said. My longings mostly remained unfulfilled.

Once I read in a magazine whose name I forget, that "The sense of security that little girls develop in their relationship with their father leads to success in life." I think that sense of security can only be developed by the attention paid to life decisions. Or, no approval that's lack of affection produces a lasting effect in life.

In my life, I was courageous enough to make hard decisions and to accept their consequences. For example, I decided to leave Ankara, the city where many young people came to study, and to go to Antalya for a degree in tourism. After my decision, I was looking into my father's eyes, waiting for him to ask, "My daughter, did you consider carefully?" Yet he said "It's your decision," with his usual indifferent manner. Yes, it was my decision but I needed to know how much I was loved. I was making the decision to find that out. I assumed that if I were far away, he would feel freer to express the love that he was unable to express when I was close to him.

Poet Can Yücel used to miss his father who traveled a lot while he was a little child so much that he said "My father is the person I love the most in life."

In the same way, I hoped that my father would realize how much he missed me, and finally say "My daughter is the person I love the most in life." How mistaken I was... I was making courageous decisions to get his attention but I was hitting against a blank wall each time.

I must have fallen asleep with these thoughts. When I woke up, I found my father sitting alone in his armchair in the corner of the living room. That big man had lost weight and shrunk. He did not use to have many close friends, even in his youth. I knew only one. "It's the only friend who understands me," my father used to say. I think he knew that it wasn't easy to understand him. When I saw a postcard showing the old walled city of Antalya, I had realized that his friend was living in Antalya. "You have to see this beauty," the friend had written at the back of the post card. Yes, there was someone who understood my father and he lived in Antalya. How strange that the view of the walled city had affected me deeply and turned the direction of my life.

Even though I knew that my father was responsible for his current condition, his extreme loneliness made me sad. It broke my heart that no one was calling on him, no one cared whether he existed or not. Softly, I approached him.

"Were you able to rest?" he asked.

"Yes," I said, while trying to determine what to say him.

Actually, there was a reason for my visit. I wanted to tell him that I would have a child. I didn't want to inform him by telephone, with a few sentences. Was this an effort to emphasize the importance of the child that I would bring to the world? I wonder if I was trying to make him feel his fatherhood, by telling him I was becoming a mother. Suddenly, the words escaped me.

"Dad, I came here to tell you something."

He looked into my eyes with surprise. He knew I couldn't be comfortable when speaking with him. He was rightly surprised that I had started a conversation so abruptly. After a short while, he said,

"Of course. Go ahead and tell me."

"I am going to have a child. I wanted you to know this."

I had rendered this happy information, in the manner of an announcer reading the news. Yet I was so filled with excitement ever since I had found out that a small heart was beating inside me. It was such a desired child. My husband Ricardo and I had waited for this child for five years. On the day when our doctor gave us the good news, we walked through the narrow streets of Rome, to Trevi, the "Fountain of Love". It was the most meaningful place for us, to greet our baby and say to him "Welcome to the world." Because he would be witness of our love.

On the other hand, I was witnessing something else in my father's eyes that had gained a deep meaning since I told him that I was going to become a mother. I wondered if I was imagining this depth in his looks. Had I been affected by all the father-daughter scenes I had watched in movies? But no. He continued looking in the same way, and then he said,

"I'm very happy."

"Really?"

"Of course. I wish your mother could have seen her grand child."

My father who had said nothing about his feelings or longings about my mother, since her death, was now saying he wished she could have seen her grand child.

I could only mutter, "Yes. I also wish she could have seen him."

Could it be that the tight knot that had been made years ago was beginning to come untied with his words?

At that moment when I was at a loss for words, my mobile phone rang. It was Ricardo, my husband who was always beside me at my difficult moments.

"Ricardo," I said.

"Hello my darling. I miss you," he said.

On the phone, he always spoke in this way, no matter how far away from each other we are. His saying "I miss you," was a way of saying he loved me. We had also nurtured the love in our hearts while nurturing our longings.

"You are very close to me Ricardo," I said. "The distance does not matter at all. I miss you too."

Years ago, I undertook the risk of leaving the house where I was born, so as to feel that I was loved. Then I met Ricardo. I understood that love was very close to us - at the distance of a heartbeat.

I was about to graduate from Tourism High School when I met him. I was working at a fair of the school during my last year. He owned a tourism company in Rome and had come to our university from Rome, as a tour operator. Since I could speak Italian, it was my job to look after the Italian guest. While I took him around Antalya, he was telling me about his professional experiences. I was asking him so many questions, with my eagerness to enter that profession soon.

"Tourists should not be made to feel like customers," he said. "You have to make them feel like guests in your country, exactly as you are doing with me now."

Sometimes, my language skills were not enough to express what I wanted. He would surprise me again, and say "What your tongue can't express; can be expressed by your heart... The heart comes before words."

On his last evening, we were sitting at the marina, watching the sea. The sparkling lights on the sea and the heaps of stars in the sky seemed to be talking for us. .

"You are very quiet this evening," he said.

"It's the night that's talking," I said. "Look at the stars."

Suddenly he said, "Yesterday, I fell in love with a girl speaking a foreign language. Remember, I had said the heart comes before words..."

Was the furious beating of my heart a proof of love?

Ricardo returned to his own country, but he had entered my heart. We were talking on the phone frequently. All conversations began with his "I miss you." During one of our talks, he said "Marry with me. Let's miss each other while we are together..." That was when we promised each other that we would never quench that longing.

"Yes," I said without thinking much. On this occasion, I had made a decision for myself. This decision, made with the guidance of my heart, would take me to unknown lands. After a short while, I told my decision to my parents. My mother got saddened to think that I was going even further than before, but she was consoling herself by saying that I had learned love. To my father, he felt as usual, that this was my own decision.

Ricardo came to Ankara to take me away to Rome, the city which is the intersection point of all roads. He was eager to meet my family.

My father said "Welcome" in his usual distant manner. Ricardo was showing me how it was possible to communicate in an unknown language. Communicating with my mother was easy, as usual. This new relationship with my mother was exactly what I had expected. Ricardo never neglected to praise my mother's cooking. I had told him about the sensitive points of Turkish women. He found our way of living close to his own, and immediately understood every indication of love. One evening, while we were drinking tea after a meal, he asked me:

"Do you know that there are many kinds of Italian coffee?"

"Yes, I do. But do you know that the meaning of a coffee shared, is strongest in our country?"

He was surprised. How could he know that the meaning of the coffee that he had been drinking for forty years, was hidden in this land.

Perhaps all stories begin with the house where we were born. When I left that house, I had not imagined that I would travel so far..."

When the day of separation arrived, I, who had never liked traditional ceremonies of farewell, suddenly realized for the first time how important they were... "To see someone off by hoping that they'll return one day... To pour water behind them to wish a smooth journey..."

When I glanced behind for the last time, I saw that my mother was crying and my father was biting his lips. As for me, I had suppressed most of what I wanted to say. "I'll miss you," I had muttered.

What I really wanted to say to my father was: "Perhaps there are no other tomorrows to postpone love. What I needed was only your affection."

I took the hand of the man I loved, to start a new life. I was conditioned to miss someone, as soon as I knew I loved him and understood that I was loved in return.

Missing, longing were my choices any more. My first days in Rome were fairly difficult. I had joined the ranks of those who say "The one who has not lived far away from home, does not know how painful it is..." At daytime, I was working in Ricardo's tourism company, at the Turkey counter, telling foreigners about the country that I was longing for. I was speaking about that country with such joy that people who heard me often decided to visit Turkey at once. It was as if people who sat before me as clients were becoming friends who shared my longings.

In the evening, when I took a glass of well-steeped tea, the tiredness of the day would withdraw from the tips of my toes. But the weariness of my heart was not easy to live with, even though Ricardo kept saying "I'll make you love this place." On Turkish holidays, I wanted to prepare a special dessert, even though I knew that no one would visit us. If I didn't, I was unhappy. Something was missing. It was not easy to give up responses that had grown through a lifetime. That's when I also found out that a classical mode of Turkish music could make me cry.

But there were things I could not understand. My father must have had his reasons for remaining so distant from his family. How I would have loved to be in the place of that old friend of him - the one who had been able to understand him. As you know, sometimes you couldn't understand anything from a film when you were a child, but if you watch the same film years later, you realize that you have a full conception of it. Since you can conceive that old film in a different way, that film gains a new meaning for you.

When, just before Ricardo's phone call, my father said he wished my mother could have seen her grandchild, he seemed so different from the father I knew. Would the rest also come, in spite of many years of our shared past?

I said goodbye to Ricardo and returned to my father.

"I see how happy you are," he said.

"Yes," I said. "I'm happy."

He added: "I have been silent for a long time haven't I?" He said, "Because I could not take responsibility for my life, I chose silence. Perhaps that was my way of using my right to choose."

I couldn't understand anything from those words.

"I would have wanted to build my family myself," he said. "Things would have been different if I had been able to do that..."

"But we were your family," I said.

"We cannot re-live the years that are in the past," he said. "But all stories have a beginning."

He began to tell me his story.

"While I was a young boy, the purpose of my life was to become a star football player. In the 1950's, I was playing in the youth team of

Ankaragücü. My coach told me I was talented, and that if I continued to work hard, I could be transferred to one of major teams. But at home, my father wanted my love for football to remain a passing whim. No one expected a future from football at that time. To chase a ball meant idleness. As for me, I felt such a sense of strength when I played, that the moment filled me with happiness. One day, the coach told me my agreement with the team was cancelled. "What do you mean?" I mumbled. He said that my father had spoken to him, and since I was not eighteen, he had to accept my parents' wish."

It was my turn to share my father's disappointment of many years ago.

He was sharing with me, the dreams of a completely different life that had been denied to him. Now, I understood better, the words of Rochefault: "A person suffers because he lives more than one life." My father, who once hoped to become the star of football fields, had spent his life in an armchair in the corner of the living room.

He continued to thaw out.

"After I was torn away from football, I was almost dead inside. I had no idea how to own up to my life. I finished high school with difficulty and completed my military service. I became a bureaucrat to fulfill my father's wishes. Now, like all honest young man, I had to find a decent girl for marriage. We asked for the hand of a girl my mother had met in our neighborhood, according to the will of God. That's how I married your mother, my dear. I never had a say in the decisions affecting my life – even one that was so central to my happiness. So, I lived out my life to spite my father. It was as if I didn't really have to be alive in my own life because I had not built it myself. The truth is that your mother was a very good woman. But I was so angry with my own father that I stole from your happiness as well."

My father fell silent.

He had let out the poison that had gathered inside him through many years. I could no longer get angry with him. After a moment of silence, I swallowed hard, as though a lump was stuck in my throat:

"Not only from our lives, dad," I said. "You stole from your own life, too."

"But my regrets are more for what I failed to give you, in the name of spite..."

"Yes, I would have wished that you could have been happy with the cologne I gave you that holiday morning. But I now see that a bottle of lemon flower cologne was not enough to make up for what was taken away from you."

"It should have, my dear. I apologize to you."

My father now needed tenderness. I softly put my head on his shoulder. "For the first time," I said, "I really feel that you are my father." We stayed like that for a while, without speaking. Now, our silence was peaceful. That brief moment that I wanted to keep forever belied all the years of our past relationship.

Suddenly, I understood why he had that manner I thought 'indifferent' when he used to say to me, "it's your decision." My father who never had a say in the decisions that shaped his life, had left me completely free to shape mine. In the way that a slave lives with the dream of freedom, my father was dreaming of experiencing freedom by offering it to me.

When I lifted my head off his shoulder, I saw him smile with a warmth I had never seen before.

"It's time to water flowers," he said.

"I don't understand."

"While your mother was ill, in bed, she asked me not to forget to water her flowers after her death," he said. "I promised her to water them everyday so she could rest in peace. The truth is that even her last wish was made for me. To give me a purpose for living."

Ah, my dear mother. I hope you are watching and seeing this love that you never knew while you were alive.

"Come on dad. I'm sure my mother needs more peace."

Together, my dad and I watered the flowers on the balcony. On this occasion, my mother's flowers were not being watered out of loneliness, but out of a wish to make love grow. I turned to my dad,

"They say flowers grow on love..." I said.

"Yes," he answered.

We blessed each flower that we watered on that day when together we greeted life.

Suddenly, he began to recite the lines of Behçet Necatigil that I have sealed in my heart.

"There were flowers that bloomed in your secret garden.
At night and alone.
You didn't have much to give, or perhaps you didn't have time..."

Now, we have plenty to give, but will the time that we lost ever forgive us?

Time, I beg you, give us permission!..

Time, please, let us a little longer...

Praiseworthy Prize

Bekircan Tahberer / Canada

He was born in Adana in 1961. He was graduated from German Language and Education Department of Çukurova University in 1984. He studied for master degree in Medicine Faculty, Deontology and Medical History Department of the same university (2005). He has translated various books including *The Sand Castle* of Iris Murdoch. He was registered to Adana Museum and started to collect ancient coins and archeological artworks and to carry out researches regarding Cilicia Numismatics (history of coins and medals in the ancient world). In addition to various conferences for the introduction of Ancient Anatolian coins in Turkey or abroad, he has held the course of Ancient Numismatics in the Continuing Studies department of British Columbia University. His novel, "Defineci", is ready for publication.

This story is translated by its own author and edited by Linda Walsh.

A Journey Back Home

BANG! Everyone in the room was startled by the sound of the hammer as it hit the desk. Their faces exhibited a range of feelings - from excitement to nervousness.

"Going once, going twice, gone!"

Bang!

"Lot number 67, silver tetradrachma of Alexander the Great; sold to the gentleman with number 265".

The tall middle-aged man felt both great excitement and contentment. He had finally completed his holiday shopping about two weeks early. A happy smile took the place of the nervousness on his face when he thought about his son. It was not difficult for him to visualize the astonishment in his son's eyes when he got his not so ordinary gift.

When Mustafa exited New York's famous Waldorf Astoria hotel, where the annual coin show was being held, he felt his gradually balding head burning from the freezing temperature. He had never felt such exuberance. It was not like the way he felt the day he got married, nor was it like the feeling he had the day his son was born. It was something else: completely different from all other experiences he had had before. He had read about such experiences, watched them on television and in movies, and heard about them from friends, but he had never experienced one himself.

It was the first time he had attended a live auction-and he had been successful! The item he had hoped to buy -the only item he had bid on- was sold to him. It was an unexpected dream come true. When the auctioneer pointed at him, he looked around, wondering if he was pointing at someone sitting beside him. He then checked the number he held in his hand to make sure that he was the one addressed and not the people around him. He heard the thick, self-confident voice of the slightly bearded, fat auctioneer looking through glasses that were far too small:

"The gentleman with number 265!"

Everything had happened much faster and, to his surprise, much easier than he had anticipated. Walking on the sidewalk after he left the bourse floor of the international coin show, his hand was trembling as it gently wrapped around the little velvet purse in the pocket of his overcoat – the purse that contained his new treasure. The weight of the pure silver piece from about 2330 years ago sent hot waves throughout his body against the cold outside.

He felt like he had accomplished a very important task. The magic words of a philosopher from ancient times came to his mind:

In appearance many people want to accomplish a good deed, but very few have the courage to attempt to do it, and among the ones that attempt one only a handful are able to complete their task.

He thought he had accomplished a good deed in the sense that the old philosopher had suggested.

Mustafa had been born in a small village surrounded by vineyards near the Taurus Mountains, about half an hour's drive from Tarsus, a major town in southern Turkey. He finished high school in Tarsus and went to university in Adana, 35 kilometres to the east.

The plain where cities like Tarsus and Adana have existed over several millennia is surrounded by the Taurus Mountains to the north and the Mediterranean Sea to the south. It has always been famous for its enormously fertile soil and hot climate. The village where Mustafa grew up was half-way up to the mountains and therefore cooler in the summer. The houses in the village had natural fences of prickly-pear cactuses instead of barbed-wire or other types of fences. The cactus plants, with their beautiful flowers, were not only natural protectors of the gardens, but their fruit was also a good product to sell in the summer, since it was considered to be very healthy. After all, it grew completely naturally.

As a boy, Mustafa and his friends loved to visit the two nearby ruins, even though they had no idea who had lived there and when. The village people named the ruins in relation to their location to the village: The "the Lower Ruin and the Upper Ruin". The kids loved to play there because they constantly found colourful pieces of earthenware jars and plates, pieces of glassware or jewellery and occasionally some bronze coins, items that the elders of the village thought worthless. The Lower Ruin was the official pasture of the village but the Upper Ruin was just a levelled area right in front of a high, rocky hill. Young Mustafa loved to oblige whenever his father asked him to take their small herd of goats to graze. It was a good opportunity to visit the ruins. His father found it strange that Mustafa was so eager to tend the animals. Most young boys preferred playing soccer instead of taking a herd to pasture, associating with goats instead of their friends. However, he was happy about his son's cooperation in family chores.

From an early age, Mustafa collected his finds from the ruins in a small box under his bed. He had three bronze coins with some figures and inscriptions on them and many small painted pieces of earthenware jars. He also had a glass finger ring, along with many broken pieces of brightly-coloured glassware. It gave him joy and excitement to look at the items in his small collection and he dreamed about the people who had lived there before them and left those artefacts.

There was no longer any trace of ancient buildings in any of the two ruins because whenever a villager needed some corner or threshold stones while building a house, they would simply go and pull out one or two well-cut masonry pieces from the ruins. In fact, there were not many stones left (because of abandonment and devastations during previous calamities). Mustafa knew all the village houses with walls that contained two or three pieces from the ruins, and tracing the ancient stones on the walls in the village was a kind of game that he really enjoyed playing.

As he got older, he realized that the carved stone bath-tub-like container that his father had brought from the Lower Ruin, and which they used to feed goats in back yard, was a child's sarcophagus. He had always found it intriguing to see the floral ornamentation and the representations of cupid - not so artistically carved but nonetheless impressive - on the sides of the family's special goat-feeding trough.

During his early secondary school years Mustafa developed an interest in collecting stamps. He saw many nice stamps with highly interesting pictures and designs on letters sent to village people from relatives abroad. Many Turks had gone to Europe to work as 'guest workers' in the early 1970s. He sought out the discarded envelopes throughout the village. He would cut the stamps from the envelopes as carefully as if he were creating a work of art then place them between the pages of a book.

His fascination with foreign stamps led him to a new duty: unofficial letter writer for the elders in the village. His reputation as a good letter writer spread quickly after a couple of letters he wrote from the mouths of an illiterate elderly couple to their son who lived in England. He was happy to assume this role because that way almost all letters were brought to him, so he could get stamps without running after them.

He did not have any difficulty in answering letters or composing new ones for others, as he knew everybody very well in his small community. Mustafa could always find more things to write about than could the people who actually were supposed to be writing, and regularly added more news - about the census officials who came to the village, about the snake that bit Hasan the Shepherd, about how wonderful the white and red oleander blossoms looked that Spring, about the bugs that infested the grape vines, and so on.

Letter-writing, foreign stamps and ancient coins all increased his interest in foreign languages, and he went to university to study English. There he met a woman who was studying agricultural engineering and who would later become his wife.

His enthusiasm for collecting ancient artefacts began to take on a more serious form during his time at university, and the ever-growing number of ancient artefacts he had in his possession made him to decide to become an "official" collector. In Turkey, it was forbidden to keep antiquities in one's possession without a licence, so he applied for a licence from the local museum.

He worked as a teacher for a short time. After a while, with the encouragement of his wife, who was by then an accomplished agricultural engineer, he felt he should return to his village and establish a co-operative in order to better organize grape-growing and marketing.

He knew that all growers in the village complained about the endless abuse they endured from the grape merchants. Soon afterwards he began to export the raisins that were produced in his village and in other villages nearby. That year he had exported a large quantity of raisins to some European countries and then he had come to New York to establish new contacts with importers in America. He had timed this business trip carefully so that he would be able to attend the ancient coin auction while in New York. He was extremely happy to get the special coin that he had wanted for a long time.

Alexander the Great, the king of Macedonia, is very famous in the western world for the great military success he achieved in his short life, and as a result, his silver tetradrachmas have become some of the most sought after collectible items in the world. Whether by chance or because it was a very frequently seen type, lot number 67 had not attracted many bidders. There existed a small counterstamp on the reverse of the coin which was not identified by the auctioneers. Perhaps that was the reason many had not bothered to bid on the coin - there were plentyof Alexander tetradrachmas in extremely good condition that did not bear this unidentified counterstamp.

Mustafa felt he was the happiest person in the world at that moment. Not only had he established very good contacts for his raisin business, but he had also bought a great piece of art and history. He hoped to impart his enthusiasm for collecting to his son with that special gift. Now he could not wait to return home.

•••

CLANG! That was the sound of the heavy metal hammer as it hit a piece of metal which in turn slammed into another piece of metal. It was followed by another sound, a sound not as strong as the previous one. This time it was just the sound of a small piece of metal falling into a basket with other small metal pieces. The second sound caused the man sitting by the window to turn his head and gaze toward the gloomy side of the room that was dimly lit by the fire from the furnace. He was a rather dark-skinned, somewhat overweight man in his early forties whose hair was beginning to thin.

The man who hit the hammer pulled out the dirty piece of cloth hanging from his waistband and rubbed the sweat on his forehead that had mixed with soot from the furnace. He then folded the cloth and used it to pick up the small piece of metal that had fallen into the basket. After examining it carefully on both sides, he raised his head and called to the man sitting by the window.

"Come Master, take a look at this!"

The Master dropped the graver and the somewhat egg-shaped piece of hardened bronze flattened at one side on which he had worked since that morning and hurried toward the two men that stood around the anvil. He took out his handkerchief and after folding it several times, took the small piece of metal that the other man was holding with his dirty handkerchief. He walked to the table by the window without taking his gaze from the metal piece he held between his fingers. He examined it very carefully, flipping it this way and that, weighing it in his hand and looking at it carefully once again while holding the now cooling metal piece between his thumb and forefinger. A contented smile spread over his face. That was a good piece of work. Without doubt, the young king was going to like his creation.

"Carry on", he shouted to the workers: the men who stood by the anvil with hammer and thongs and the ones who worked by the furnace casting melted metal into round moulds, "but be very careful! Don't strike them off the flans; centre the dies very well. There is no need to hurry this time. Heads and tails, as well as the inscription, must look as sharp as possible and they must feel like a thorn in the hand. Let us strike ten pieces for now, the rest we will take care of later."

Sandan was a member of the family known to have been master engravers for at least seven generations. He lived in Tarsos, a city known and famous for its founder, the hero-god Sandanos. Master Sandan was one of the most prominent and colourful personalities in the city, involved in all kinds of artisan work, including sculpting and painting as well as his primary profession of seal-engraving. His father had named him after the hero-god Sandanos of Tarsos so he would be respected, but as an extremely accomplished artisan he never needed the additional respect his name could command.

Sandan learned the craft of engraving from his father, and his father had learned it from his father. Traditionally, a rare skill like engraving, which required artistry and knowledge as well as imagination, was only passed on to very close family members, as older masters would not want to let the secrets of the craft slip through the hands of their families.

Personal seals were an indivisible part of life at that time, as they were used instead of signatures on all kinds of documents. Master Sandan created seals from small pieces of precious stone such as ruby, turquoise or serpentine. Customers could choose from hundreds of different images for their seals. Master Sandan could easily carve many different figures of gods and goddesses, scenes from popular myths, or countless other religious or authentic symbols. That was a tremendously fulfilling job that proved to him each time he completed a commission how meaningful his life was.

An ordinary customer usually did not know what to ask for. Master Sandan, who could speak both Luwian and Aramaic, which was the language of diplomacy in those years, usually decided himself what to engrave on a seal, depending on the occupation of his customer. Of course, an illiterate tavern owner or a sandal maker who dealt with ox hides all his life could have little idea of what to have on their seals. However, rich merchants who imported precious metals and grains from Phoenicia, Cyprus and Egypt and exported wine, linen, silver ore and cedar lumber from the famous Taurus Mountains were a different group of customers. But tax collectors, governors and their officials were his primary clients. They always brought the most precious and hardest stones and demanded the most sophisticated and hard-to-engrave compositions to be carved on their seals.

Sandan's father had worked for Datames, the Persian governor of Cilicia(1). His superior engraving skills brought him to a new position and he was appointed official coin die engraver for the city mint at Tarsos. They gave the position to Sandan after the death of his father, even though Sandan was quite young at the time.

Governor Datames was replaced by Mazaios, who during the earlier periods of his tenure employed die engravers from Smyrna.

---

(1) Cilicia was the name of a region in what is now southern Turkey.

Nevertheless, it did not take very long for the new governor to realize the superior artisanship of the local die carver. Just like his father, Sandan was not employed to carve dies only for the Tarsos mint; he also worked on dies ordered by the nearby cities of Mallos, Issos, and Soloi, and even Kelenderis and Nagidos farther west in Cilicia Trakheia(2).

Mazaios, 361 - 334 BC. AR Stater, (10,99 g.)
(Courtesy www.coinarchives.com)

Mint Master Sandan decided to honour the Governor by designing a very special coin die for his reappointment to the mint. This new coin die was to include the longest inscription ever written on a coin to that date: ***"Mazaios Governor of Transeuphrates and Cilicia"***.

Creating a sophisticated coin die required not only great artistic skill and ingenuity but also superior carving tools and new types of equipment. Sandan possessed everything that was needed. His linguistic skills also gave him an advantage over other coin die carvers, as many of them were illiterate and could not even transform a given script onto a die.

The delta where the River Kydnos(3) emptied into the Mediterranean provided a safe port for the city of Tarsos and it became a major stop for merchant ships from all over the eastern Mediterranean region. The goods that were brought from various parts of the plain and the territories beyond the Taurus Mountains would be offered to seafaring merchants at the Tarsos port.

---

(2) Cilicia Trakheia is the western and mountainous part of Cilicia in southern Turkey.

(3) Modern Tarsus (Berdan) River in Southern Turkey.

However, when the weather got hot at the beginning of April, many wealthy merchants and the nobles of the city would move into their summer houses in Mopsukerta in the foothills of the mountains, about half a day's ride from Tarsos. Therefore Tarsos would seem like a deserted city during the summer months.

The engraving business was not the only source of income for Sandan and his family. With the profit from the seal-making business, his grandparents had bought a small vineyard in Mopsukerta, where the weather was cooler in the summer. At first they had only intended to grow enough grapes for the needs of the family, enough to make some wine and raisins for the cold and rainy winter months. But thanks to his position at the mint and the increasing number of orders for coin dies he was receiving, Sandan was making much more money than any of his ancestors had ever earned. Therefore he decided to invest some of his money in vineyards and bought a vast area of land in Mopsukerta to grow vines.

Now he was able to grow much more produce than his family needed. While they kept some for their use in the winter, the majority of the grape crop was used to produce wine in the cellar next to his mountain villa. Sandan packaged his wine in distinctively designed amphorae. He even created a special stamp – a bunch of grapes – which he placed on the handles of the amphorae. The bunch of grapes was to become his own badge for his products – his trademark. Before long, the wine in the grape-stamped amphorae became renowned for its exquisite taste and flavour and was not only sought after by the people in Tarsos, but also merchants coming from Cyprus and Phoenicia were placing substantial orders for it.

That summer they had moved up to their villa in the highlands. The Master was both working on the seal orders that he had received from numerous Cilician cities and supervising the men tending his vineyards. He sometimes got seal orders from places very far away, which helped him learn what went on in those far regions. One day, a merchant from Galatia stopped by and while there had mentioned about a large army coming from the west.

A few days later, at dusk, Sandan noticed a messenger running toward his villa.

"Master Sandan, Master Sandan," cried the messenger, panting fiercely, "gather up your things and run immediately. The Macedonian army is about to cross over the Khilakku Pass(4) and they are advancing this way. The governor Mazaios has already fled Tarsos!"

This was something Sandan had been expecting for a while. He had heard the news that the Macedonians, under a ruthless commander called Alexander, were marching throughout northern and western Asia, capturing every city in the Persian Empire. Rumour had it that this man, King Alexander, was a son of Zeus, the king of all gods. They even said Alexander was reincarnated with the powers of the legendary hero - the god Herakles - except that, unlike his predecessor, Alexander was immortal.

As happened before all military campaigns, the governor of Cilicia had recently ordered a significant number of coin dies and the mint workers had been working from sunrise to sundown. The coins that would be made would be used to pay the mercenaries during the upcoming war. To carve the last order of three sets of dies, Master Sandan had to go down to the plains in the middle of the summer heat, when the sun was so hot it could boil eggs. The strict mint rules demanded that he carve all coin dies at the mint itself. That was quite an unbearable task for him in the summer as he had become used to the comforting, cool weather of the mountains.

The pending invasion could have a substantial impact on everyone. At first Sandan didn't know what to do. Running away would not have been as complicated for him as it was for other people, had he wanted to do so. He only needed a handful of tools to exercise his profession wherever he went. He could easily flee with his family, carrying all his coins and precious stones in a bag and settle somewhere else. However, it was not easy to leave the land of his ancestors, who had lived there for generations. Moreover, he was a very good craftsman and a new king might mean a new job for him.

After dark, he saved some coins that would be enough for their needs for a month and put the rest of the family's coins in a goatskin bag. He buried the bag in a spot in the pine grove behind the villa where he thought no one would think to search for anything.

---

(4) The narrow passage that gives way to the plains of Cilicia in the Taurus Mountains.

He asked his wife to get servants put one of their best amphora of wine near the door of the cellar. Instead of fleeing, he decided to welcome the invaders. It was a great risk but he believed he could take it.

Sleep escaped them. His wife and young son were sitting in one corner in the house, nervously waiting, without knowing what would happen. Although it was by now quite late, Sandan had not extinguished the oil lamps; in fact he had servants place two additional bronze lamps at the gate to the front yard. It was an invitation to passersby and before long the invitation was accepted. About ten horsemen from the scouting forces of the invaders stopped in front of the gate. They were looking for provisions and wanted to learn about what was waiting for them ahead in Tarsos. Sandan respectfully invited them in and offered them his best wine, some oat bread and the delicious goat cheese traditionally stuffed in goatskin.

The commander of the scout force reassured their host that his King Alexander had not harmed those who did not stand against him but was merciless to those who were hostile. Sandan felt greatly relieved. He was not a warrior and absolutely not hostile to anyone. As a skilled craftsman he could be of great help to any king.

It was going to take two months for Sandan to meet the Great King. The King had become severely ill when he, feeling suffocated from the heat of the Cilician summer, had plunged into the cold streams of the Kydnos River that was flowing swiftly from its sources in the Taurus Mountains and would not recover for a long time.

While his army collected provisions on the fertile plains, the Great King, having heard about the fame of the master seal maker and his master works at the Tarsos mint, summoned Sandan to the palace of the Cilician governor, which now served as the residence of Alexander. Sandan, who had been eagerly anticipating this call for some time, had prepared a special gift for the king. He had engraved the head of Herakles, clad in a lion's skin, on a big almond-shaped, light green serpentine that he had reserved for a very special customer. Then he had embedded his precious craft work on a gold ring. He knew the myth of Herakles strangling the Nemean lion and that the young Macedonian king was associated with the hero-god.

With this special gift, he would both show the king how well qualified he was in his craft and gain his trust. And that was what happened. Yet the biggest surprise was to come when he actually saw the king's face. The likeness he had meticulously carved onto the precious stone was exactly that of the young king.

•••

THUMP! Thump! ... Each time the axe hit the dried out tree stump, it kicked back as if it was hitting a rubber ball. Even though Adem was only in his thirties, he sighed heavily as he gazed at his calloused hands grasping the handle of the axe. "Oh my God," said Adem to himself, "removing a stump is a lot harder than it looks!"

At least it was now autumn and the weather was not quite so hot. Nevertheless, Adem was exhausted from the heavy work. And it was getting dark. He had worked all day to cut down the dry almond tree that stood in the middle of the small field he had inherited from his father. Now he was trying to clear away the root.

That tree had caused him problems the previous spring, breaking the blade of the plough several times, which prevented him from completing planting on time. He had postponed the job of removing the tree as long as possible, knowing that it would be an arduous task without a tractor. He had never had the money to buy one; instead he had a horse that he used both to pull his cart and to plough his small field. He would have to remove the tree himself, and that cool cloudy day was perfect for such hard labour. So, that morning he had sharpened his axe and pickaxe, taken the food his wife had packed for him, and then gone to his field to cut down the dry almond tree.

His grandfather was once the wealthiest landowner in their village and his father was no less wealthy than the grandfather. When the old man died, his vast fields were divided among the eight boys, the four girls getting none of the land. Adem's father inherited two hundred hectares. When he died the land was divided among the five brothers, each getting only forty hectares. The worst was that Adem was a still young boy when the father passed away and his elder brothers had allotted him the part of the land that was full of stones and broken pieces of earthenware.

He learned about farming while working with his brothers. He married Meryem, whom he had first seen at the age of eighteen and with whom he had immediately fallen in love. After coming back from his compulsory military service, he argued with his brothers and began farming on his own. For the last ten years, he had barely gotten by on his not so fertile share of field.

Adem had three daughters and he loved them. However he could not help lamenting the fact that God had not given him a son. He often thought, "If my eldest girl were a boy instead, he would now be a young boy of twelve and we could work shoulder to shoulder." On the other hand he sometimes thought it was better that way because he had only a very small piece of land. The girls would each marry a boy and leave home but what could a boy do with that small field? If he had three boys, it would be unimaginable to divide the land and expect them all to survive on their share.

Unfortunately he had no ideas of any alternative plans for his children. It did not occur to him that his children could go to school, learn a craft or run their own lives. That was not something he had seen in his family. His father and uncles had divided their father's land and his brothers and he had done the same with his father's land. Therefore he was completely unaware of the concept of doing something other than farming on one's father's land.

So every year he came to his field with his wife and three daughters and tried to clear it of the stones and broken earthenware pieces, piling them at the border of the neighbouring field. He had never understood why there were so many stones in his field but none in the fields that flanked his. A larger part of his land constituted rather a bumpy area and that was the main reason why his elder brothers left it to him as it was not as fertile as the other parts. That was the main reason his elder brothers had given it to him. But he had worked hard to improve it over the years and now the root of the old almond tree was the last obstacle left in the field.

"They wouldn't have left it to me if it had been fertile land," he muttered. When darkness prevailed he stopped working, attached the horse to the cart and started for home. He ate little for dinner before he fell asleep without even turning on the television. Television was the only form of entertainment not only of Adem's family but also of the majority of the village people. It could even be said to be an addiction.

When he woke up in the morning he still felt tired. His wife and eldest daughter were already awake; they had milked the two cows and fed the chickens. Meryem quickly fixed breakfast for the family, serving green olives that she picked from the tree in the backyard and cheese she had made from the milk from their own cows. Since they sold most of the milk after occasionally making cheese they usually drank tea at breakfast.

As he packed his tools, he asked if his wife would like to go with him, because pulling out the root wasn't going to be easy. She instantly agreed.

"Let me just get some boiled eggs and a loaf of bread for our lunch", she said.

"Well, that is your problem", said Adem in a tired voice. Another hard day was ahead. While his wife packed the eggs and bread, his elder daughter filled two plastic bottles with water from the well in front of their house.

Since they grew everything they needed, either in their field or in the yard around their small house, they paid for nothing except for tea and sugar.

His wife was a clever woman, growing all kinds of vegetables in the back yard every season. The chickens were producing eggs and multiplying and the two cows produced enough milk to make their own cheese and to sell the rest to make a few extra lira.

As was traditional in many parts of the rural Anatolia, village women gathered several times a year to make bread for each other. Adem also grew the tobacco that he was addicted to as was almost every male in the village. Thanks to the well in front of the house they did not pay for water either. Their village, surrounded by all kinds of vines and trees, was located near the Syrian border in the province of Antakya, near ancient Antioch, capital of Roman Syria.

"Hopefully we won't get rain today; otherwise it will be really difficult to cut and pull the roots in the mud", said Adem.

"Don't you worry", said Meryem, "now that I am coming with you, we can finish it quickly!

"Sure, you are the daughter of Hercules!", mocked Adem.

"Go ahead, laugh at me. Don't you know that for years I have been tending the vegetable gardens in our yard? Do you ever wonder who digs the soil and who plants all the vegetables you eat?" said Meryem angrily.

"I know who does. I know very well", said Adem with a slight smile, falling into deep thought. He knew how hard she worked for the family. He felt sorry that he could not provide with the life she deserved as his hard-working, honest and loyal life companion. Unlike many husbands in the village, Adem got along with his wife very well. Just like his mother, his wife was a very hard-working woman. Thankfully their daughters were also very hard-working. Because everyone worked hard, they had never had a shortage of food on the table.

After arriving at the field and working for a while they decided to dig around the tree roots so they could have more working room. The roots spread both diagonally and vertically. They worked long and hard. Adem would take a break each time his wife was emptying the dirt he had dug up. Then he would dig again. They were both so focused on the work that they did not notice the dark clouds beginning to cover the sky.

"WHACK!" That was the sound of the pickaxe as it hit a stone.

"Oh my God! Look at this, isn't that stubborn root enough trouble? Now we have a stone at the same time", grumbled Adem.

It also began to sprinkle. "Keep going!" Meryem demanded, "it is just a sprinkle. No quitting until we have finished the job!"

This is what Adem admired most in his wife: her determination to complete a task.

The rain got heavier as he took the shovel from his wife's hands and began to empty the dirt he had dug a couple of minutes earlier. It was not a big stone but it took time to clear it from the dirt and the roots that surrounded it.

By now the rain was soaking them both.

"If we quit now, the rain will loosen the dirt and cover the hole. We'll be right back where we started!" warned Meryem.

"Now that we are already soaking wet, we might as well get this stone out", said her husband. "And this woman won't ever let me get out of this pit until I'm finished," he added to himself.

"Pass that pickaxe to me so I can shove it under the stone and try to lift it", Adem instructed. It was very difficult to move the stone from where it had rested for thousands of years. He couldn't help but fall backward when the pickaxe handle broke.

"Oh, my God", he said, panting nervously, "obviously the angels of God are not on our side today!"

"Don't blame this and that", retorted Meryem angrily, "get out of the way so that I can lift that damn stone. It is already loose from its place!"

"Take it easy, you are going to hurt yourself", said Adem, "let's use both the handles of both the shovel and the axe to pry the stone from its place."

The worst was that neither handle could be shoved completely under the stone. There had to be something else blocking the handles. Maybe the stone had a shape that extended downward. Adem pushed the broken handle of the pickaxe as far as he could and then stepped on it using all his body weight and his wife tried to pull the stone from the other side. She pulled so hard that when she suddenly lost her grip she fell backwards into the now extremely muddy pit. All her clothing was not only wet but completely covered with mud.

"Look at all this filthiness and misery. I don't know if we should laugh or cry!", said Adem, confused.

Meryem, trying to get up from the mud pit she was sitting, said happily, "Laugh, laugh! What will you gain by crying? We've got the stone out now. Once we take it out of the pit, the job is over!"

While both were trying to roll the big stone out of the ditch, Meryem's foot stumbled upon what she first thought to be another stone.

"Oh my God, there is another stone here!"

"For God's sake, leave me alone now. I cannot deal with another stone today. I feel miserable from head to toe!"

"Okay then, you go ahead and roll this stone to the edge of the field while I try to get the other one out. It looks much smaller. You know how much trouble they cause when you hit the blade of the plough. That is money we spend then, money that we can better spend on our girls."

As in many families, the needs of the family were primarily the needs of the kids. Meryem never thought of spending money on herself or her husband. It was the kids that mattered, only the kids.

When Meryem reached into the mud to put her hands around what she thought was a small piece of stone, she realized that it was not exactly a stone. "What could this be?" she asked herself. She continued to work around it and before long she could see that it was not a stone but almost a round-shaped earthenware jar about the size of a small watermelon.

Even though there was no one else around, instinctively she whispered to her husband, trying not to make any loud noise:

"Adem, come over here, right away!"

"What is that? Didn't I tell you that I won't get any more stones today?"

"Don't shout so much and come here at once", ordered his wife with a very serious look on her face.

Adem, completely exhausted and wet, with mud dripping all over his body, reluctantly got up and began to walk toward his wife. Meryem, who was not in any better condition than Adem was, pointed at the round object she had dug out of the muddy ditch where she knelt.

"What the hell is that?"

"Come here and see" said Meryem who was now more angry than anxious to see what was inside the jar.

Adem knelt beside his wife and reached for the jar. It was not as light as he expected and he needed to use all his strength to lift it from the pit that was rapidly filling with rain water and mud.

"Oh what a heavy thing this is. I think it weighs about ten kilos. I wonder if there is lead in it".

When he rubbed the mud from around the rim of the jar he noticed some smaller round stones in it. He picked one up, dipped it into the water and rubbed it with his fingers to see what it was. He could not believe his eyes!

"It's a coin! It's an old coin!" he exclaimed, trying to keep his voice down.

"What coin? Don't get too excited right away", said Meryem, "let me see". She grabbed the small object from her husband's hand. It really looked like an old piece of blackened metal.

An instinctive nervousness replaced their initial confusion and excitement. "Hurry! Go get the food bag from the cart. Let's put this jar into it and then go home right away", said Adem hastily.

Adem took the coins to his friend he knew from his army days who now happened to run a jewellery shop and a tractor business in a nearby town, and explained to him how they had stumbled upon the little treasure. His friend knew the hardships Adem and his family endured and offered to exchange the coins for a used tractor. At first, Adem thought his friend was joking but he was overjoyed when his friend reassured him that he was serious.

When he parked the tractor in front of the house, Meryem couldn't believe her eyes either. She never realized that those old coins could be worth a tractor, even a used one.

They were never to realize that the coins they found were the savings of a farmer of ancient Antioch who married a girl from Tarsos about 2300 years ago.

How could they know that one of the first coins the master engraver Sandan made for the Macedonian king and saved for him was among the coins in the jar that they found? They would never know that the Sandan's granddaughter had fallen in love with the son of an Antioch farmer and that special coin was given to her as part of her dowry, which a devastating earthquake had buried along with everything else including the jar that contained the family savings.

As Mustafa's plane began its descent to the airport in Adana, he still excitedly clutched the coin in his hand. No one would ever know that the coin he had bought in New York was one of the first coins master engraver Sandan of Tarsos had made for Alexander the Great from the silver mined in the Taurus Mountains. They would never realize the meaning of the counterstamp in the form of a bunch of grapes on the reverse of the coin or even the fact that Sandan had his summer villa and vineyards where now Mustafa had his house and vineyards.

None of these people knew that, in fact, the artefacts they had found reflected their own heritage. These items had belonged to their ancestors and not to a foreign people. Many of these artefacts had been destroyed, either intentionally and unintentionally, and others had been smuggled out of the country. However, many others still remained in the ground, awaiting discovery. The ancient settlements, traces of which still remain in every cubic centimetre of Anatolian soil, belonged to their ancestors, who had lived there thousands of years ago.

a coin of Alexander the Great struck in Tarsos

Praiseworthy Prize

Sinem Elkatip / USA

She was born in İstanbul in 1974. She was graduated from Chemistry Teaching Department of Boğaziçi University in 1996. She studied for master degree on chemistry in England. After working as a chemistry teacher for a while, she went to New York in 2002 for studying for master degree in philosophy. She is still living and studying for doctorate in New York.

Immigration

"There is also an attic storey above. It is very neglected and full of junky things. I cleaned it two months ago for the last time. But if you decide to rent the house, we will certainly discharge furniture and give the house a thorough cleaning."

While looking at pines and deep blue sea beyond branches through the window, I lost my concentration in the conversation. I recognized that there was a question directed to me at the last moment. I continued looking at the sea while I was saying that "That's okay" without even knowing what I had approved. Did I behave shamefully since I didn't look at her face? Was it so important? I was outside the time, and got fascinated with dark blueness of sea. I was surrounded by and dug deep into the past. Looking through the years, I could see streets through which I had walked, houses in which I had lived, offices where I had worked, reunions to which I had attended. However, I failed to see myself. I certainly knew the house in which I had lived and the office where I had worked. But where was I?

I remembered that we had talked with Çiğdem on this topic three months ago. We could understand each other without depending on words by the virtue of our friendship lasting since secondary school. She was more social than me. She decided to end dependence of our existence to streets, houses and offices. She would create a life meaningful in itself. First of all, she would go to India. I asked her "Aren't there any streets and houses in India?" Then she said, "Well, let you seek the ideal solution and flog a dead horse. This is what I can find for this moment. It is not important whether I will be exactly satisfied or not. At least I will see India. And this is not so bad, is it?"

Three weeks after her departure, I was notified that she was attacked by fatal malaria, and couldn't be treated on time since she didn't have medicines recommended to tourists. And I received a post card forwarded by her from New Delhi one week after this incidence. Up to then, I had never received a card from a dead person. She wrote that she found out an excellent type of tea which she was drinking while writing the card. She wrote that flavor of tea relieved her from thinking about general matters of life. It was so fresh and delicious.

"Come in, come in... Pardon, excuse me. Are you well? I was talking about attic storey. Will you look it? You shall ascend this stair..."

Homeowner was calling me again. How long had I been lost in thought? Hadn't she talked about attic storey lastly? I had to find an excuse and hinder her in thinking that I was really strange.

"Oh, excuse me. I am a little bit anemic; and hence I get abstracted and exhausted if I fail to eat my meals regularly. And I didn't have breakfast."

"Oh, dear! Then, please eat something immediately. I had better prepare a sandwich for you."

This time I felt myself under the weather. She got anxious in vain because of my lie. Furthermore, she took trouble for me. Suddenly, I remembered biscuits in my bag. I told homeowner not to trouble herself since I didn't have so much time -this was another lie- and further told her that I always had biscuits with me for such situations. While ascending stairs, I had to eat one of those stale biscuits which had been in my bag for two weeks.

Particles of dust flitting within beam, clacking wooden stairs could easily meet expectations about an attic storey. I only wondered that whether attic storey also provided sea view, or not. However, I forgot this curiosity as soon as I reached the attic storey and saw deflated furniture thrown around. I felt sad. I was walking very carefully. I didn't want to hit, stress, push and break that furniture which had already been brokenhearted. Before being dusted in such a manner, they also had a bright era in their lives when they had been bought, removed from their packages, touched and smelt for the first time, and when they had been treated with great respect. But then, it was decided that they had been consumed. They even didn't have the right of speak. Nobody could hear the voice of a bag saying that "Yes, my handle was detached, but you can fix it. I have been carrying your letters, photos for a long while. I have hid your years in my cells. Will you throw your history aside?" Have you ever heard a reading lamp saying that "Don't you remember that I lightened you patiently while you were reading Arabian Nights? While all householders were sleeping, when my own light was even too much for me, I remained lighted just for you. And now, will you eclipse me evermore since this glass hat above me has cracked?" Humans never hear such voices. Furniture of attic storey and their screams were covered by a dusty silence in time. Just as years covering us, and soil covering Çiğdem...

I caused a bundle of buckled and fade paper on a round table with a broken leg to fall down even though I was walking carefully. Then I had to tread on a Brown-grey toned shawl which, I thought, had been white once upon a time. When I took papers in my hand, I saw these faint sentences:

My dear,

Almost all tales have happy ends. That's why I wish I could tell a tale to you just as in the past, but you aren't an infant any more. You become an adult child just as all of us.

I didn't want to read remaining part of the letter while I was exposed to prying eyes of homeowner. All of a sudden, I put my bag on my shoulder by overturning stable lives of dust particles. Homeowner would certainly think that biscuits answered the purpose because my motions were lively for the first time since I had come.

"Oh, yes attic storey is fairly well. Pardon me, would you mind if I take these papers? I'll inform you about my decision tomorrow morning. Actually, I like the house, but you know, I must think anyhow. I want to live in the island for a long time. I'll bring papers back tomorrow. Is there any problem for you?"

Homeowner hesitated for a short while.

"If you wish, I can still prepare a sandwich for you, and meanwhile you can read papers," said she.

I try my luck for the last time by saying that "As I said, I don't have much time. Otherwise, I can stay some more. If possible, I'll read these papers in the boat." Hereupon, homeowner told that I could certainly take papers. Then, I thanked for everything and wished her a nice day.

I got excited for the first time long since. Idea of settling in the island started yielding its results. I compared myself to birds migrating to protect themselves from cold weather in winter. But I felt cold not because of weather, but because of the city.

With papers in my hand, I walked towards the wharf along streets of island after reacquiring my liberty and abstraction, and being sure that I wouldn't be exposed to curious eyes any more. I started to read while waiting for the boat which would carry me back to the city.

> *Do you remember? You used to come by me at nights of strong euroclydon which frightened you. Without saying anything; you climbed the bed, covered my neck with your tiny hands and went on sleeping. As you had grown up, your visits became less. You also approached thundering euroclydons with an increasing interest and love. You became friend with them despite their frightening nature. While I have been decaying day by day, your rapidly increasing enthusiasm is the most important factor that has sustained me. But still, I am not able to desist from worrying about your being exposed to an unknown euroclydon one day. What if I fail to be with you in such a period?*
>
> *Please my darling, do not take it amiss! I certainly have faith in you. I am sure that you will never loose your enthusiasm for life. I am writing such things because I don't want you to have any suspicion. You will be on the right way, I feel this already now. I love you very much.*

At first, I remembered that spring day when I had run in a garden full of daisies and corn roses. I also felt like this on that day. I was running as if there had been somebody waiting for me at the end of the road. I believed that life expected my running towards it so as to share its secrets with me. But of course, I couldn't express my small game in this way. I only felt that somebody who I loved very much was waiting for me and would talk about matters which were unknown to me. It was obvious that I didn't meet with anybody at the far end of the garden. I enjoyed running so much that I already forgot that I had been running towards somebody when I reached the far end.

I had thousands of questions in my mind. Was this letter received by its target? Who did write it? S/he said that s/he was decaying day by day, I wonder whether s/he is still alive, or not. Who was the target of this letter? Should I deliver it to its target unless it was received by him or her? Or, did this letter belong to its finder? In other words, did it belong to me? Of course. Perhaps, it was written for me. I myself also got surprised at my staking out a claim to this letter just after such kind of thoughts. How could I be related to this letter? I felt or wanted to feel as if this letter had belonged to me, wasn't it enough for proving my absolute loneliness? I started chilling. I watched steamship's approaching to the dock, intaking its passengers patiently and moving away. I stood still.

I last came to the island with Çiğdem just one day before her departing for India. We couldn't think that the steamship approaching to the cost was the last one which would return to the city. We looked each other for a while after steamship's departing from the dock, but then we said that "Come on! It can't be the last steamship. It is still too early. There are at least three more services." We didn't see any other steamship for next two hours, and then we tried to give money to the dock officer. Seemingly we were self-assured, but in fact both of us were worried and hid our feelings from each other. When ticket seller said that "You must wait for tomorrow henceforth," we were first left dumbstruck. It was obvious that we weren't residents of the island. But then we started laughing just as we used to do in case of similar instances. Çiğdem would go by airplane next day and had planned to pack suitcase after returning from the island. When we went to the cafe at coast for drinking tea once more, she said that "Take it easy! May be this is better." "And this is also appropriate for the purpose of our voyage. Let everything emerge naturally." Who knows, perhaps she forgot primaquines due to her hurry during preparation.

I read the letter in my hand once more. I didn't know whether I was on the right way, or not. I decided to find the writer and target of this letter. I wanted to be acquainted with those persons. Perhaps, they could tell me whether I was on the right way, or not. First of all, I would have a talk with the homeowner. If necessary, I would dedicate my weekend entirely for this purpose. Strange to say that, people dedicated their lives for great ideals whereas I talked about just a weekend. I wondered what should we undertake for what, and of course how long should we maintain these undertakings? I was sure that people, who dedicated their lives for a purpose, didn't ask such questions. On the other hand, duration which could be spared by people like me could not exceed one weekend in sum due to such kind of irrelevant questions. We couldn't go forward. We started from scratch again and again with our unanswered questions and the lost time while asking these questions after the end of each week. "I wonder what shall we undertake for what, and of course how long should we maintain these undertakings?"

While moving along uphill and silent streets of the island, I decided to consider myself as a detective. They're free of emotions. The same was also true for me. I wouldn't have any expectations in case I could find writer or target of the letter.

I wouldn't request to have long talks with them, and wouldn't try to be a part of their great love. Everything should occur in a natural way.

When I arrived in the house, homeowner stretched out his calloused feet to a taboret; held a newspaper in one hand and a slender waisted tea cup in the other, and enjoyed herself in the balcony. However, as she said, her own house was located at five minutes walking distance and she didn't live here. I was somewhat vexed at this. Now, she might consider that I aimed to control where she was really living. Homeowner was amazed at seeing me. After huddling with herself, she shouted at me from the balcony.

"What is the matter? Do you forget something? Or, are shipping services cancelled? Southwester may come up. But not now, perhaps in the evening."

"My business in the city has been cancelled. If you are not busy, I want to ask some questions about the house?"

"Of course, you are welcome. We can also eat hot pancakes together, and hence your blood glucose will increase," said her smilingly. She didn't consider that I was controlling her as I had expected. When I entered home, smell of pancake penetrated into loops of my brain and suppressed all of my perplexing thoughts. I heaved a sigh of relief.

She said that "Would you like to drink a cup of tea?" Without even waiting for my reply, she came with tea and pancakes on the tray. I looked her face carefully for the first time.

"I think you have some questions. In fact I also wanted to speak with you, but you were in a hurry. I had better talk with you now. Otherwise, I can forget. The island is extremely cold in winter. As you notice, this house is not so much protected against winds. And southwester of here is reputable. In fact, you can easily warm up the house, make no doubt about it. Believe me; I have never lived in a house more comfortable than this. However, I fairly admit that all of my tenants complained of howl of southwester. As you know, I can't do anything for this. What we talk about is wind. So it is impossible to prevent its blowing. Besides, I have learnt very much from winds, but it is a matter of choice. I don't want to disturb you, but I must inform you about this issue. Do you want more tea?"

Although I didn't drink even half of the tea, she stood up so abruptly that I couldn't say anything. I heard her breathing deeply in the kitchen. After a while, she returned with a relaxed face which always had an ambiguous smiling expression. It was an expression of smiling which was peculiar to people knowing the real meaning of grief.

"Thank you for these delightful pancakes." One of pancakes contained cheese and the other one contained minced meat.

"Bon appetite. It is an old custom. I cooked pancakes for five o'clock tea on Tuesdays and Thursdays. If you like, I can give some. I fail to adapt myself to new circumstances, I always cook for two persons and some of them remain. May she rest in peace, she liked pancakes very much."

"May god rest her soul, who is she?"

"She is my daughter. God forbid, it is the worst grief one can experience."

I couldn't find anything to say. She gave me a hand while I was looking at her helplessly.

"Oh, look! Here is Black Pearl," said her and pointed at the gull settling onto the roof of next house. "It is too old and extremely prideful. It also likes pancake very much." She broke of a small piece and threw it towards the roof. "But when we look at it, it never eats. Let's act as if we weren't interested and so it can eat smoothly."

"Did you give this name to it?"

"Yes. But in fact my daughter gave this name. Because of its eyes. Please, don't look at it now. You can look later and see that its coal black eyes are as sparkling as beads."

Even if I wondered, I cared not to look at it. May well be, it wanted to ensure that nobody was looking at it before reaching pancake.

"You told me that you had some questions."

My questions? Yes, my questions! Strange to say, but I forgot about the letter since I had come to the house. "Yes, yes... I want to ask who had lived here before. The letter I found in attic storey..." Then, I took out pale papers from my bag. "... actually I wonder the owner of these letters. Or the writer of them."

I had to explain myself in details. I had to specify reasons of my curiosity, but how could I do this? She gave me a hand once more.

"I probably understand you. Let me first bring you one more cup of tea. Then we can talk at length."

I got relaxed. I reminded the last card sent by Çiğdem. There she told how she got pleased with the new kinds of tea she tasted. I was also very pleased with continuously refilled tea. While I had just eaten half of cheesy pancake, I did not think anything. I didn't have any questions and the sea was deep blue. I was waiting for the story to be told by homeowner.

"Here are our teas. I had to think so as to remember people living here before. But if you essentially wonder the writer of that letter, its answer is very easy. I wrote that letter. I wrote to my daughter. She was so lively. On the other hand, I was struggling against an illness decaying me. Fate! I feared her standing all alone. I didn't want her will to life to be harmed. I saw many cheerful, enthusiastic people who became cross with life and went on in this way; I saw how they turned into completely different persons. I don't know whether a letter can prevent this or not but I didn't have any other chance. And so I wrote it. It is act of god... Not later than two weeks after this letter, I was the one who stood all alone. And my health has got better as if challenging with me."

She gulped, and covered the tea cup but couldn't drink. I couldn't dare asking what had happened. But she achieved to continue.

"She had a high fever… Within just a week... We couldn't understand what had happened. It was said to be an allergy. It was because of a very rare kind of insect. We learnt this after her death. Bitted part of her skin swelled like a balloon. As I said, we couldn't understand in the beginning. Some people came and controlled her. We boiled herbs. None of them could be effective. Finally, we decided to rush her to hospital. Yes, we decided but... We couldn't lead her to the city on time. A southwester broke out. An incredible southwester. A murmur which I had never heard before."

I couldn't achieve to say anything other than "I am really sorry," an ordinary sentence which failed to represent my depression. I said that "I had a friend and he also…" But I couldn't complete the sentence. She was looking away. Neither could I see where she was looking at, nor could she hear what I told. Finally, she brought the silence between us to a close once more.

"I'll take a glass of water. Would you like, too?"

I also wanted to benefit from these short breaks in the kitchen by saying that "Of course, let me help you".

Kitchen was filled up with the soft sun of nightfall having petite arms.

"As you see, there are lots of pancakes. I'll certainly give you some in a packet while you are leaving."

After drinking water and taking a deep breath in the kitchen, we started walking towards the balcony. She went on talking by a freshen voice, "I haven't been able to chuck the letter since then. I hoped that she would come back one day. I didn't chuck it, in fact I couldn't. I moved from this house. I hired it out for two times. Seven years have elapsed since then. I have recently started accepting her death. Second tenants also vacated the house. I cleaned the house for hiring it out once more. I last met these letters then. I smiled at this amazing faith of the letter. It has insisted in reaching its address, but it was finally received by me. It wrinkled and paled more each time, but still waited for being read insistently. I couldn't chuck it any more even if I wanted so." For a while, she stopped and looked at me without taking her eyes off. "It means that it has been waiting for you. When you entered the attic storey, I felt that in my bones. And you dropped those papers among so many articles just as I expected!"

For the first time, she called me like a friend of her. I put the letter on table. While I was taking the tea glass, I had already decided to rent the house. Just then I heard a murmur in the air.

"You see! They said that southwester would break out, but this is the voice of northeaster" said the homeowner. When I tried to understand the source of murmur, my hand hit the glass and tea poured onto papers. I tried to clear papers away the table immediately, but papers have torn very much due to elapsed years. They broke into pieces as soon as I touched them. It was impossible to read them.

My homeowner was looking motionlessly at the table with frozen eyes. I was really in a flap. While trying to piece papers together, I also apologized to her. But, the more I touched papers, the more they broke into pieces. Small pieces stuck to my hand. All of a sudden, homeowner kept my arm rigidly, and said that "You had better stop now. I could do it."

I stood up silently.

"Hımm, as I said before, I'll inform you about my decision tomorrow."

She also stood up. She didn't have any similarity with the woman smiling a short while ago.

"Of course. You must be fast. Northeaster will break out soon. Shipping services can be cancelled."

I started walking towards the dock. Services had not been cancelled yet. While waiting for steamboat, I put my hands dirtied with tea and pieces of paper into the sea. I compared myself to birds which fell sick while migrating to hot places. Steamboat arrived a little later. I returned to the city together with the crowd.

Praiseworthy Prize

Suna Keleşoğlu / France

She was born in Çankırı in 1971 and graduated from the department of Electronics and Communication of Yıldız Technical University in İstanbul. She got married in 1998 and moved to France. Some of her stories were published by *Kahve Molası (Coffee Break)* electronically, and also in the print version of *Kahve Molası*.

That's Life Sister, Today is a Holiday, The Taste of Caramel Candy that I Almost Forgot

I turn back for one final look. His eyes turn red. I notice that he is biting his lips as he raises a hand to wave at me. He is trying hard not to cry. He is probably embarrassed. I understand that. As for me, I'm not embarrassed at all. I start to cry, not knowing when we'll ever see each other again.

My brother calls out: "Call me as soon as you get there." His hand remains hanging in the air. He is looking at me. I am looking at him. Tears flow down my cheeks. Time stands still...

– Sister, sister...

– Zehra, don't run so fast, you'll fall down...

– Sisteeeeer...

Once again, I hear the voice of a child, Zehra, running after me. Her childish voice echoes in my ears. I see that my brother Osman, now left behind, continues to wave at me.

"Passengers traveling to Paris on TK flight no. 1572, please proceed to gate no 18."

I return to my senses, with the voice of the woman making the announcement. I take my ticket out of my purse and head towards the boarding gate. I look back at my brother once again, sobbing.

Why Zehra, why? Why you?

I'm on my way back to Paris. On the way to the plane, as I give my ticket to the stewardess, I notice from her expression that my face must be a mess. I have a runny nose, and I sniffle, indifferent to everyone around me.

My seat is beside the window. The plane seems to be full. There are still people filing in, looking for their seats. I wonder who will sit beside me. I hope it's not someone who likes to chat because I'm not good at saying "No." I usually strike up a conversation with my neighbors on buses and planes, but today I'm not at all in the mood to talk. I hope my neighbor will keep quiet. I turn to the window, as if I might be able to watch my own life through that small pane.

There is an age difference of two years between Zehra and me. Since I became thirty-five years old last week, she must be thirty-three. I have not celebrated a birthday for years, but last week, my friends at work gave me a surprise party and reminded me of my birthday.

So, it's been ten years since I moved to Paris. How quickly time flies. It seems only like yesterday that...

After childhoods spent in squatter houses, fortune had smiled at us. First my elder brother, and then I had done well at exams and won bursaries for boarding schools. My elder brother Osman was a very successful student. He had gone to university with a bursary, and graduated with the top award. As a student, he also worked to contribute to my education. Ever since high school, I had only one aim: to study chemistry. Not only did I want to respond to the efforts of my chemistry teacher, Ms. Nazlı, who had introduced me to chemistry, but I also was impressed by the lab experiments we conducted. I wanted to become a great chemist, like the scientists whose life stories I had read. To make discoveries, to advance in research...

After successful university years, when I was offered a job at the headquarters of the French cosmetics firm where I had been working, I was only twenty-five years old. I was very excited, and made up my mind without any hesitation. When I told my parents that I would work outside the country, they didn't oppose my decision at all. My father had worked on boats for many years, and traveled far and wide. My mother, who knew the world from the postcards he used to send, was always curious about foreign countries. Through the years, their main aim had been to support our education for granting a prosperous life to us. My elder brother Osman became an economist, and began to work at a bank. When he was promoted to rank of bank chief in the same bank, he bought a spacious apartment and moved our parents there to live with him. He had married a girl working in the bank. My elder brother Osman, his wife Sevim and their twins had an ordinary but happy life. At the time when I moved to Paris, my sister Zehra had already flown away from the nest. She had rushed to marry a health care worker that she met while she was at the last class of nursing school, and she had given birth to three children in rapid succession.

Zehra had spent her whole life in struggle. She never found the life she had longed for. An unhappy marriage, a mute child (whose muteness remained unexplained), and finally an unemployed husband who gambled the family into debt. At first, Zehra sent her daughters to boarding school. Then she devoted herself to the care of her little son. Even the doctors and health care workers in her circle were unable to understand why her little son Mert was unable to talk. The child could hear all sounds. Yet at age four, he had not uttered a single word. The relationship between Zehra and her husband, that was already strained, reached its breaking point one day, when the man raised his hand against Mert. When I saw Zehra for the last time on New Year's Eve, she looked thin, and complained of chronic headaches. My mother had started to care of Mert.

When my elder brother Osman telephoned, three days ago, I was at a meeting where I was making a presentation on a new product to the firm's bosses. Even the secretary, who interrupted the meeting for the sake of an urgent call, was sulking. After receiving the news that Zehra was diagnosed with a brain tumor, and that she had to undergo surgery urgently, my face had taken on such a dark expression that my colleagues were concerned. I collapsed in a heap on one of the armchairs. I excused myself, but promised to return for the presentation to clients that would take place in four days.

As someone who had always made a priority of work over personal life to the point of postponing marriage to my fiancée, I was breaking my own rules for the first time. I took the first available plane to Ankara. And now, I'm returning to Paris.

Just as I was thinking about these things, I heard a young girl's voice:

– Yes mother, this is our seat.

The woman beside here smiles at me,

– Hello, Bon Voyage.

She is holding a straw bag under her arm. The girl settles between the mother and myself. We greet each other. I smile,

– Have a nice trip.

I wonder how my eyes look. I'm sure they must have guessed that I've been crying. The woman takes out some tissues out of her straw bag that resembles a beach bag, and offers the tissues to me.

– It looks as if you need these.

Then, her eyes tell me "I understand you, you need to be left alone," and she and her daughter turn their attention to the newspapers in their hands. Just before turning my head towards the window, I glance at the newspaper in the girl's hands.

I see the headline:

"Happy Holidays!"

Strange to say, I even forget that today is a religious holiday.

I was the child with green eyes banging on the wooden door with my fists. Scratches and scars on my knees.

– Aunty Saadet, open the door, it's us...

My elder brother Osman and Zehra were with me. On holidays, my mother would dress us identically, and she would send us to the neighbors to pay our respects by kissing hands and touching them on our foreheads. On that particular holiday, she had continued her tradition and bought Lacoste t-shirts for all three of us. She had bought rose colored ones for Zehra and me, whereas grass green for Osman, from the draper's shop in neighboring district. We were hardly making ends meet. My dad had not returned from his trip. My dad was a cook on boats. We used to see his face about twice a year. Sometimes he stayed home for several months but we never knew when he would appear, or disappear.

My mother was a midwife. Almost all the children of the neighbors were born in her hands. Yüksel, the son of aunty Saadet was among those children. My mother had realized during Aunty Saadet's delivery that something was wrong, but she couldn't make Uncle Cafer understand the necessity of taking her to the hospital. Shortly after birth, Yüksel had high fever, and by the time he was taken to hospital it was too late. Something was wrong in his nervous system - or the connection between his nerves and his brain. In those days, it was not treatable. He couldn't run, he couldn't talk, and he couldn't use his hands and arms like other children. My mother used to say that Yüksel had to have a wheel chair as from the time when he was four-years-old. Yüksel and my elder brother Osman were coevals. Yüksel also had an elder sister named Münevver. Münevver was an odd girl. She didn't like us to use her name. If we ever called her as "Münevver *Abla (elder sister)"* around the neighborhood boys, she used to get mad and shout at us. On a given day, she had chased me all the way down the road, wielding a high-heeled shoe as a weapon.

Nowadays, in the squatter neighborhood where we used to live, they're destroying the houses one by one. During my last visit around the New Year's Eve, when I visited Necla Abla, to express my condolences after her husband's death, I saw how they had torn down the houses. It broke my heart to see the ruins of the neighborhood where we had lived for many years. We had moved into an apartment in the Sincan district of Ankara when my elder brother Osman took an employment. I left the most vivid memories of my childhood in the squatter neighborhood. Our house was on top of an uphill road. Two bedrooms and a living room, with a small garden. My mother used to grow tomatoes and parsley. Every summer, flowers would bring color to our world. Aunty Saadet was our next-door neighbor. She used to work as a dressmaker and as a cleaning lady. Her alcoholic husband, Uncle Cafer was a worker in a factory. Some say he died in an accident, and some say it was suicide. No one really knew the truth. During a night shift, an iron cable had strangled him. People said he would not have died if he had not drunk so much. Aunty Saadet never talked about Uncle Cafer. She never referred to his life or death. She used to refer to him as the father of Yüksel and Münevver.

Whenever my mother said, "Your late husband was insensitive,"

"Unfortunately, the father of these children was so, my neighbor..." Aunty Saadet would answer.

On that particular holiday, as I banged on the closed door of Aunty Saadet's place, thousands of thoughts were crossing my childish mind. I was swimming in a jean skirt that my mother had bought for Zehra and me at the marketplace in Ulus. My sister, who had plump cheeks and who was sturdier than me even though she was younger, looked great in the same skirt. Zehra always had a few more kilos than me. On that day, my elder brother Osman was also wearing jeans. My father had brought those jeans for him from Italy for the previous holiday. On this holiday, he was not with us - he had sent us a postcard from one of the countries he had gone.

– Aunty Saadet...

All three of us were banging on the door by now.

– Here I am. You'll break down the door...

She let us in. Her special brown cardigan on for the occasion, her graying hair tied back, wearing brown slippers that we hadn't seen before.

Zehra nudged me:

– Look, Aunty Saadet has bought new slippers.

– Be quiet.

Zehra was only seven but she could notice everything. She paid attention to who was wearing what, and she would ask for clothes that resembled those worn by adults. She would spend hours before the mirror, combing her long brown hair. Some days she would not undo the braids that my mother made for her, and the next day, she would gather the curly hair on two sides of her head. Her hair was certainly more beautiful than mine. My hair was fine, straight and took on a greasy look very quickly. I looked pretty small for a child of nine. I used to wear a headband to school. I remember one time when everyone thought I was a little boy because my hair was cut short. Ever since that day, I make a point of wearing my hair long, but they never grow lower than my shoulders. I never had long brown hair like Zehra's.

The face of Aunty Saadet looked tired. Once inside her living room, each one of us kissed her hand and touched it to our foreheads. She stroked our hair and made us settle on the couch. Yüksel was sitting in the wheelchair obtained with difficulty from public insurance, with a vacant expression. Our childish minds could not make sense of why he was in this strange situation. We kept asking my mother why he couldn't walk like all other children. Yüksel was one of those who had the first goal scored against him by the time he was born.

While Aunty Saadet was pregnant, she was beaten frequently by her husband. The women in the neighborhood used to say that was the reason why Yüksel was like that. When we were young, we heard the women whispering such things, but they never said anything to Aunty Saadet, herself. Yüksel *Abi (elder brother)* would move his head this way and that, unable to hold his arms straight. He was fed by Aunty Saadet or Münevver.

On that holiday morning, it was obvious that Aunty Saadet had taken some time to open the door to us because of this. There was some food around Yüksel's mouth. After welcoming us, Aunty Saadet had headed to the kitchen, and emerged with a damp rag and a bowl of candies.

When she called me, saying "Canan, come and offer candy to your brother and sister," I found that I was unable to take my eyes off the candies in the bowl.

She went up to Yüksel and wiped his face with care before attentively cleaning his restless hands.

My elder brother Osman was unable to sit still. His face was full of puberty pimples. He was wondering where Münevver was because he was secretly nurturing a platonic love for her. Zehra, who loved to chat, relieved him of his misery.

"Aunty Saadet, isn't Münevver around?" she asked.

"She's gone to her aunt to pay her respects," said Aunty Saadet. "She'll be back this evening."

Zehra was let down. She had hoped to show her flowery hairpins to her Münevver. I remember how Zehra had made my mother go round and round in the marketplace to look for these hairpins which were identical with those owned by Münevver. Zehra used to want whatever Münevver had or wore. This was something that made me a little jealous. I worried that Münevver might be a better elder sister to Zehra than myself.

I have an impulse to turn my head towards the young girl sitting beside me on the plane. I notice her fashionable hair band, her color coordinated clothes and her painted fingers. A sparkling young girl like most of her peers. She must be around fourteen or fifteen. She is trying to sit up straight to show off her breasts. I remember myself at fifteen, and how I would curve my shoulders to hide my breasts. My sister Zehra, on the other hand, wanted large breasts like Münevver. Münevver represented the ideal young woman to her. She had usurped the role that should have been mine. When Aunty Saadet said Münevver had gone to visit her aunt, I was secretly glad. Childhood...

Once again, I glance at the newspaper in the young girl's hands, and notice the headlines announcing the holiday. Once again, I return to the past.

Who knows why the adults in our neighborhood did not make holiday visits. They would send us, the children to greet the neighbors and friends. It must have been because the adults who were always trying to get something done never had time for visits. Holidays were no different. Cooking, cleaning, dishes, and laundry took up the entire day. Most of us did not have fathers. In our neighborhood, perhaps one or two women had their husbands at home. The husbands of some worked on ships, like our father, some worked in Germany, and some had died at a young age. Apart from a few old men, only the knitter Necla, Sülün Abla and Aunty Türkan had husbands around. Oh yes, there was also our grocer Uncle Hamdi. His wife had departed from this world at an early age. So if we didn't count the snotty children and the boys at puberty, ours was a "Neighborhood of Women".

It was the children who got the utmost pleasure out of holidays. Those were the days when the fatherless children of our neighborhood, who were sometimes happy and sometimes sad, would dress up in their best clothes. On holidays and the first day of school, we were all squeaky clean. We tried to keep our faces clean, and didn't even play hide-and-seek, in order to get more candy at the houses we visited. We almost forget our childhood, in order to keep clean the clothes that our mothers put on us in the morning. Instead of running, we walked with deliberate, careful steps.

When my father was in town, on the first day of the holiday, we would go to visit my paternal grandparents who lived in Sincan. Next in line would be a visit to my paternal aunt's house, and then one to my paternal uncle's house. When my father was away, my mother could not take us to make these visits by herself. On the second day of the holiday, my paternal Uncle Seyfi would drive down in his pick up truck to get us. But the first day of the holiday, my sister, brother and I would visit all the neighbors one by one, we would first kiss the hands of the elders, and then continue with the younger folks, while our mother waited at home.

While I'm lost in the memories of past holidays, the cabin crew makes announcements, preparations and the plane takes off. I smile at the young girl beside me, and just when I'm about to turn to the window again, I notice that the stewardess has arrived with a tray of chocolates, and is serving me.

"Have a good trip," she says, "and a happy holiday. Won't you take one?"

I take a chocolate with a smile. "Have a good trip."

Then I turn to the girl beside me and I wish her a good trip and holiday. When I unpack chocolate and put it into my mouth, I see that we are flying towards clouds.

On holidays of my childhood, we used to go from door to door, until our cloth bags sewn by my mother were full of candies. Some neighbors, like Aunty Saadet, would invite us in. Others would serve us some candies and send us home. By late afternoon, all the children of the neighborhood would gather before the grocery store, to show each other our loot: the pocket money and candy. It was a childish competition. My favorite was caramel candy. Sometimes we used to exchange candies-each taking more of her favorite kind. I first tasted chocolate when I started primary school, on the first day of the Sacrificial Holiday. Zeki, whose father was working in Germany, had distributed chocolates to all of us. After tasting the chocolates that came in a shiny wrap, I no longer liked the taste of caramel candy which I used to collect too avidly until then. But chocolate wasn't a usual visitor of our holidays. My father would bring some when he returned from his trips... So we had to make do with caramel candy wrapped in shiny paper.

Every holiday, Aunty Saadet used to buy those caramel candies. We were not shy with her. She would say, "Take more, children. Take more," and we filled our pockets by handfuls. Aunty Saadet seemed to like us. One time, she had bought my elder brother a shirt, and some fabric to make dresses for us. She also gave us some pocket money as much as she could afford. She often hugged us as if giving us the affection that she was unable to demonstrate to her own two children.

All right, we knew Yüksel Abi was sick. But I couldn't understand Münevver coldness towards her mother. At one point some rumors spread in the neighborhood that Münevver was Aunty Saadet's stepdaughter. My mother said it was completely nonsense. "Münevver is Saadet's own daughter," she said. For some reason Münevver Abla was distant from everyone in the neighborhood, including her own mother. It was as if she disliked the neighborhood because she disliked our poverty, our way of living and us. The only person towards whom she was nice was Yüksel Abi. She helped to feed him, and took him out for a stroll in his wheel chair from time to time. Her face brightened with a smile when she was with him. She even hummed a song as she pushed the wheel chair in the streets.

Zehra was very fond of Münevver. Disregarding her coldness and her manner as if putting us down, Zehra would cozy up to Münevver, whenever she could. As a little girl, she so admired the adulthood of Münevver, that she watched Münevver clothes, nail polish, and romance novels, eager and impatient to grow up like her...

Why were you so impatient to grow up, Zehra?...

It wasn't for nothing that I was remembering that childhood holiday with so much detail. It was the last holiday when I saw Aunty Saadet. She had suddenly fallen into the paws of a vicious illness, just like Zehra who is fading away before our eyes now.

I remember when we jumped out of bed at the voice of Münevver shouting at our door:

– Aunty Meryem, aunty Meryem!

No sooner had my mother greeted Münevver, that "my mother has taken a fall," Münevver said, and fainted at the doorway.

While my elder brother Osman and I tried to bring her around, my mother had rushed outside in her nightgown, Zehra skitting after her. The husband of the knitter Necla was a cab driver. They had taken Aunty Saadet to hospital in his cab. Aunty Saadet had not returned. Now it was

Münevver who looked after Yüksel, and who did all the housework. From time to time, to visit her mother at the hospital, she would leave Yüksel with us.

One day, my mother got us dressed up to visit Aunty Saadet. She was at a hospital in the district of Ulus, and we, the children enjoyed going to Ulus. We were eager for the visit as if we were going to a fair ground rather than to the hospital. My mother bought some lemon flower cologne from our corner grocer Hamdi. She took our hands and we got on the minibus. The hospital yard, hospital corridors and waiting rooms were packed with people. My mother asked several attendants where Aunty Saadet's room was. The door of the room was wide open, and inside there were more visitors than patients. When I saw Aunty Saadet lying in bed, at first I thought she was dead. Her head was covered with bandages. My mother had told us that she had had an operation, instructed us to be quiet and not to ask any questions. Aunty Saadet had opened her eyes at one point; she had even smiled at us. I've never forgotten the smell of antiseptic that filled the halls of the hospital that day.

I found myself in the corridors of that same hospital this morning. The face of my sister Zehra who was beside me during the visit to Aunty Saadet, years ago, and whose hand I had held tightly, is in my mind.

We were at her bedside-my parents, my brother, aunt and Zehra's former husband, while she lay unconscious, her long brown hair spread out on the pillow. No, I imagined her long brown hair. They had shaved her head in order to operate for the tumor. Yet, when I looked at Zehra's head covered with bandages, I kept seeing her long silky hair. My mother was holding her hands. My father was seated in a chair, silently weeping. None of us said anything. The fact that Zehra was a nurse had helped us get a private room in the hospital with the help of doctors who knew Zehra. Now, when the doctor arrived, my mother, my brother and I headed outside. I had wanted to stay in the room to hear what the Doctor would say but my father who is a cardiac patient, was so upset that I wanted to spare him from further pain. My aunt went downstairs to phone her children, and Zehra's former husband Mahmut went outside to smoke.

I held my father from his arm. Throughout our childhood, we had not had a chance to share joys or sorrows with my father because he was absent so much of the time. I suddenly realized that this was the first moment of sharing an emotion. All the pain on his face was also on mine. We were embracing each other. Even though conditions of life had kept us separate much of the time, I loved my father very much. We felt close to each other, perhaps both of us had chosen to depart from our homeland. If my father had chosen to work at a hotel instead of on a boat, he wouldn't have to go - and we would have had a completely different life.

And if I hadn't left... If I had not left my family, my childhood, my friends for the sake of career in chemistry... I thought about the career ladder I was on at the cosmetics firm where the newest discoveries were made.

My brother came out of Zehra's hospital room, wiping his eyes. It was obvious that he was trying hard not to cry, not to upset my father.

"The doctor said the operation had gone well," he said.

"That's good," answered my father.

"Let me drive you to the airport so you don't miss your flight," my brother said to me.

I gave my nod of approval. I embraced my father, and kissed him on both cheeks, and turned away to hide the salty tears that were running down to my mouth. I opened the door of Zehra's room, for one last look at my mother and Zehra. I whispered to Zehra's ear that I loved her very much. I kissed her hands, looked at her face intently, imagining her long brown hair. When my brother came into the room and gestured to me to hurry up, I promised myself that I would return, whatever it might take. This should not be the last time I was seeing Zehra.

Another wound left from my childhood began to bleed just then. The image of the first person that had died in my life -my first childhood loss- rose before my eyes: Aunty Saadet. I saw her face in the halls of the hospital. I shivered with the memory of the coffin that had come out of their house. The cries of Münevver, the sharp screams of Yüksel... I grabbed my brother's arm and walked through the hall quickly.

Now, I revisit the places of our childhood, the holidays that I shared with Zehra...

I would not have thought that the happiest days of our childhood would be darkened by the death of someone we loved, and that the memory would haunt me on this day, so many years later. I'll do whatever I can, to prevent death from snatching my sister who is struggling with the same disease as the one that took Aunty Saadet away from us. Now, I'm on my way back to Paris. But I'm making some important decisions. Whatever it takes, I'll put aside my career for a while, to be with my family at this difficult time, at least until Zehra gets well. If my fiancé wishes to return to Turkey with me to get married in Ankara, we might do that. But Zehra's health is my highest priority now.

I'm fiddling with the pack of the chocolate which was served to me by the stewardess for a short while ago. My mouth is covered by the taste of a bitter chocolate. I keep folding the yellow piece of paper in all kinds of shapes, and discreetly put in my purse. I smile to myself, thinking about the caramel candy Aunty Saadet used to serve us.

As the plane goes towards the skies of the city where I had built my life and my dreams, the capital where I've left my family and my sister Zehra behind is wrapped in the darkness of evening, and I watch the smoke rising from chimneys.

I take a sip of the water the stewardess has served me with the candy. The aroma of caramel candy has replaced the slight bitterness of chocolate in my mouth...

Praiseworthy Prize

İlke Susuzlu / England

He was born in Gazimagusa, TRNC in 1979, and graduated from East Mediterranean University Department of Turkish Language and Literature in 2000. He interrupted his postgraduate study on Folklore in University of Hacettepe since he gave up of being an academician. He lives in London and is the editor of the Turkish news paper called *London Society Post.* He writes texts for theatre plays, he directs them and acts in plays. Moreover, works as a drama trainer in society centers. He is the founder of Susuzlu Theatre Company in 2003.

To the Imagination of Mademoiselle Cesar

Now we are following a yellow solitude... The smell of grief on the air arises through the melodies of a violin! The most glorious part of our memories that we can not catch even though we reach out to it cruises in the empty rooms. A cloud takes what we have what belongs to us... A star falls! Other stars accompany it... The day loses its color. The sky dresses up a black veil. I know that a new day comes in few hours! We will add a new one to our past. We will pass by the past ones one by one. Our souls will go away. Rivers will flow until they become one with the others. Our bodies will memorize the gaps of the uncolored and breathless rooms on and on. We will gaze at the birds flying away under a red vault. We will say all the payers that we know to make the ones return who left us. Our tears will burn the empty rooms like a fire. Only the birds crying for freedom will ring at our ears. And also the flaps that we hear but never see.

Flaps... They hurt me deep inside since "she" flew away. By the way, how long it has been since she has gone? I mean Cesar... How many days did I greet smiling painfully after the day she performed her dance of departure? How many weeks have turned into months when I waved at the birds that fly away one by one thinking that Cesar might have been there with them? I don't know. I removed them from my memory since I have to forget the number of the weeks that I was worn out hoping that she will be back at the evening! Boggling that I have to leave the doubts about what happened to her, I finally learned to say "life goes until the last minute and the last point you can live".

Thank you Cesar, you left our lives with your little body after you taught us many things. I still couldn't get used to the fact that you left... While I still remember the day when you come home, I don't even want to imagine you leaving shouting and screaming. Well, when did you come home?

I guess it was two years ago. Maybe it's been longer. I don't exactly remember the date; it was September. Somehow, when I think of September, I visualize the autumn leafs vanishing silently through the flames. I still love 'September' since it is the birth of the ending springs! I guess my love is reciprocal. When love is reciprocal, it hurts more; since we aggrandize the love. As it aggrandizes, we set one part of us more on fire, and we turn into leaves of autumn. As one of those leafs, I was torn away from my branch and waiting for the day that I will burn... This fire was shadowing forth also the new life as if the grain of a mystical air! Every familiar thing was going to absent from me in a cold day of September. Like birds, I was going to shake the dust of my feet to the climate of different worlds that I have to acclimatize.

Thoughtful and absent minded, at the evening of a day that I was going to say good bye to where I live and I got used to leave the determined days behind, in the living room of my house which have been witness to my childhood and my dreams, there was a fearful and silent bird inside the blue cage. Obviously she was from another world. She wasn't familiar with the air that she was drawing in. She was not acclimatized the geography that she was going to live. I was able to understand her well. She attracted my attention as one might expect since she was something new within my knowledge.

My eyes examined at once my parents watching the cage! What was this bird doing in our house? The respond to my question was short and clear-cut; this bird would be the new guest of our house! By touching its cage with my fingers, I greeted this bird which would be a member of our home after months. However, it ignored me as if I had been a figurine. A further living thing was added to members of house from which I would depart in a few days. In all fairness, I was very happy. Mostly for my mother.

Since I am the single child of my family, it was my mom with whom I had shared my secrets, my bliss and sorrow, my hopes, my dreams, the TV serials that successfully ended up at the most exciting moment, songs, my caprices in the examination days, the news and naturally my struggles. Always, my mother had suffered from my depressions and resentments. She worked hard to make it up when I was offended; and I quarreled with my mother. I always expected her to make it up when I was offended. We had become the best friends of each other! Compulsorily, this friendship had to go on in different territories, where the seas separated us. Naturally, it affected also my father much. He was going to miss my obstinacy and his state of mind between me and my mother. Who knows, when we were going to come up with something, I and my father never ended up a discussion successfully! Through these dreams, I started to attach a different importance to this bird. Dreams would have remained forever, but my parents used to need a new living creature to maximize their happiness. Because they couldn't stand keeping their love inside. That's why the silent bird in the blue cage had been sent. It was a sign; a symbol of the blue canopy indicating the continuity and power of love and ability to love.

Few weeks before my departure, I observed the bird whose cage was left from pillar to post. First days of the tiny bird at her new home had passed in fear. Her presence was indistinct. Only "the volume of her cage" used to remind her presence. She was totally quiet. It used to seem as if she had taken an oath to stand still. She used to eat something only by force. I could never see her drinking water. She was obviously missing the territory where she was born; and suffering from departure. She was offended, but she had nothing to do but acclimatizing the territory she came... Suddenly I began to consider that we were of identical faiths. I hit it off with her. She turned into my toy when I was at home; I used to like annoying her. It was a pleasure for me when she used to react to the things I did. Just like a sibling... Anyway, she also left her resentment away and all the family was fascinated by it. She was quite successful in planting the flag at the top. She was dignified as much. She didn't used to let anyone get closer to her cage and didn't even used to allow anyone to reach out.

After several days the bird was still lack of a name. Formerly, I wanted to give the name "Cesar" since I was told that it was a male bird. After, when it was understood that it was female, its name was altered as "Mademoiselle Cesar". Then, I departed for dampening under the rain of another country; leaving behind my own country where I had collected my house, my streets, city and memories; my mom, my father, and also Cesar. This journey caused my longings to increase. Cesar was among my longings. When I dial handset on hook the number of my parents to hear their voice from a distance of kilometers, "Cesar" used to be the first "person" that I used to ask about. I personalized her in my mind. Despite her lacking of hands, she used to have a huge heart full of love!

And again in one of my calls from a distant country, I heard that Cesar flew out of her cage, settled on my mother's hand, and kissed her. That day, the 'wild' bird, which didn't allow anyone to come close to her cage, had been friend of a hand – but a hand which tried to caress her everyday. We were as pleased as Punch because of this act of Cesar. My mom succeeded to tame a bird that it used to be thought not to get rid of its wildness. Now it was my fathers turn, however Cesar was too chary to choose a second hand as a friend. Maybe Cesar used to expect that my father might have caressed her, and this might have been true since she settled on my fathers hand when she got it. Flowing side of love warmed up my father inside so that he had grown used to remise of his sleep and wake up very early in the morning with the first ray of light just to gather 'purslane' for Cesar. Strange to say, but I also adopted myself to the fact that there were three people living at my home. My mom, my father and Cesar.

Formerly, it used to seem very funny. How could a bird attract two hearts? How could it love at the risk of resisting against the nature? How could it make the others love? It was against the laws of nature. However, I would have understood that it wasn't an 'ordinary' bird. Speaking lips aren't required to express our love. Cesar didn't have lips; however she used to have glances whispering her love. Cesar wasn't only a part of our family through her glances; she also captured all voice of our family. It used to bite off more than it could chew. The strange thing was you were not able to counter her even though she was defenseless! You were not able to be angry with her because she was so tiny. Her glances were as clean and reassuring as those of a child. I guess I will never have the piece I used to find in her trembling breath.

Cesar was a heroin just as the ones in dreams. She used to have a sacrosanct beauty. Most probably because of her heroism, this beauty used to be perceived despite all the interruptive obstacles. Being far away didn't mean lacking of the close feelings. I may fail to express what I want to mean since I am ambivalent now; I'd better give an example.

One day, when I was far away and trying to get rid of my tiredness, I communicated with my parents. We absolutely wrote to each other everyday; it was nice to get news! My mom wrote the messages; somehow my father was unfamiliar with mobile phones. Anyway, the response of my mother to what I wrote was not sincere and warm. As though the words were melting on air! They were sentences written cursorily. They had been written just to be written. As mentioned before, I know my mother well. Under these circumstances, I always consider that something bad has happened. Distance should be something which consumes somebody up faster and more.

I held the phone with numerous speculations and questions eating me up; I decided to get rid of my anxiety pressing the numbers of the phone. Soon after, I heard her voice saying "Hello" at the other side of the phone; however it wasn't her voice as usual. It was as if the bitter symphony of the emotions reflecting on the voice of a sad person! Then I interrupted the concert with the question asking "What happened?" to prevent the symphony to continue. The smell of grief on the atmosphere might have been caused by the fall of Cesar into silence... My mother told what had happened trying not to cry.

To find answers to the questions in my mind when I hung up the phone; I had to wait for three days until Cesar got better. Well, what had happened to Cesar? The bird that we tried to make survive behind the grills by giving it water and food, had tried to express her internal and exceeding emotions by keeping silent. Through its tiny body it had tried to show the power of love and then the miraculous side of care. Each creature in nature needs love; I guess nobody can survive wholesomely without care. Cesar, realizing that love do arrive through care had kept her silence for three days. She had experienced three long mornings and endless nights without eating or drinking anything. She could eat just a little. My mom have had given her medicine by force opening her mouth, and never left her tirelessly and caressed her silky feathers as if bringing a child back to life. She had touched her feathers through her fingers being cut to her heart, abandoning herself to despair and on the other hand, keeping her hope. She had given her love, and care... and Cesar began to move and increase her reactions slowly, and after few days, she was again the cheery bird we got used to. My parents were bursting with happiness. This was the first accident which Cesar had. Isn't it like a fairy tale? However it is true. A bird which can't speak in any language have reminded us the forgotten and mostly denied side of love. For the first time, I had learned the silent mood of love.

And days followed one another! I departed from a "distance" towards the quarters that I used to stride through their streets leaving a long year behind and adding a new age to our time of life. After a flight of six hours, while I was enjoying attaining the lemon tree which I missed and bitter coffee which is drunk under this tree every morning, it attracted my attention that Cesar have been treated as if she were a human being standing in the first place. Everything was happening in a way she wants. Furthermore, she had known the household to get what she wanted. She was trying to avoid looking at my face most probably since she understood that I was observing her moves. I guess she was afraid of losing her sovereignty! Since I discovered her weakness, I kept taking on her and annoying her until I heard my mother warning me "That's enough!" Naturally, the bird took an oath not to sidle up to me. We were just like two siblings who were not able to get on well with each other but also not able to keep away from each other. I didn't used to have another sibling; I was an only child. Cesar was a good chance for me to experience this feeling.

My summer holiday of three weeks has ended up with sentences including the word of "Cesar". Cesar, waking up the household with her voice as soon as the day shines on the window, was going to be included in my longing even though she used to interrupt my morning sleeps in my summer holiday. The bird which used to wish to wander around the house with free steps leaving the cage as soon as my mother greets it through the grills of the cage, on the day of my departure, came to my hand and bent its head to let me caress it. It looked at my face as if saying 'I will miss you too' and saw me off!

Time periods that sometimes fast steps had been confused sometimes oars had been pulled slowly had come between. While my longing hardened, encircling part of love like iron armor continued to prevail in the house of my childhood. Cesar began to eat at the same table with my parents. Tiny pet which was not able to stand on when there was someone missing at the table used to love to take a nap climbing on the top of its cage after the dinner. Moreover, it used to drop asleep with my mother at noon, and even if it woke up earlier, it would keep silence not to disturb anyone until she woke up too. When it was bored, it used to go to the bedside of my mother or my father to stand sentry silently. Sometimes, it used to fall asleep on the leg of my father; this time my father didn't used to move until Cesar woke up. Well, there was such a love between them. Reciprocally and completing one another...

Cesar got over a number of accidents until the next summer holiday. Especially, she used to react on the voices with high volumes at night banging her wings to the grills of the cage. In such a case, my parents used to calm her down staying with her, caressing her and making sweet noises. Cesar was a very sensitive bird. She was full of love. She used to call my parents to account in case she stands clear of them for a minute; if this standoff took longer; she used to turn her back and expect to be pleased like a human being. Her susceptibility was caused by her fondness for care.

Cesar was aware of everthing necessary. She used to cognize the footsteps of my parents. She used to hear the noise of my fathers car and used to serenade until my father park the car in the garage. When my mother went to another room, first she used to listen to the voice; if there was not a sound to be heard she used to follow her, and making different voices she used to ask using where my mother was. Strange but true; Cesar have had become a human being without hands who wan not able to talk.

In the second summer after I departed for far away lands, I met once again with the bird which enters the cage only during the sleep hours or in case my parents were out. However, I took someone with me that it would get on well. Cesar, the fellow of my parents, stroke up a friendship as soon as she met the person with whom I experienced deepest love in my life. Also my husband, who greeted her every morning, and raised the love kissing and fondling her every night, considered Cesar as one of the family members. Cesar accepted that we were a family with five members even though she didn't used to like crowd and didn't used to share the love of my parents.

Once again the page of the calendar displayed the day of separation. I left Cesar saying "see you next year". The days passing without knowing what time might bring lost their colors after the message informing that she has "gone". We began to face the moments of this colorlessness, this blurry state of mind. As soon as my parents uttered the words "she has gone" on the phone, the word of "losing" threw up to me on and on. My mother tried hard not to cry. The tiny bird that she loved have succeeded to draw the Picture of separation form y mother, however my mother was indecisive about the color of grief. It seemed as if all the fundamental and intermediate colors of the rainbow have had worn the sorrow.

After Cesar had gone all the lines have been wiped away. My parents, who used to be backing home in hurry just not to leave her alone at home became unwilling to enter the house. The house lost its breath. My parents still couldn't get used to the sudden abandonment of Cesar. They couldn't confess it. They still take a look at the open cage of Cesar in the hope that she will return! Because people can not accept easily the fact of the loss of a living creature that they loved really much.

Cesar had gone. She flew away leaving two couples of eye locked up in the blue sky. After she has gone, my parent began to do something that they would never do before. They began to leave birdseed in the garden. It makes them happy when the birds in the nature become happy. Cesar was a signal! An innocent friend knocking on our door to remind of the word of "merit".

In a midday time, Cesar ran away shouting and screaming from the house that she filled with memories just after my father left to house to buy newspaper. My mother, not getting what was happening, stood in bewilderment after Cesar who flew away raising over her shoulder from the door of the kitchen towards the blue sky! The hardest moment of the grief stop; to stand in bewilderment and not to be able to do anything! It may seem just consolatory but everything happens as they should happen. In the end, Cesar has gone away, but where? Someone caught her or did she die?

Cesar wasn't used to live alone. Furthermore, the day when she went, the entire city fell in darkness as if they all were in mourning, and an endless rain has had begun to fall on the city. In each flash of lightning brightening the sky; pieces of hope torn from the hearts of my parents gathered in a depth that they were not familiar. Oh Cesar! My tiny! Did you want to enjoy the freedom, or did you dash yourself unconsciously to the water of the city? I don't know, we don't know!

Cesar might have wanted to leave! Her eyes were already staring at outside the window before she left. May be she remembered the freedom that she has forgotten for a long time, or she returned to her origin.

After all, my parents and Cesar enjoyed and shared the free side of love! For a period of more than two years, they taught each other what they had forgotten and had never learned.

I don't know how long it has been since Cesar went away, but all these left days displays that this departure has no return. My parents suffer their grief really much but only inside. Still, they are at ease; they gave all their love to a living creature that they hosted in their house. There are plenty of things to tell. Unfortunately my parents keep their silence. They are listening to the sound of loneliness. Their eyes look around in the sky! Knowing that she won't be back, they still don't want that darkness falls on the city. The door of her cage is open! Everything remains the same as the day she left. Only thing that changed is the lack of her existence... my parents missed her gaze. And they also missed her climbing somewhere in a courtesy of Mademoiselle.

I also missed her really much. She brought the second spring to our house after I left home. Now I accept... Yes, I was jealous of her secretly! May be she was very tiny but she used to have the power to share the loneliness of two people. She was a two-side mirror reflecting the whole life through short and confident steps. She was the living creature of both her life and our lives. And I accept; Cesar was more than a breathing bird. She was a source of life, voice of hope, symbol of forgiveness, mother of silence, meaning of all passing days, cure of difficulties, companion of loneliness, confidant of the eyes which have sworn not to speak, leader of motivated screams, inimical to anger, inspiration for hearts looking at the day, fragrance of flowers blooming at night, and may be most importantly, a deep love reminding us of the existence of many things that we have to discover...

She was a 'human being' for us... She was a life. She was a treasure which was able to reflect its shadow on our hearts. A treasure that diamond, ruby, or emerald could not compete with. As you watched it, you were getting lost in its depth. I learned firstly from her that words are not enough to explain the feelings. I enjoyed the pleasure of silent talk with her. Through her existence, I caught on holding the life with its different sides and not leaving it anymore.

And she went away...

She said goodbye leaving the eyes behind gazing at the flying birds...

Her toy plate, her detached wings, her beak stone, sprays, bird seeds, the traces that she left eroding the walls and books, and her eyes in the Picture remains.

And also her open cage with the hope that she will be back someday...

Praiseworthy Prize

Mustafa Cebe / Germany

He was born in Malatya in 1965. He was graduated in 1987 from the Business Administration Department of Dokuz Eylül University in İzmir, and studied for a master's degree at the University of Köln for a while. He has been living in Germany since 1989 and writes children's books.

Rose

There is no reason for the rose
It flowers because it flowers
It neither admires itself,
Nor wants to be seen.
(A. Silesius)

If only the guide would stop talking, if only the ache in his soul would abates.

It's as if inside of his brain gets shaken up with the shaking of the bus.

He leaned his head against the windowpane of the bus going along the coast, and watched the sea. His troubles were also traveling with him. In the last two days, anxiety had shaped his heart and turned into the malaria fever in his bed each night. He would wake up with a voice saying, "You're looking for a different tomorrow." It resembles the voice of memory, the voice of warning. He was dizzy, his insides were clammy. Yet, for six months, he had so looked forward to these two weeks he would spend in his country. Where did this anxiety result from on the second day of his vacation? He had hoped to get rid of it, by taking a day tour. He made his reservation for the tour on the previous evening and went upstairs to his room. In the morning, he woke up in pain, and started the day in pain as if hanging on to a specific memory...

When the bus stopped, the passengers seemed to be in a hurry to get outside. He got off reluctantly after the bus had emptied out completely. The guide had gathered everyone around, to give information in German about the places they were going to see. He listened without interest. "Let's meet at the bus in two hours," the guide said, and then the group got going.

The sun was getting more influential. He stood still for a while, watching the group. He turned to the other side and glanced at those sitting in the shade of a tree. He wanted to drink tea in that shade, and to sit there lazily.

He started to walk on the earth road. Passing beside a stonewall on which rugs were spread out to dry, he stared at the rugs for a while. At the moment he was leaving, one of the rugs attracted his attention. He approached slowly and began to inspect the rug from one end to the other. He stroked its surface, as if caressing it. All emotions and memories inside him started bleeding first, and then mix with the colours of the rug. He felt as if there had been violins broken in his soul. His hurts were turning into a tune, sang in chorus by broken pieces.

The carpet seller rushed to his side. "It's our own hand-woven carpet sir," he said. He pulled his hand away abruptly. He rubbed his burning eyes. The bleeding inside him had stopped. His eyes had started to shine as if he was watching a rose he touched return to life.

"We have many others inside," said the carpet seller. "You may also see them in our weaving section while being woven."

His hand and his eyes remained hanging in the air. He gathered together the broken songs inside, and followed the carpet seller.

When they entered the section where dozens of looms stood, the sounds of weaving tools and scissors seemed to be singing the same refrain. He felt as though he had passed beyond the threshold that separated reality from dreams. He could no longer separate dreams from realities. They stood beside the loom where a young woman with long hair was weaving a carpet. "This young girl is the one who weaved that carpet you were looking at," said the seller.

For some time, he looked at the carpet, and the hands that were weaving it. He was struck by the speed of young woman while working. He was looking at the carpet and her eyes successively, as if hoping to find shapes of carpet in her eyes.

The salesman had started to pour out information on the carpet to the man who was staring at the weaver as if he was mesmerized. A whole series of information covering everything from shapes to colours. The only quality the carpet didn't have was the power to fly. "If you would allow me, I just want to watch the weaving," he said. The salesman answered "Of course," in an offended manner and walked away.

He was left alone with the young woman. He kneeled to watch the flying hands. "May I touch the carpet?" he murmured. The woman blushed, "of course," she answered, her voice hardly audible.

He gently stroked the carpet for a while. His hand stopped on the burgundy coloured rose design at the center. His eyes seemed to grow large. The light filling his heart shimmered. The distances seemed to shrink. Gates swung open. Questions multiplied. The rose that was fading in his heart revived, multiplied, turned into words.

He asked with a quivering voice, without looking at the girl: "What is your name?"

"Rose," she answered.

Rose, he repeated wordlessly.

"My mother seems to have given me that name after the rose your hand is on."

Your mother!

"My mother wove many carpets in her youth. She created all the designs. She wove this one with the rose motif, for her trousseau. It has a sad story. Whenever she tells us that story, her eyes fill with tears."

"Is your mother still weaving?" he asked in a soft voice.

"No, when she was young, she wove for her trousseau but never again after that. My father was a carpet merchant. They say he used to go from house to house asking for carpets. That's how he met my mother. When they got married, they settled here."

"How long have you been weaving?"

"Three years."

"Would you tell me the story that your mother has told you?"

The young girl looked around, "I don't know she said.

"Don't worry; I'll buy the carpet. But I would like to know the story of the carpet I'm buying..."

"My mother was around fifteen or sixteen. My maternal uncle was at high school then. One day, he came home with the teacher's son who was at the same high school. The teacher's son had grown up in a large city so he had difficulty getting used to our town. He was bored. When they arrived at home, my mother was alone, weaving a carpet in the living room. "As soon as he entered the entrance hall, my heart lit up," she says. "It was as if a bright light entered my heart to melt away all the longing that had collected there." The boy couldn't take his eyes away from my mother either. He looked at her long and deeply. When my paternal uncle took his friend upstairs, my mother was upset. In her heart she was pleading "I hope they'll return downstairs to sit beside the fire." Before ten minutes, her wish came true. The two young men threw some logs into the fire and began to talk. It was my paternal uncle who was talking while the guest was listening. My mother says "he was not talkative but he used to have such a beautiful way of looking at you..."

With that look, the sparks of a flame began to burn my mother's body. When my uncle went outside to pick up something to drink from the grocery store, he came near my mother to watch the carpet that she was weaving. He touched each ball of wool, and then he picked up the burgundy coloured ball and said "why don't you weave a rose with this one." On that day, my mother began to weave the rose into this carpet with that ball of yarn.

The next time he arrived, he was very pleased to see the rose in the carpet. He came and went for months. One day, he told my mother that he was leaving town soon because his father was going to work in Germany. At first my mother was devastated. She wanted to with him but it wasn't possible. "I'll come back one day to get you," he said. So my mother finished weaving the carpet, working on it day and night. He gave it to him as a gift when they saw each other for the last time before his departure.

As she began to choke, she looked at the man who was lost in her story, with beads of perspiration on his forehead, "This isn't some story I make up to sell the carpet," she said. "Not even my boss knows about this. It's the first time that I'm telling it. The first time to you..."

He turned his eyes away from the burgundy coloured rose, to Rose's green eyes. "All right," he said. "If I want to thank the lady who is the owner of this story, how could I reach her?"

The young woman shrugged a couple of times. "I don't know," she answered.

The cab was advancing quietly under a vast sky, and the wind that came in through the open window and struck his face was whispering some things he was trying to forget. He was on his way, burdened with a heavy load. With the images he had gathered, he was traveling from exile, making his way towards his own bed.

Driving across hills covered with olive groves, he was staring at one single point, like a sparrow that forgets all on the branch where it is perched. When he descended to the shore road, words spilled on the sea, along with the points of sunlight. Words that said "in my heart is the weariness of walking burdened with a different fate."

The sea was agitated. The sparrow whispered its song. The boat near the shore moved away. He was flowing towards a different solitude than his own.

The cab driver nudged him, "Sir, we've arrived at the address you gave me."

He pulled himself together, like awakening from sleep, and he got out.

He stood before the door, his body stiff.

His quivering hand reached the doorbell.

Soon the door was opened.

Her eyes were touching his.

The boat was rising and falling in the waves.

From the eyes that had met at the place where pain had gathered, silent tears flowed towards the sea.

Encouragement Prize

Serdar Özkale / Germany

He was born in Balıkesir in 1965. He was graduated from Political Sciences Faculty of Ankara University in 1986. After working as an assistant in the faculty for two years, he started business in Türkiye İş Bankası as a Training Expert. He has been serving as Nürnberg Branch Manager of İş Bankası since 2001. This story which was awarded a prize in this competition had been read aloud in Nürnberg-Association of Kemalist Thought; and also in Nürnberg Turkish German Women Club respectively in November and December 2006.

If You Have a Heart, Give My Cat Back

She was attracted by a small placard stuck to the corner of a shop having a window, in which curtains made of lustrine and decorative furniture were exhibited. The shop was at ground floor of the historical building which was the intersection point of Oberewört Strasse and Unsschlittplatz. Although she wanted to return home as soon as possible, she slowed down and desired to see what was written due to a mysterious curiosity. She was startled as soon as she read the first sentence of the placard. She began reading the advertisement attentively:

"To the reader of this placard,

Liz; my dear cat, my darling, my basis of existence has got lost as from the second day of Christmas. Liz, my cat and darling, got lost as from the said day on which I led her out of street door so as to provide her to take air. On the basis of my long-lasting experiences, my age and my heart filled with love of God, I know that she is still alive and she is in your house. Yes, you, the reader of this placard, I certainly know that you are also a woman; you take my cat and keep her in your house. However, I see my cat in my dreams every night. In my dreams, she is lying down on the couch in our house, thinking deeply just as she rarely does, and looking at me sadly. I feel that Liz is alive and miss our house very much. You also know that she misses me. If you have a heart and a tiny love in it, please give my cat to me back. Just allow it to go out the street for returning her to me. I suppose that you are living in an adjacent quarter, but if you carried it too far away, please bring her to our street and leave it. Liz can easily find the correct way and her own door. There is a special entry under garden gate, she can easily come in and find her mother through it. I thank you in advance since you will do this. I write my telephone and address for all eventualities. I wish absolution for all of us and invoke God for granting passage to heaven.

Best regards, Gisela Beck."

She read the placard excitedly and rapidly. She mopped her brow and peeped around. She continued walking swiftly just as she had done a few minutes ago. But this time, she walked as if escaping from something, but not trying to arrive in somewhere.

That night, Gabriele Schmidt failed to sleep until the morning. She fell asleep at dawn for a while and started dreaming a little later; in her dream, a white cat was talking to her and tried to nuzzle her even if Gabriele pushed her back. She waked up during this scuffle process, her dream turned into a nightmare. When she got out of the bed, the new day had just dawned. She lit up a cigarette. She had never thought that this could happen. What could she do now? Should she go on her life as if nothing had happened, or should she send Gisela Beck, owner of the cat, a message telling the truth? Should she apologize to her for everything? Okay, but for what would she apologize? She was entirely blameless. She didn't want to remind that night which she had immediately removed from her life, but again she reminded it, it was the second night of Weihnachten. She had gone to her friends' house for meal; she had drunk more wine than as usual. This was the first Weihnachten without him. She couldn't forget. Although she said that she could. Let it be admitted that she had entertained with her friends. But she had felt lovelorn and lonely again as soon as she had left her friends. She went to the car park in tears through the street which had been entirely illuminated. She continued crying for a while after getting on her car. She didn't deserve any of these experiences. At the very time she turned the corner of that baleful street, she noticed beauty of snow falling under the light of street lamp. Snow which was precipitating piece by piece fell onto the bicycle locked to the beam of street lamp in a pretty nice manner. She stopped her car and looked at pieces of snow falling onto the bicycle for a while. When she operated her car, she heard a wheezing sound. Liz which couldn't be seen among snow was crushed under the wheel of car. Strange to say, she hadn't thought that this cat had a name and what her name was. Poor Liz… Poor Liz... When she got off the car, the cat was crushed under the wheel and was dying in agony. Her eyes turned upside down and she was growling oddly. She didn't even remember how she could dare to take dead body of the poor cat from the ground and put it into the baggage within a shopping bag. It should be the courage provided by alcohol. That night, she carried the cat to Fürth Forest and left it at the bottom of trees in the bag. Afterwards, she went to home and slept as if nothing had happened. As soon as she got out of the bed in morning, she ran to the toilet and heaved. On that third day of Weihnachten, she felt herself as a murderer and cried all day due to both this unfortunate event and emotion of lornness.

She had recently forgot this incidence, but until she saw that placard. What would she do now? When the new day dawned completely, she decided to write the letter below:

"Dear Madam,

I am writing to you because I have a heart and love in it. First of all, I am also a woman and own emotions of a woman. Emotions like maternity, loneliness and love. I nourish different types of love in my soul and I certainly want to love and to be loved. However, God doesn't always treat its subjects equally, and rarely grants me to taste some emotions. Moreover may God absolve me, he has almost never granted such emotions to me. However, I really suffer from the lack of them...

No, don't take it amiss, I am not ugly, psychopath or strange as can be expected. My only fault is that I don't know how to behave coquettishly. In other words, I haven't met with the correct man so far. But, I don't aim at telling such things while writing to you. I want to talk about Liz. On the second day of Weihnachten, God granted Liz, or Barbi as I call her now, your cat to me. She was like a Weihnachten gift presented to me with her white hairs, azure eyes and red tape. I gave her this name because of my hunger for Barbie babies which my mother had never bought for me in my childhood even if I wanted very much because she spent almost all of her money for buying alcoholic beverages. I assume Barbi as a gift sent by God by the mediation of Santa Claus, and I have never considered returning her.

My house is her new house any more. She is sleeping deeply in her room inside. Within the elapsed time period, I am accustomed to her so much that I can't return it to you and desist from the greatest happiness in all my life. I certainly know the meaning of stealing happiness of a woman since I have experienced similar incidences... I have always promised myself not to treat somebody else in this way. Now, I feel as if I failed to fulfill my promise. But, I think that it is a somewhat different condition. As you would appreciate, Barbi is not a boyfriend, but a congenial companion.

Dear Madam, please acknowledge that I am right on my side. I require her so much that... I wish patience for you. Please believe that I will take care of her very well.

Sincere regards."

Since she knew that her letter would be replied soon, she controlled the wall to which the placard had been stuck for some days. She wasn't wrong, but she didn't dare to go and read it. She decided to read the placard at night when there was nobody in streets.

That night, Ms. Schmidt went out after dressing herself just as a burglar. Before leaving home, she had drunk two cups of whisky so as to pluck up courage. Probably, she got drunk. Finally, she came in front of the placard. She read the letter which had been written and stuck to the wall solely for her more rapidly than she expected. She had never been belittled and deflated so much before. She started walking towards her house swiftly as soon as she read the letter.

Ms. Beck wrote in her letter that:

"You, the woman who seizes an entity, a very valuable entity, which belongs to another people; you can't have a heart. You can't have any bits of love in your soul. You are a poor burglar. Besides, I don't think that you take care of my cat well. I also don't expect that my cat can love a woman like you. Liz is a noble animal. I don't have a disposition to request something from a woman like you. However, you presently capture the most valuable thing for me. If you don't let her return, please at least give her (x) branded feed. It is expensive, but Liz like these feed. If you can't afford to buy them, determine a place for me to leave money. Somehow, you are accustomed to take entities of other people. So you can also take this money easily.

Furthermore, I want to say that Liz likes listening Bach. She will be happy if you play Bach's albums from time to time. I am sure that you have never listened Bach before."

The letter had been written abruptly and brashly contrary to Ms. Schmidt's expectations. She wrote the below letter swiftly and angrily as soon as she went to home:

> *"Dear Madam, I neither seized Barbi nor stole it from somebody. The cat was a gift of God for me. You, the woman who left the cat outside in that cold Weihnachten night, how can you know the meaning of mercy and love? The music you listen is enough to prove that what a depressive woman you are. I haven't had a cat until now. But you must know that I am not so bowless, and I can't make her listen to Bach. Nowadays, Barbi listens to Mozart and Vivaldi, and I can easily understand from her vamping murmurs that she is enjoying very much. I make her listen to Brahms immediately before she sleeps. I am sure that, in her whole life, she has never enjoyed as much as now. Moreover, please don't worry; I have enough money to buy the best feed for her. I also don't have disposition to request something from you. However, I have only one plea from you. If you write Barbi's favorite toys to me, that will be very kind of you. I wish you good days."*

Within a few days, Gisela Beck stuck her response to the usual street corner. She again belittled the woman who deforced her cat. The object at issue doesn't comprise only Liz, or so-called Barbi, but also music, cat care, fancy, love and special emotions particular to a woman. These correspondences in the form of letter and placard went on for a while. Meanwhile passerbies, employees of surrounding shops and residents of street read letters stuck to the wall curiously and followed the developments interestedly. Once, a curious reader requested Ms. Beck to issue letters received by her as well. This incidence became so reputable that Nürnberger Nachricten, newspaper of the city, published a short announcement on this topic. Gabrielle Schmidt, who noticed that going further into this topic will be meaningless and needless, decided to end the discussion by a writing a final letter.

In her last letter which she dropped into different mail boxes in various parts of the city, she told that Barbi went out of the house since she forgot closing the garden door on a Saturday and that Barbie didn't return since then. Although she had been very nice to her, and had loved her very much, Barbi showed nonsense ingratitude. She also made a request. Was it possible to inform her if Barbi returned to her old house? She really wondered whether or not the cat was alive.

It was the end of winter and beginning of spring in Nürnberg. April had just started. Despite the elapsed months, no placard had been stuck to the wall of curtain store located at the intersection pointof Unschlittsplatz and Obereworth Strasse. The topic came to an end.

Shortly after the last letter written by Ms. Schmidt, she bought a Turkish Angora of six months old to herself. A completely new era started in her life with this snow white cat. As can be easily understood by the reader, she read books on cat care and gave her (x) branded feed each day so as to control wildness and everlasting naughtiness as much as possible. But, naughtiness of the animal had never ended. She scratched fabric on seats; she caused various furniture to be broken by jumping onto tables and armchairs. Wildness of the animal could not be removed even by making her listen to Mozart and Vivaldi.

Ms. Schmidt who was not only looking at very green parks and colors of spring through her window across Pegnitz river, but also reading the newspaper in her hand immediately after completing her breakfast on a Sunday; noticed that she didn't hear sound or noise of the cat at all. It was clear that there was a problem. She started looking for Barbi at once. However, the cat was neither far away from nor aiming at acting unruly. She nuzzled to the seat and focused at outside. She was thoughtful as if a philosopher. This was really strange! She started talking with Barbi. But the cat went on wheezing as if saying something without giving up her thoughtfulness and solemnity.

Ms. Schmidt, who didn't go outside that day, had such a silent and peaceful day for the first time after a long period. Music which they were listening from the radio, granted both her and her cat a special quietness within a single day. Next day, she went to a music market immediately after the work, and bought a set of Johann Sebastian Bach's CDs.

That year, Ms. Schmidt spent a wonderful summer during which she discovered Johann Sebastian Bach together with her cat at her home across Pegnitz river in Nürnberg.

Encouragement Prize

Birol Uzunmehmetoğlu / Canada

He was born in Kastamonu in 1968. He was graduated from Boğaziçi University in 1990. Since 2000, he has been living in Toronto with his family. After working as Quality Control Official at a company that produces software for trains, he works at the Ministry of Social Services of Ontario as Quality Control Engineer. He is married and has a child.

Nostalgia for Homeland

It's one of those freezing days in Toronto that I have not yet grown used to. There is a sun in the sky but it might as well be made of plastic since it gives off no heat at all. While walking towards the bus stop, I tell myself to be thankful for small mercies. After the gray skies that I've seen for weeks, it's as if this sun rose in my heart. As I notice my own shadow on the heap of snow at the roadside, I discover that gray days are lack of shadows. I wonder if shadows also have their own countries, and without so much focusing on this question, I continue walking. Anyhow I feel the pleasure of coming across an old friend.

It is so perishing that a five-minute wait in the bus shelter covered with glass on three sides, is indifferent to wait for five hours. My cheeks, the tip of my nose and my ears look probably in the red. Should I sniff or take my handkerchief out of my pocket? Take off your gloves and look up for the handkerchief in your pockets... Oh, let it slide. Sniff away. I pull down my toque to cover my ears, because the worst is the ear pain from the cold.

The red tramway called as street car has finally arrived. As soon as its doors were opened, all the cars on the two-lane street stopped. Isn't anyone in a hurry?

We are two persons at the bus stop, and even so, there is a polite race between us for being the first entrant to the street car. The man I don't know and myself, we both point at the interior of the street car to each other and wordlessly, we say "you first," with our eyes.

The two steps that go into the street carare white with the salt poured on the snowy roads. As I slip my ticket inside the box, the driver greets me "good morning." While I look for a place, with a mechanical voice, the driver announces the next stop: "Dufferin."

My usual seat is occupied today, by someone from the Far East. I wonder whose usual place I occupied in the bus when I first arrived in

Canada? Finally, when I find standing room between people who are in search of a little warmth by embracing their morning coffees like embracing a lover, I'm glad. I wonder if it's the hot coffee that warms up the cold mornings of this country that creates such a dependence on coffee, or the memories of warm lands that the coffee brings? I realize that I should get myself a coffee thermos soon.

Two more stops, and the traffic has stopped flowing. On top of worrying about getting to work on time, now there's the curiosity: what has happened? I look at the faces of the people beside me. They seem to be relaxed. Although the music coming from the ear phones of the youth with long hair and a single earring sets me in motion, he is sitting still and staring at a single spot as if he is also frozen from the cold. I notice hair roots of the redhead girl sitting beside him. It's obvious that she is originally blonde. I would never wear those loose pants that the guy in black is wearing, not even in exchange for money. I think the guy in a suit on my other side is checking his appointments on his palm pilot. My friends in Turkey have had them for a long time, but I'm going to take another look at my budget after taking my next salary, so I might buy one of those.

The ads inside the street car make me notice that we're in the season of income tax returns. This year, I'm again late with required transactions. Once again, I postponed it to the last minute. I must get rid of this negligence from now on, I tell myself.

I glance at the newspaper in the hands of the man standing before me. The largest hockey team in this city was defeated this week. I do not wonder why I did not catch this news on the evening newscast on TV. There is no one firing shots towards the air, or organizing long discussion programs, or there are no car horns, no waved flags, and no anthems; so how could I know? There's never any difference whether the local team wins or loses. This quiet response, which I once longed for, now seems strange. I wonder if I should be glad that I'm quite close to the door in this crowded street car.

When the street car suddenly stops again, the driver apologizes and makes an announcement that we should all get off to walk the forty or fifty meters to the bus that's waiting for us. Anyhow, the passengers going down the steps look lazier to me.

The traffic has stopped. It's as if the cars on both lanes are stuck to the street. I grab my coat collar tightly as I walk towards the bus waiting for us. Perhaps it's time to put aside the scarf that my mother has sent me from Turkey and get something warmer. And who said these boots were cold proof?

I pass beside three or four street cars lined in the street, one after another. The multi-colored advertisements painted on their exteriors don't even make me curious. They're all empty. Their drivers are either reading a book or glancing through the advertising leaflets that lie here and there. They are calmly waiting for the road to open, as if it is something routine.

I wonder if my name is advancing on the waiting list at the Toronto Public Library, for the Turkish book that I've asked for. I had better check this evening on the Internet. I realize that while I lived in Turkey, despite the plentitude of books in Turkish, I probably did not read as much as I read here. Is it because people around me read much of the time, or because the public library system encourages reading?

The people walking on the snow-covered sidewalk resemble a line of ants. Some of us hold lunch bags and some of us work files. We move forward in an orderly line, without speaking.

Finally, we find out why the traffic had congested. A car has hit the first street car in the line, from the back. Since I've passed beside four street cars on my way to the bus, and since there is a street car every four minutes, I estimate that it's been sixteen minutes since the accident has taken place. Am I wearing myself out with another useless calculation?

From a distance, I see that the correct procedure after an accident is being followed. I notice someone being given first aid at the back of an ambulance whose back door is open. The firefighters are cleaning the shards of broken glass on the road. A police officer is taking down notes on the accident while another one is regulating the traffic. There are neither sirens, nor people shouting and gesturing. A strange calm rules the day.

Are these familiar words that I'm hearing? Yes, this is in Turkish. At this early hour in the morning, could I still be dreaming? Who would utter any words in this cold, anyway?

But no, I was not wrong. Two swarthy men were watching the unfolding event at accident site, both with their hands in their pockets, and curiosity in their eyes. I can't make out if they are much older than twenty, but I clearly hear as I pass by them that the language they're using is Turkish.

"Look man, the street car is in the right. The car has hit it from behind."

"What do you mean man, the guy put on his brakes so suddenly. You don't put on the brakes like that on icy roads."

I don't know if the police officers thought of consulting my countrymen on who was right and who was wrong. But suddenly I felt a longing for my country. I think there may be ticket sales at the travel agent that's downstairs in the plaza where I work. I can always postpone buying the palm pilot. I wonder how much a ticket to Turkey would cost?

Encouragement Prize

Beyhan O. Duffey / France

She was born in 1972. She was graduated from the Theatre Department, Dramatic Writing Subdivision of Dokuz Eylül University in 1999. She held different positions in İstanbul State Theatre and İstanbul Municipal Theatre. She had lived in Saudi Arabia and French Guiana for a while due to profession of his wife. Her travel essays and stories were published by an e-newspaper, *Kahve Molası (Coffee Break)*. She's written stories for various television series, and scenarios for children programs. She's still living in Bussieres, French. She has a daughter.

The Cherry

– What do you want to be when you'll grow up?

– I'll be a truck driver.

– But it is impossible.

– Why?

– Because I hear that you are ill and will die. Is it true?

– I don't know. But it is probably true. I always have blood in my mouth.

– If you die, who will be my friend?

– I don't know. Perhaps you can find a new friend.

– But I don't want to have any friend other than you.

– Don't cry. You'll have to cry more when I'll die. So you'd better not consume your tears.

– What of it? I want to cry now.

– Then cry as much as you wish. You are just a crybaby.

– Please Murat, don't go!

When I found them, they were saying the above to each other under the cherry within garden. In a childish manner, I immediately informed my mother about what had happened. Because what I saw was unbelievable for me. Murat kissed Zeynep from her lips.

My mother was unable to hit Murat due to his illness, but yet intended to punish him. She pulled Murat's ear strongly and tried to force him to say that "Mum, I'll never do it again! I promise you! I won't do!" On the other hand, I was looking at Murat who stared at me with eyes full of tear, and also stroked my chest and slowly said him that "It serves you right."

In fact, I loved Murat. He was a quiet and silent child. Each member of our family loved him very much since he was the only boy in our house. When we learned about his illness, we were completely upset. In the end, it was decided that he should be treated abroad. However, I was going to school where I was with my lovely teacher and friends. I would also be a teacher in the future. I would have to separate from all of them due to Murat's illness. I thought that all of these were because of Murat, and hated him in my heart.

My father had been dismissed from his job in the coal factory. In fact, it was a satisfactory incidence, because I liked him very much. I waked up each morning when "wakening siren" of the factory in our town rung just before the sunrise. Each time, my mother would have already waked up and laid the table for breakfast. I took the teapot seething on heater despite my mother's all oppositions, and served tea to him while he was looking tenderly to me. I enjoyed watching crumbs sticking to brisky mustache of my father. His mustache started turning white just as his hair. I laughed when his mustache inclined to the right and left while he was chewing the food. On the other hand, my father vibrated his mouth much more so as to enjoy me.

When siren of the factory rung at length, it meant that it was time to begin working. My father got on his thick, black coat and held its collars up. My mother, herself, clothed his head by his scarf, and only his eyes remained uncovered. He was sent off by the same ceremony each morning and he gave me two and half Turkish liras as school money. While waving my hands for him through the window of room heated by a cook stove blazing strongly; I silently begged as "My God, please let my father live at least as much as me".

As soon as he went outside, my father multiplied. The street was crowded by other workers of town, who became hunchbacked under their black coats. While the coated crowd went far away from my window with pieces of snow mixed with cigarette smokes, the street relapsed into silence as in the beginning. Even today, I have my eyes full of tears when I remind this magical scene of my childhood.

My father who was cheerfully sent off by us in mornings returned home with coal black hands and face. He was also entirely tired. He carried cans of water boiled on stove to the bathroom and stayed there for long minutes. When we sat down around the ground table diligently prepared by my mother, he again became my jocose and funny father who I loved very much.

In the end, he got rid of all these difficulties. Furthermore, when dismissing him from job, they gave him such a high amount of money that we had never seen until then. We had to buy many things. Perhaps, he could even buy shoes, school bag, and a set of sweat suit to be worn in gymnastics lessons for me. But, it didn't take long for me to understand that reality was sharply different from my thoughts. That money would be used for going to Germany.

I hated Murat once more.

One night, I overheard what my mother and father were talking about. Murat was sleeping between me and Elif, our younger sister in shakedown. I wasn't sleepy at all, but I pretended to sleep without any case. My mother sat down next to us and cried quietly while caressing hair of Murat who was sleeping and wheezing.

– Yusuf, we can be wretched in a foreign country. Let's change our mind and protect our unity as a family here in our homeland.

– It is too late, Fidan. I have already quitted my employment in the factory. We have no other chance. We must go.

– Please, don't sell our cow at least. We may return immediately. We must be take measures; otherwise we can be ruined in the end.

– We won't be ruined, Fidan. Didn't you hear what my brother said? Didn't he tell us not to be worried about future? My mother will take care of both the cow and the house. After issuance of our passports, we will immediately go to Germany.

– Yusuf, it is enough to talk about Germany for frightening me. What will we eat and drink there? How can we get accustomed to there? Living in a foreign country is really challenging.

– Yes it is difficult, but do we have any other opportunity? We must go there for the sake of Murat.

– Then, at least we can leave girls here. Esme is very sad because she will depart from her school and friends. She can stay together with her grandmother.

– Fidan, I can't go anywhere without Esme.

– My dear Yusuf, I certainly know your devotion to Esme. Of course, you know better than me.

– We must protect unity of our family. It is possible that we can't return and it is equally possible that we can't find them when we will return.

I had cried under the quilt until morning after listening what my father had said. I understood sincerity of my father's love much well. I wouldn't tell my mother that I didn't want to go to Germany any more and wouldn't cause my father to get depressed. I would certainly go with them.

We started making necessary preparations for our travel to Ankara. My father took all of us to Sümerbank one day before. He bought completely new wearing apparel for each of us. I was mostly happy with getting rid of our black gumshoes. Our shoes were a little larger for us just as every other thing, but nobody cared this.

On the day of departure, all our family ate testimonial dinner on a large table laid under the cheery in the garden. Some of our villagers even prepared viaticum for us to eat during travel. My mother was grappling the neighbor women and crying. My mother entrusted the tree which provided cherries almost enough for the entire town every summer to my uncle. Because this tree was memorial of her deceased father. My father went to the factory and took leave of them. I and my classmates cried so much that almost no tear had remained in our eyes. Elif who didn't notice anything yet was picked up and held in arms of our grandmother. She was playing with plaited hair.

Murat and Zeynep were sitting under the cheery where I had seen them for the first time and complained them to my mother.

– Will you be healthy again?

– Of course. As far as I know, doctors will take care of me very well in Germany.

– You won't forget me, will you?

– I don't know.

– Do you mean that you'll forget me?

– I don't know.

– I won't forget you, Murat. I'll have waited for you under this tree until you will regain your health and come back.

It was the liveliest scene that I remembered about our last day in the town. All of villagers and the town itself were crying for our departure.

In the end, we arrived in Ankara. My father was significantly worried when we went to the Consulate for interview. My mother tried to calm him down, and always asked him to be silent. I got very surprised because I had never seen my father so scared until then. When we stood before the officer, we also held our heads down and folded our hands just as my father.

– What is the illness of this boy?

– Cancer.

– Isn't it possible to treat him here?

– No, it is not sir. Doctors said that we should go to a foreign country. Otherwise, the child will die.

Officer of Consulate looked carefully to Murat over his eye glasses at the tip of his nose. Murat also held his head down and folded his hand just as us.

– What is your name, the young boy?

– Murat.

– How old are you, Murat?

– Five years old.

– Are you happy with going to Germany?

Murat raised his head and looked first at the officer and then at my mother with his deep blue eyes. We also set our eyes on Murat and waited for his words which might change our common fate. Murat looked at the officer again, and said "Yes" in such a decisive manner that everybody guffawed.

It was certain that they would grant visa to us, however our bureaucratic transactions took a month due to ongoing anarchic incidences in Ankara then. As six people, we had spent that one month in the small bachelor house of my uncle and retained a clear memory of those days.

We finally arrived in Germany after a very difficult and exhausting voyage.

This country was a completely extraordinary place for us. People, roads, streets and even birds flying in the sky were different. They gave us an apartment on the ground floor. It didn't take enough daylight through small windows on high walls, but it was a comfortable house with furniture inside. There were even three separate beds for three children. Furthermore, they weren't shakedowns, but they were all bedsprings. It had a large bathroom in which hot water was eveready. Washing machine, fridge... Even a color television... We, who hardly self– controlled ourselves, embraced each other and cheered loudly after almoners had left the house. Because we would live in a house which was unusually comfortable and luxurious for us at that time. We owed all of these things to illness of Murat. It was easy for us to come to Germany since he was ill and since it had been decided that his treatment should start here. So, all our family could benefit from opportunities of this country without any restriction.

My father started working within a week. He started working as a garbage man in the municipality of the county where we were living. On the other hand, we were waiting for him to return in the house for the whole day. My father was pleased with his new job. He talked about his job so braggingly that we were aligned around him just as watching a movie and hanged on his every word.

– Which job is more difficult, father?

– Being a garbage man is much easier, my daughter. I am not dirtied by coal and don't ingest coal dust as in the factory. It is a gleaming job. Do not pay attention to its name. We have gloves covering our hands, orange overalls, and masks on our mouths...

– Blimey! Do you wear masks so as not to be recognized?

– No, of course. They make us wear them so as to prevent our being ill due to wastes. Here is a civilized country.

– Father, I know what 'civilized' means.

– Bravo! My clever daughter...

"Machines accomplished every kind of tasks. Wastes aren't thrown cursorily, all of them are put into trash bags which are wrapped solidly and separated according to the materials inside them. Machine, itself, lifts and discharges huge waste cans. We start collecting wastes even before dawn; we have already completed our job until noon. When I consider the nonstop work in the factory,

this job is much more satisfactory and easy. I am completely happy with being such a garbage man. The only problem is missing my home country!"

We had listened stories of garbage from my father for months.

Our house was checked by almoners once in two days. We got a strange fright when they came; we somehow thought that they harmed us. And they wanted to take Murat together with them in one of their visits. Murat put his small arms around my mother's neck and cried for not going with them. My mother embraced her son strongly and didn't give him to them. Meanwhile, we, two sisters were crying loudly and clasping skirt of our mother. It was obviously a family tragedy. We didn't know where they would take my brother off. We couldn't understand their language. In the end, we won the struggle and didn't give Murat to them. That day, I understood that I loved my brother to bits for the first time.

Next day, almoners came together with a Turkish translator and Murat was hospitalized for the purpose of treatment. When he returned to house after days, all of his body bloated and his eyelashes, eyebrows and hair were shed partly because of medicines he had taken. He seemed to be exhausted but happy. He went to and came back from the hospital continuously for seven years.

Everything had settled into shape step by step. We were also getting accustomed to our new life slowly. My mother always said that, "May God be pleased with German government." Murat's treatment went on without any disruption. Both the job and wage of my father were very good. It was even possible to think that we could be rich soon when his current wage was compared to his wage in the factory. But my father wasn't as happy as in the past; in fact he wasn't happy at all. He had spoken less and less with us day by day. I noticed that he paid less attention even to me. The only thing he did was to count down his wage many times and to daydream with the packet of money in his hand. When he came to the house by an old, Mercedes branded, orange car after months, we were all very well pleased. Besides, my father was cheery for the first time after months. That day, he shared a decision about his own life with us for the first and last time in his life. No matter what it would cost, said he, he would stay in Germany, be retired as a garbage man and buy a first hand Mercedes car in the end. He would completely move away from our world by his first hand Mercedes after he retired as a garbage man.

My mother waked up before dawn in mornings as she used to do, and she slept again after believing that all of us were sleeping. She told that she always saw our house, garden, cow, neighbors, and chickens in her dreams and didn't hide her tears from us.

We got bored of living intra muros after months. All television programs were in German and we couldn't understand anything. We were both afraid of and keen on going outside. I sat under the highest window whole day and watched legs of passbiers. From time to time, I listened voices of children through the open window and watched their games in this unknown language.

And one day an incubus event occurred! We all had to go to school!

Elif started nursery. She learnt another new German word in the nursery each day, and when she returned to home she repeated this word to us and caused my mother to shake her sides with laughter. In my mother's point of view, Germans were speaking in a very strange manner. Why didn't they speak Turkish just as us? Why did they choose speaking this difficult language? If they spoke Turkish, they would have a much easy life.

Murat had many new friends in the hospital. Furthermore, there were lots of toys, which he had never seen before then, in the department of pediatric oncology where he was staying. Especially, there was a truck among these toys... Murat always daydreamed by looking at that truck. He imagined to be the driver of that truck and to go to countries even further than Germany. He got along well with the children in hospital even if he didn't understand their language. These children were also ill just as him. Their hairs and eyelashes were also shed and they also wore a mask on their mouths. But all of them were very happy. Murat couldn't understand why he and other ill children were taken care so attentively. As my father said, when he went to the hospital to take Murat, he even cried sometimes since he didn't want to return to home.

I couldn't accommodate myself to the school. I couldn't sleep, I got afraid, wanted to escape and rescue myself by hiding under skirt of my grandmother. I didn't want to go to school. Even if I couldn't understand the language of children, I could easily understand that they humiliated me. They looked to my face abhorrently. They pulled my braid; they put chewing gums, pins and dead insects to my desk. I couldn't withstand any more. I wanted to hurt myself, but immediately changed my mind by considering that my mother would be heavily depressed in such a case.

In the end, I decided not to go to the school. I wouldn't allow anybody to change this decision. I insisted on this attitude from the beginning to the end. When they understood that I wouldn't change my mind, almoners said that I couldn't go on living in Germany under these circumstances and if I still refuse going to the school, then I would be sent back to Turkey. I had never been so happy. I would join with my teachers, friends and school again. I accepted to return to Turkey even if I separate from my mother, siblings and father who I loved very much although he didn't love me any more. I would stay with my grandmother. I wouldn't annoy her as in the past. I would strictly obey all of her instructions. The only thing I wanted was not to go to Germany once again.

I got very surprised when I noticed how I had changed after living in Germany for some months. I was in doubt about accommodating myself to Turkey again.

We regularly received information from Germany. We called each other by phone once a week. I missed my mother and Murat most. I committed myself not to cry before each of these phone calls; however I started crying as soon as hearing my mother's voice.

Murat and Elif had already adjusted themselves to school. They were learning German rapidly. They also had many friends. Especially, Elif had almost forgotten how to speak Turkish. While talking with me by phone, she also used some German words, and learned their Turkish correspondents from my father when I failed to understand her. Owing to her, my father had also learned some German words and started saying "good morning", "good evening" to his colleagues.

One day, we were shocked with the voice of my mother who called us by phone. She was crying a lot and couldn't even tell what her problem was. We first thought that something bad happened to Murat. Finally, we understood the reason; they also forcibly registered my mother in a course for learning German! It was obliged to continue the course at least for six months. Then she could continue if she wanted. My mother didn't know how to write and read. She couldn't understand anything from lessons of German, and she said on the phone that "as such an old woman, I hardly chocked back my tears in the class." She also decided to come back to Turkey just as me for rescuing herself from this language lessons which turned into a nightmare. However, this wasn't possible.

After a short while, they decided to remove her from the course due to her health's failing day by day. So, she relived herself of a serious problem. On the phone, her voice was happy any more. She told that she would sacrifice an animal for God when she would first come to Turkey since she was quit of such a great trouble. Now, she just wanted to stay at home and not to go to a course or any other similar place. She achieved what she wanted. My mother neither went to a course when she had been in Germany, nor learned German a little bit.

Murat frequently fell behind in his studies and sometimes repeated the same class due to his illness. They prevented spread of the disease; however they couldn't remove it from his body completely. Murat grew up more slowly than his fellows, and didn't grow up in length or weight. However, he learned German perfectly and was very successful in mathematics. Only if he didn't fall behind in his studies due to treatments in the hospital, he could be a very successful student.

I couldn't stay in Turkey for more than six months. I became only skin and bone because of grief and I got sick. I missed my family very much. Especially, I felt as if I were dying whenever I heard my mother's voice. In the end, they bought a ticket for me and sent me be back to Germany. I never shared this emotion with anybody else, but I had never been so happy before then and it was my best trip.

We celebrated my returning to home enthusiastically. My mother had cried for almost two days due to her happiness. She cooked flans and patties for me ceaselessly. I rarely went outside. Despite this, I started learning German slowly. Because none of us could understand Elif any more, since she always talked with us in German. Although my mother insisted on not understanding her, I could easily learn words. Murat hadn't changed so much. He didn't grow up in length, but he seemed healthier than he had been in the past. My mother hardly changed. She always told how she had relieved of the school, and then guffawed. My father didn't even embrace me. He kissed me from face and started watching television. He never asked me what I had done during six months when I hadn't been with them. On that day, I certainly understood that my father moved away from our world.

My fears weren't groundless. The second and most troublesome nightmare would start soon. I couldn't meet requirements of my class, and hence had to start my education from the lower class. Since I couldn't adjust myself even to the lower class, they transferred me to the class of youngest students. I was too older than my classmates. Everybody joked about me. I felt embarrassed, but couldn't say anything since I was afraid of being sent back. From time to time, I wanted to leave school due to my despair; but a foreign person inside me, who even graveled me, told that I had to withstand and I would be successful.

– You, the dirty Turkish girl. All of you smell like garlic!

– Our apartments become sniffy because of you. God knows, how terrible meals you cook and eat!

– Go away from our country!

– You will also serve us and collect our garbage just as your father. Turks couldn't do anything else!

I gritted my teeth and bore such insults of my schoolmates. I made up my mind on those days. I would continue my education. I would have a first– rate position and chasten them.

My mother returned from the holidays in Turkey very sadly any more. She thought that she was alienated from everybodyand everything. She knew that it was impossible to return her life in the past. She also didn't want this. She was unhappy among Germans in Germany; and she was unhappy among her relatives in Turkey, too. She looked people in Turkey with alienated eyes; and people in Turkey looked her with alienated eyes, too. However, my mother had a single desire; she wanted to be buried in her hometown after her death.

We had been belittled and humiliated by our neighbors, men and women in the street, students in the school, sellers in the market, in other words by everybody in Germany for years; and hence we couldn't accommodate ourselves to this country. But the startling point was that we were also treated as foreigners in Turkey. We were rootless between two countries. We couldn't desist from either of them. We were foreigners for both...

Elif was the one who was in the worst condition among us. She became wholly absorbed in German mode of life. Since she started school too early, she stroke up early friendships and got estranged to our family. She was also ashamed of our ignorance and my father's being a garbage man. She ran away from home for two times before the age of fifteen. We couldn't find her for months in both incidences. After a long time, she was found and turned over by German police while she was living in the street by her German friends.

My father retired into his shell since he had bought his Mercedes. He didn't guide us on any topic, and didn't talk with us in a fatherly way. Perhaps, he didn't know what to recommend us. He didn't know whether he had made a right decision about coming to Germany, or not. However, if they said him that "Come on! You can return to your country together with your family whenever you want", I was sure that he wouldn't.

In fact, Elif rebelled against my father by her acts. Because she couldn't be as lucky as me. She didn't even know what paternal love was. I knew this, and persuaded my father to help and talk with Elif. It was useful. Elif got tongue-tied against advices of my father who hadn't talked with any of us until then. She embraced my father and kissed him many times. My father also embraced her and kissed from her brow. I thought he did so partly because he felt this was a requirement.

Elif promised not to run away from house again on that day when she talked with my father. She reminded the period when she helped me for German lessons. She told that I had a great difficulty in understanding my lessons; however I overcame this difficulty in time. It was obvious that she was a little bit jealous of my success. However, this jealousy promoted her to advance in her education.

Murat had been already accommodated himself to live together with his illness which had a lifelong treatment. Besides, he had already learned not to occupy himself with her body which didn't grow either in weight or in height.

Murat could overcome his illness mostly owing to the great circle of love surrounding him since the first day on which his treatment in Germany had commenced. Whenever he returned from hospital, he had a happy and smiley face even though his face and hands bloated and his hair, eyebrows and eyelashes were shed. He had been never worried about staying in hospital during his seven– year treatment period. He always went there willingly. In my opinion, he recovered from illness due to love rather than medicines. Both our and hospital staff's love. I think he chose being at the place where he was most happy even if he was ill, and hence became a doctor. And he rendered thanks to doctors who took care of him fondly in his childhood by choosing pediatric oncology as his specific branch. Now he treated ill bodies of those young children as fondly as his own doctors.

By the time Murat decided to work in Turkey and returned to his home country; Zeynep had recently completed her university education and became a teacher. We held a chaste wedding ceremony for them under the cheery where they promised each other to meet one day in any case. My mother couldn't see that happy day, but I am sure that she enlivens with the love of Murat's son in the place where she was buried.

I feel chilly, it is very cold nowadays. Elif, who visited us some weeks ago owing to the judiciary recess, was really lucky because it was sunny during her visit. Now, it is so cold that it may snow in a short time; however we haven't seen autumn rains yet.

Who was that old man under the cheery? That man who suddenly appears as if he had got out of time tunnel... His cheeks are really distorted. His shoulders fall down. As far as I see, his hands enlarge as he gets older. Maybe, this is a misperception of me. My dear funny father who used to shake my heart with his love, whose bushy moustache shook while eating his meal, who gave me two and half Turkish liras as school money each morning, who made me the happiest person of world when he kissed my face, who had his eyes shine with joy while laughing, for whom I begged to God so as to provide him not to die before me...

What was the reason of my father's changing in Germany? What caused him to be covered with silence and to retire into his shell...?

He inflicted a forbidden love upon my mother for years. If he didn't leave us one day, perhaps we could never learn the truth. My rugged mother... She bowed to her fate so as to protect unity of our family and not to separate her children from their father. She endured and shut her eyes to his forbidden love for years, but couldn't accept his departure.

When my father came to my university in Germany after my mother's death, it was as cold as today. It wasn't so hard to see the penance in his eyes when he was standing in front of my room's door and looking at me. But it was too late. We summarized the elapsed years with a few sentences. Afterwards, a farewell peculiar to strangers.

Years are elapsing too fast. It is very difficult to believe. I remember our going to Germany as if it had happened yesterday. Our happiness when Murat became a doctor... Elif's forcing my mother to wear her gown at graduation ceremony and taking her photograph... My father's leaving us... Death of my mother... My deciding to settle down in Turkey after giving up my post in the university... Birth of my daughter...

I promised my mother to forgive my father if he really returns to our world one day. In the name of all of us!

– What do you want to be when you'll grow up?

– I will be a mother just as my mother.

– But first of all, you must attend school and be as clever as your mother.

– Why?

– Because you will be as strong as your mother then.

– Is my mother very strong, grandfather? Hum, is she strong enough to remove this cheery?

– She is even stronger.

– Hum, are you stronger than my mother?

– I have never achieved to be as strong as your mother, my little girl!

– But, men are always strong.

– You're right.

– Will you leave us, grandfather?

– I don't know. Will you sadden if I leave you?

– I'll sadden very much. But my mother will sadden even more. My mother loves you very much, grandfather…

– I also love your mother very much, my little girl. I love her even more than she guesses…

– Please, grandfather, don't leave us and stay here...

When it is raining heavily, I am sure that all three of us have seen my mother who is standing under the cheery and waving her hand to us smilingly…

Encouragement Prize

Bahattin Gemici / Germany

He was born in Nallıhan, Ankara in 1954. He completed Hasanoğlan Atatürk Primary School Teacher Training School, and had worked as a teacher at Ilgaz and Kurşunlu for two years. He studied German at the Gazi Educational Institute. Since 1977, he has been teaching in Herten, Germany. He has been involved in efforts against racism and xenophobia in Germany, and for equal rights for the Turkish people in Germany. He worked in the Herten Parliament of Foreigners, and as an honorary judge as the Recklinghausen local Court. His poetry and stories have been published by various magazines and newspapers, in schoolbooks and broadcast on the Radio of Western Germany (WDR).

His published books are: *Yarım Bırakma Türkünü, Poems for Primary Schools, Sing'weiter dein Lied, Schweigend... Aufschreiend, Esinti, Unheimisch fremd, Şimdi Vaktidir* and *Almanya Öyküleri.*

His Awards: *Georg-Tappert award; Herten City award, Literature grant from the Ministry of Culture of Northern Ren Westfalia Province, Köln VHS poetry competition award for first rank,* and *TRT-INT award.*

He is publishing his essays and products in www.bgemici.de. He is married and has two children.

New Neighbor

The news dropped on the neighborhood like a bombshell: a Turk had bought the house no. 15 on Waldgasse. The residents who heard the news rushed to their neighbors', Michel and Jutta Weber's, house.

The people on this street had not let even a foreign tenant come to their corner. Now, a Turkish family would settle for good in this street that they had protected so carefully against anyone who might be different from themselves. What are Turks doing among them? Germans should live near other Germans, and foreigners should live near other foreigners, and no one should disturb the peace.

"What did you do Mr. Weber? When did you sell your house?"

"If only you had told us... We would have found a proper buyer for you."

"Believe me, a Turk is the last thing we need in our neighborhood. Now our houses will lose value..."

Mr. and Mrs. Weber were astonished at the sudden arrival of their neighbors.

"Calm down. Please sit down..."

"Mr. Weber," started Ms. Simon, "Now, how are we going to get to sleep with all the noise of children? These children will break windows, and even steal things."

Mr. Kupitz: "There'll be people coming to visit them everyday. Our neighborhood will be full of Turks now..."

"Probably the wife wears a headscarf and she'll fill the balcony and the yard with hanging laundry," said Ms. Leppak.

Mr. Zimmermann looked as if he would explode from the force of his irritation: "From now on, no one can enter this neighborhood because of the smell of garlic," he said. "You'll see. These people will plant beans in their garden, and the crooked bean sticks will destroy the aesthetics of our neighborhood. This is where the problem begins. This is one of the main reasons for the dislike of foreigners..."

Mr. Peters spoke with a whiny voice, "Mr. Weber, why did you do this to us? What have we ever done to you? You've burnt us up, really. Now see if you can improve things..."

Mr. Weber who had listened patiently to all the complaints now exploded: "Enough! That's enough! I can't understand you. Everyone knew I wanted to sell the house. No one came forward. You all got excited when I sold it off to a Turk."

"You are right," said Mr. Peters. "Very right. If only we had known that a Turk would buy the house, we would have done something to prevent it."

"What could I do? He paid up, and I let him have the house. The house is mine isn't it? I can sell it to whomever I want. The buyer is happy, the seller is happy. What is it to you?"

"Don't say that Mr. Weber. We were at fault but please be reasonable. Is there no way out of this situation?"

"What are you saying? Of course not. All the paperwork is done. The people are moving in within a month."

His wife, Jutta Weber joined in the conversation: "You are opposing the family without even knowing them. You are making a mistake. This is prejudice. Yes, this is what they call prejudice." Mr. Zimmermann got really angry at this comment. He blushed, his hands began to shake. "It's not prejudice Ms. Weber," he said. "These people are like that. We know. You've known one, you've known all..."

"No, no!" answered Mr. Weber. "You are wrong. Look we're seven people here. Do we all have the same character? And, do you know what I'm going to do with the money I got for this house?"

"How would we know? Excuse us, in this confusion; we forgot to ask about that..."

"Of course you did. You're filled with the fear of the Turk. Gentlemen, we aren't living in the Middle Ages. Put your swords back in their scabbards. We are living in the 21st century. Change this mentality... We are going to buy a house in Turkey with the money. We're going to settle in Antalya."

"Oh God! You are going to Turkey?"

"What else? If you're smart, you come too. Of course there is some time yet to your retirement, but you would do well to start preparing. From now on, we want to live in peace, near the sea."

The residents of the street were astonished that their old neighbors had made such a decision. It seemed crazy! Mr. Weber had lost his mind. When they went outside, everyone was sulking.

"The guy is obsessed with the Turks," said Mr. Zimmermann. "On the one hand he sells his house to a Turk, and on the other hand, he talks about settling in Turkey. So people get senile in old age. Oh my God, bring Mr. Weber back to his senses..."

Mr. Kupitz: "My friends, I have the impression that we're making a mistake. Why are we so afraid of a Turkish family? Maybe Mr. Weber is right..."

Mr. Zimmermann gave a sour look at Kupizt. "If that's how you think, why did you not rent your empty apartment to a foreigner?"

"That's different," answered Mr. Kupitz.

"No, it's not different at all. It comes down to the same thing..."

Mr. Weber had never guessed that his neighbors would have reacted so strongly to his decision. "What is it to them?" he muttered, "Isn't it our house? We can sell it to whomever we wish." Then he called out to his wife in the kitchen, "Do you see, our neighbors are filled with a fear of the Turks," he said. "The Demirci family knows nothing about this. They're such good people. The man is a social consultant. His wife works at the factory. Their children are well-behaved and loveable. They're still in primary school."

"Oh, yes." said Ms. Weber. "But before going to Antalya for a holiday, we used to think that way about the Turks, too. After seeing the hospitality they extended to us in Turkey... Anyway, I think we really did well. It's a good thing that we sold the house to a Turkish family. We were the ones who invited the foreigners to work here - and now we're rejecting them. And then we say 'the Turks are forming ghettoes, they're not teaching German to their children,' and we use them as campaign material before elections. We should blame ourselves a little."

"Yeah, well. It's hard to explain this to our neighbors."

"Let's get prepared to leave as soon as we can."

"We'll leave my dear. We'll go to the sea and the sun very soon..."

Waldgasse Street was in an upheaval with the fear of the Turks throughout the month. Finally, the long-feared day had come. On a Saturday, a red Volkswagen stopped in front of the house numbered 15. A well-dressed man and a woman whose head was not covered got out of the car first. Then two children, a girl and a boy appeared. People who lived near the house peered at the newcomers from behind their curtains and concluded that the newcomers didn't look so bad. But this family could not consist of these four people! Didn't the Turks have several wives? Where were the other wives and children?

A few days later, a truck loaded with furniture stopped in front of the same house. Carriers took the furniture inside. That night, the lights of the house remained on until late at night. The Demirci family got settled in, while their neighbors kept gossiping about them. How could a Turk put together enough money to buy a house?

The next morning, Mehmet Demirci walked to the nearby bakery. Inside, people were waiting for fresh buns to come out of the oven. He got in line, and heard the conversation of some people standing in front of him. "A Turkish family moved in yesterday." He kept quiet. The Turk in question was obviously himself. How quickly the news had spread! That meant that the people who lived on this street were close knit, and they were aware of the comings and goings of other residents. "It's a good place, we're fortunate," he thought. It wasn't for nothing that there was a saying "Don't buy a house, buy a neighborhood." Once they were settled, their neighbors would probably come visiting to get to know them. He picked up the warm buns in a paper bag and set out for his house. He saw an elderly woman in the yard of a neighboring house. He was glad there was an elderly friend for his children. "Good morning neighbor," he greeted her with a smile.

Mrs. Leppak turned her face away.

Mehmet Demirci was disturbed by this. Why had this woman rejected his greeting? If a person refused to greet a neighbor, who would she ever greet?

He entered his house with a frown on his face. He told his wife, Ms. Ayşe what had happened.

"It's an old woman, you say," said Ayşe. "She probably does not see or hear well. She might not have noticed that you greeted her. Why else would she refuse to return your greetings? Don't think about it."

A month had passed. Everyday, Mehmet Demirci was taking his children to school, dropping his wife at the factory and going to his own business place. Gradually, they had grown accustomed to their new house, but there was always something else that was needed. It wasn't easy to get settled in a new house.

The month of March had ended, it was early April. Flowers began to bloom and leaves began to unfold on tree branches. Now they could plant their garden. Mr. Weber had planted a lawn on one third of the garden, flowers on the second third and had left the last third empty for vegetables. That space would be for onions, garlic, beans peppers, cucumbers and zucchini. The Germans didn't understand the Turks' eagerness to grow vegetables in their gardens. "If they knew the taste of the fresh vegetables from the garden, they would plant more than we do..." said Mehmet Demirci.

All was great but although it was more than a month since they moved into the house, none of the new neighbors had showed up to welcome them. Whenever Mehmet Demirci greeted a neighbor in the street, he noticed the neighbor turning away. What was happening to these people? What kind of a neighborhood was this? A home had no comfort without neighbors and guests. If it had been in Turkey, they would certainly have had a knock on the door, and the neighbors would have arrived with small offerings. Boreks would have been warmed up in the oven, the tea would have been steeped, coffee would be made, the children would play with each other. Mehmet Demirci shook his head, "difference in cultures..." he said. "Different countries, different traditions. For us, the adults it might be alright, but it's really hard for the children. The children need friends, games..."

His son had asked "Dad, why don't the German children want to play with us?" He hadn't known what to say in answer.

The people who had lived on Waldgase Street for years watched their new neighbors for months. Now, they knew when they would leave home, when they would return, on which side of the street they would walk, and what they would wear. There was something odd about this family – not at all what the residents of the street expected. There was a Turkish proverb: "When they got garlic married, it did not smell for forty days," the best was to keep watching and waiting. No one visited the home of the new comers. The neighbors hadn't observed any misbehavior of the children, either. Where were the other wives and children?

Ms. Leppak went outside into her yard one evening, and started to wait for the Demirci family. She wouldn't be able to go to sleep, if she couldn't ask some of the questions on her mind. A little later, the Turkish couple returning home, greeted her shyly.

This time, Ms. Leppak returned the greeting with a "Welcome."

Ayşe and Mehmet Demirci were very surprised. How was it that Ms. Leppak had returned their greeting? "Thank you neighbor," they said. They were happy that finally someone had welcomed them.

"Did you get outside to walk around for a while?"

"Yes," answered Ms. Demirci. "We decided to get some air while the children study. We walked in the park a little further. We enjoyed it."

Ms. Lippak paused. "I want to ask you something," she said.

"Please go ahead..."

"Herr Demirci, where are your other wives and children? When will they come? I just wondered."

Ayşe Demirci looked at her husband's face.

"Mehmet, what's this woman saying? Do you really have another wife and children?"

"Of course not. What are you talking about?"

"Well, obviously this woman knows you. That's why she is talking about these things in your life."

"My dear wife, you speak as though you didn't know me. Wait. I think this woman is trying to say something else..."

"Excuse us neighbor, we can't understand what you mean..."

"I mean... Are you just four people in your family?"

"Yes. What's wrong with that?"

"You mean you do not have other wives and other children?"

"Of course not. Don't make me laugh. It's a bad joke. My wife would kill me with a knife..."

"What? You wield a knife against each other?"

"No, no. You have misunderstood. If I had another wife, my wife would divorce me immediately. She is very jealous. You know, since the period of Atatürk, we have a single wife. No one can take more than one wife. Men and women are equal before the laws."

"Really? We had thought... How could we have known..."

"You are very humorous neighbor. You don't know us Turks at all, do you? Excuse me. I don't know your name yet."

"Leppak, Frau Leppak."

"Our family name is Demirci. In German it means "Schmiedt." Ms. Leppak, please come to our house, let us offer you a coffee."

"No, no, I wouldn't want to disturb you."

"You wouldn't disturb us, we would be happy. We're neighbors."

Reluctantly, Ms. Leppak went inside the Demirci house. The children one by one kissed her hand. She was surprised:

"What gentlemen," she said. "They both kissed my hand."

Ms. Ayşe said "that's not being gentlemen... It's our tradition. When a guest arrives, the young ones kiss the hand of the elders. Please make yourself comfortable Ms. Leppak. I'll make tea right away. I have already made some *börek*(*), it's cooking."

Ms. Leppak was a widow, who had lost her husband five years ago. She had a son living in Stuttgart with two children. Ms. Leppak could see her grand children about twice a year. They were the same age as these children. She asked some questions to these children, she stroked their heads.

Ayşe served her guest the warm börek that she took out of the oven. They drank tea. They got into a warm conversation, and even joked with each other. The happiness of Ms. Leppak, who had missed such a warm family environment, could be seen on her face. The Demirci family were doing all they can to please their first guest.

Mr. Peters who lived across the street had seen Ms. Leppak enter the Turks' house, and was anxiously waiting for her to come out. The woman had stayed inside for more than two hours. Could there have been something wrong? Should Mr. Peters call the police? After a while,

(*) Pastry.

he called on other neighbors, and all together, they went up to the door of the Turks.

Mr. Demirci opened the door. At first he was surprised, then, he invited the neighbors in. "Please come in, have a coffee."

"No, we haven't come for coffee. We have come to pick up Ms. Leppak. She didn't come outside."

Hearing the voice of the neighbors, Ms. Leppak called from the kitchen:

"Come on in, they're going to kill me."

So Mr. Peters was right to be worried. He grabbed his telephone to call the police. The others pushed each other to enter the kitchen. Mr. Demirci didn't know what hat hit him.

"What's going on?" he asked. "Neighbors, wait!"

Ms. Ayşe didn't know what to make of the noise at the door. Then she showed the newcomers the kitchen, "Welcome," she said. "Please come in."

The German neighbors stood still when they saw Ms. Leppak holding a börek in one hand and a glass of tea in the other. Ms. Leppak turned to them,

"I'm going to die, my neighbors," she said. "The *börek* are so delicious. I have to get the recipe for those... Ms. Ayşe, please stop putting more on my plate, I swear I'm going to explode!"

Ayşe offered seats to the new comers. "Please sit down. There are lots. Enough for all of us."

Mr. Kupitz started to say something, "We had thought..."

It was obvious that the neighbors were very embarrassed.

"What had you thought?" asked Mr. Demirci.

"We... When Ms. Leppak did not come out... We thought you had cut her up."

Upon hearing this, Ayşe and Mehmet Demirci, the children and Ms. Leppak began to laugh out loud.

"We only cut up some börek," she said. "C'mon, let's offer some to you."

"No, no, we should go."

Ayşe Demirci was now annoyed.

"If you don't sit down, then we'll be upset. Who knows, we might cut you up then..." The newcomers smiled uneasily at these words. Then, they sat down. But after a short silence, Mr. Kupitz stood up:

"The Demirci family, we wish you happiness in your new house! Welcome to our street, our flowers will come later" he said.

The guests had started to drink their tea when a police car stopped in front of the house. Mr. Zimmermann who lived in the house at the corner, and who saw the police car in front of the house of the Turks began to shout: "Look! It was obvious that this would happen. Mr. Weber, you did such harm to this street. They brought trouble to our neighborhood. Shame on you Mr. Weber!"

Encouragement Prize

Ali Özçelebi / France

He was born in Kilis in 1943. He was graduated from French Language and Literature Department of Atatürk University in 1967. While studying for doctorate in Ankara University, the faculty provided him to continue his education in France. Afterwards, he had worked in Spain for a while. In 1993, he was appointed as the dean of Uludağ University, Educational Sciences Faculty where he had been working for some time then. He took part in establishment process of Bursa Philharmonics Orchestra. His stories were published by various magazines such as *Türk Dili, Adam Öykü, Çağdaş Tük Dili*. He was awarded the third rank in 1992 Ömer Seyfettin Story Competition which he had attended with one of his stories.

Ali Özçelebi who had lived in Toulouse after being retired in 2001, and who arranged various programs regarding Turkish Art thereof passed away on November 3, 2006. His academic studies and literature works are published by his children on www.aliozcelebi.com.

We Don't Have a Child to Return From School

The man is on his wife. When he wants to lie beside her, her wife doesn't untie her arms embracing him.

– Stay there some more, says her. We have neither a child to return from school nor food baking in oven.

– I don't want to crush you, replies her husband.

– No, I am fine, says the woman, at least for now.

Despite her being almost as tall as Dayanç, her husband; she is extremely delicate. Poor man has always been afraid of hurting her whenever they make love during their thirty-year coupling. It is obvious that, if she were a greased wrestler, she wouldn't be permitted to approach wrestling track since she is too thin and puny. However, they took a shine to each other when they met for the second time. During her first visit to her husband's family for the purpose of being acquainted with them, her prospective mother-in-law said that "Oh, my son! Can't you find a better woman? She is like a bean pole. By Jove, they will draw your cartoon," when she was in the kitchen. But in the end, she liked her smile and being deft; and hence approved their marriage. During her wedding gown trial performed before many people, grandmother of her husband looked at her wasp waist and said directly to her that "It is very difficult to carry a baby in a waist like Üçgül's". This old generation lives only for having children.

Now, thirty years has elapsed in an instant. They want to make love after siesta.

The woman regrets to say that "We don't have a child to return from school." She was thinking. Once more, she slips out unintentionally. They don't have a child. In the first years of their marriage, they didn't want to have a child. Both of them are from Ankara. The woman completed her education in a troublesome university by overcoming all difficulties; and she was so lucky that she was appointed to a vocational school for girls in the centre of Ankara as a candidate tailoring teacher. In the second year of their marriage, when she became pregnant accidentally, her husband passed the exam in which he participated so as to be a Turkish teacher in France. Üçgül got very bored because of self-asked questions such as "Shall he go, or not?", "Shall we go together?", "What will I do there?", "If I don't go with him, will we be alienated from each other?", "Shall I resign my office, or not?", "Will it be possible for me to be appointed to school in Ankara after coming back?" After deciding to go, she suffered a miscarriage since she had held heavy goods while quitting the house they had rented. Afterwards, she had an inflammatory disease since she couldn't rest well and was lack of a good care. Then, she had never become pregnant. They had visited many doctors and left no stone unturned. They were in France and state of the art examinations had been applied.

When it became evident that "She is faulty", she offered her husband to get divorced. He could marry again and have a child from another woman. The man had always refused this offer. In fact, he somehow accommodated himself to this fact even if he felt sorry about it. However, her mother-in-law and father-in-law wanted descendance as it should be. That time, her brother-in-law got married. He was working in Sweden as an engineer. He got married with a Swedish girl three years after their marriage. A year after that, his wife had a son. And two years after that, she bore twin daughters. Her husband said his family that "Now, you have grand children even more than you wish! Please leave us alone..." but he saddened inwardly even if he didn't unbosom himself.

Perhaps, he always puts off returning to Turkey for this reason. He came to France as a Turkish teacher and extended his term of office for two times. When he was said that "It's impossible to extend your term once more", he preferred to stay there as a translator-worker. He had been already dealing with problems of workers and he was invited to places such as factories, social security organization, and police centers even when he was a teacher. Although her husband was extremely busy, she started feeling bored for a while later. Therefore, she intended to sew. They could also make friends as a result of her working. When

French neighbors started visiting her a few months later, she was registered to a free course for foreigners. Afterwards, she proceeded on her way easily and quickly. She also noticed that there was a gymnastics course in the same building and she was registered to it, too. She began reading books; going to cinema and theatre as she improved in French. Still, there was something lacking. Primarily, she considered that she couldn't take a step in her job. While she beat her brains out to find a solution, a French customer showed her a fashion house which was looking for "a skilled tailoring worker". She applied for this job and was immediately accepted. When her husband delay returning to home country for a long time, she opened a small shop for herself, and as from then she was an employer. Now, lower storey of the house has turned into a fashion house where five covered workers are employed.

If you work in this country, you will get the worth of your labor in spades and live as a human deserves. Although a great portion of their income is used for compensating heavy taxes, insurance premiums, she gives her blessing to this country. Because the state spends its income again for public. It constructed parks, schools, cultural centers, libraries, highways and sidewalks. As is seen, they can acquire a car, a house, and a fashion house in this country although they are foreigners. They aren't afraid of either the police, or being ill, or becoming unemployed. If they stayed in Turkey, they might have had a car only. That's why; they forget returning just as in Fatih Akın's movie. They went to their home country just in holidays and feasts.

They buy a beautiful house having four rooms and a garden, but rooms remain empty. This is really unfair. God grants too many children to poor people, but doesn't grant even one child to people who can sustain three or five children. In fact, they want one or utmost two children.

She got numb legs and her thigh started aching.

– Let's change our places, said her to him.

– What do you mean?

– Lie on your back, and let me lie on you.

Her husband lies beside her first and then takes her on him just as a feather pillow. The woman pushes her body some more upwards and reclines on wide chest of her husband; she sticks her brow to his face and her chin to his neck. While the man is pulling the linen over them, Üçgül falls into a brown study again.

In the end, they loose their hope about having a child, and bow to fate. It isn't easy to have a child nowadays, especially in a foreign country. If children become French citizens, stay in French and go to French schools; it is really a problem. Do they attend school? Can they? Can they and their grandparents, parents, aunts, uncles, relatives compete with native born French children? Who can help them? She learned French too late, can this knowledge be enough for children? Their father isn't at home everyday. Even if he is at home, he can't help them in all their lessons. She learns this from her neighbors. Here children attended lessons which are different not only from their fathers' but also their elder brothers'. Information improves and refreshes continuously. Generally, children of foreign originated families can not progress further than primary school in this city. Even if they can, they hardly receive bachelor's degree. They can go vocational schools at the most. They immediately loose their courage. Fortunately, education is compulsory here until the age of sixteen.

Mothers coming for fitting always talk about their children and schools of them. They aggravate and take pride in their successes, and complain about problems. They mention injustices which their children are exposed to. They never consider that they never read neither a Turkish nor a French newspaper, magazine, or book. Forgetting that not only do they speak with each other in Turkish, but also they watch local series in Turkish channels by means of rotary dish antennas day and night; they accuse French teachers of causing all the problems related with their children.

Confessedly, children of immigrants can't be successful due to various and complex reasons. Their parents are mostly graduated from primary school. Matrimonial troubles are dominant. Their children are as if soldiers of matrimonial wars. Sons of these parents withdraw from their family relations by saying that "I don't mind what you are doing" for a while later. Most of the mothers who only go outside for shopping in supermarkets or visiting neighbors; are traditional women from rural areas. Some of them were not graduated from even primary school and, in some instances, they don't know how to read and write although they were graduated from primary school. Who did determine and send them here? Even people who go on a pilgrimage to Mecca receive a brief training and learn what to do during voyage and in Mecca.

These people are not stupid, but they are ignorant. They don't permit their children, especially their daughters, to participate in everyday life in the street and even in the school. Unemployed housewives waste her children's' time so as to spend their leisure time egoistically. They engage their whole attention to foolish fears such as "They can eat pork meat unintentionally", "their morality can collapse, don't you dare!", "We can be gossip subject of neighbors." "My daughter doesn't know such things; she directly comes to home after leaving school..."

"Our children doesn't like meals supplied by the school. They make a bolt for house in the noon since they like my meals." In fact, four different meals are supplied to them. These meals are examined in terms of health, and their calories are calculated according to necessities of different age groups. Besides they are very cheap. By doing so, mothers obstruct their children to talk and play with their French oriented friends and other people. They can't notice that they dull perception of their children for whom they can easily give their lives. They prevent their socialization. Children, who sometimes go to fitting with their mothers, can't response questions not only in French but also in Turkish.

How can children remember names of food, vegetables, fruits which they neither eat nor drink? In lessons and exams, how can they mention books which they don't read, theatres which they aren't taken to, holidays which they don't go on, games which they don't play? Besides, some of Turks send their children who are at school age or who are graduated from primary school to Turkey, these children attend school and marry with somebody there.

She sees that eyes of her husband are closing slowly. She asks "You don't sleep, do you?" and budges her body back and forth. Hereupon, the man finds her buttocks and caresses them by his long fingers.

If they had any children, they wouldn't send them to Turkey. Even if they want so, it is very difficult to decide to whom they send their children. Parents of both are alive. No matter to whom they would send them, the other party would reprove. If they separated their children and sent each to one of their parents, then this would be even worse. And the worst is that sending their children to their parents means sending their children to the past rather than the future. Children who are sent to their villages or towns can hardly improve their skills and knowledge. The next step is the conflict of generations. No, if they had any children, they would go through fire and water for them and get them educated in best schools up to the highest level here in Germany. But they have never had a child. They have pretended not to want to have a child for preventing other party's feeling sorry; they consoled each other by defending favor of childlessness. Children could be problematic, for example they could be ill-doer or predisposed to bad habits. Perhaps, they couldn't adapt themselves to the life here. On the other hand, in case of achieving to adapt themselves, then they could dislike their parents and home countries. Military service of sons; maidenhood, womanhood, pregnancy of daughters might have imposed problems on them. They might have died as a result of accident(s). At worst, they could be born disabled. There are children born disabled within the family of man. This possibility is the one she fears most. Above all, she isn't sure whether she and her husband can come to a common mind regarding education of their children. Somebody, whose name is forgotten by her, said that "having children means encumbering your life with a mortgage".

Her husband, whose caresses are not responded by her, asks:

– What are you thinking?

– Nothing!

– You can't stand still without thinking.

– I am thinking that we are aging.

– But, what is the problem with this!

– I don't say that there is any problem! Every age has its own beauty. You are also handsome at the moment, says she, before kissing her husband's lips.

– Didn't you go downstairs? asks the man between two kisses. You told that you would have some visitors for fitting.

– Yes, after an hour.

– Let me get out of the bed.

– But, why? It is Saturday…

– I'll take a bath and go outside. I don't like being at home during your fittings. I'll walk for a short while. Then I can drink a glass of beer in the shop of Mr. İbrahim. If you want, come and find me there. We can eat Trukish Doner there and then go to the cinema.

– Maybe. I suppose that my work won't last long.

– You always say similar things, but even if fitting lasts ten minutes, you listen to their troubles for almost an hour. I am confined to upstairs.

– My visitors of today don't escape from the man as others do.

– Who will come?

– Handan and her daughters... Oh darling, wife and daughters of Mr. Ferit, the constructor.

– Why will their daughters come?

– It is hard to believe!

– First tell the reason, who knows, maybe I can easily believe.

– The older daughter will be engaged. I'll sew her engagement suit...

– It is impossible! I can't believe! She is too young, and hasn't completed high school yet!

– They will marry after her graduation. Then, they will open a bakery in Turkey…

– Then, her intended groom is Turkish.

– He is her aunt's son.

– Then, this will also be a consanguineous marriage! How can it be in the contemporary world? I may understand if they are uneducated, ignorant and bigoted people. They are somewhat educated and modern…

– I feel sorry about the daughter, she has different dreams.

– Why are they so impetuous? You know, she told that she would go to university, open a "patisserie" here and be a business woman. Why do they marry her off so hurriedly?

– Response of this question is subject of gossip. As you know, I never gossip.

He knows that she never gossips. He covers her from shoulders and tilts her over. Then, he gets out of the bed and goes to the bathroom.

When his hairy back disappears, she starts reconsidering the subject which she defined as gossip. What would they do if they had a daughter and experienced a similar incident? It depends how they bring her up. In the first years of their marriage when they didn't give up their hope yet, she talked such issues with her husband. They wanted their children to be bilingual and bicultural. They would provide their children to absorb positive sides of both countries. Somebody who ignores his/her own history can't benefit from anything. Further, if a value judgment or a virtue is really common and consistent, then it will certainly become universal. If not, it isn't worth of being protected. They wanted their children to be European citizens. Dayanç said that "Children with Turkish sub-identity and European super ordinate identity". Why not? European Union aims to realize this. European Union is printed above and French Republic is printed below on the cover page of French passports. There are Turkish originated and named representatives in German Parliament. Borders between countries have been removed already. They went to visit her brother-in-law in the previous summer by train. Nobody asked their passports or identity cards until they arrived in Stockholm. Children of her sister-in-law speak both Turkish and Swedish as their native languages. Besides, one of them knows German and others know English. The elder son had started his university education in Stockholm, continued in Wien, and completed in Göteborg. Would their children also be so successful? It seems that children of mixed marriages are more successful. Is it really so? When she is trying to remind mixed spouses she knows, their marriages and children, her husband comes in. He has one large towel on his back and one on his shoulders as in Turkish baths. He bound small head towel behind his head after getting it through his ears.

– What if we had children, asked she.

– What do you mean?

– Would they have a good education? Could we bring them up well?

– We would try our best...

-Is it enough? You know that everybody try their best and even more here, but you also see the result...

– My brother got ahead.

– But your brother got married with a European woman...

– Do you think this is important? I don't think it is so much…

– But, children learned Swedish from their mother…

– If we had children, they would learn French together with their teachers and friends in the school. Afterwards they could learn other languages. As you know, it is enough for a child to go to day nursery or infant school for two years so as to learn a language. But of course, if their parents let them attend such schools…

– We would certainly let them attend. We would never be inhibitive parents. Yes, their mother wouldn't be a French woman, but they could have French, English, or Spanish friends or lovers. Since I was also working, we were obliged to send them to infant school…

– It is not a matter of obligation, we should send them voluntarily.

– If you had a daughter and fell in love with a French boy, what would you say? asks the woman after a short silence.

– What could I say? I would tell her to be careful, in other words I would tell nothing different than what I would tell in case of a Turkish lover…

– Could we get along with each other?

– On which topic?

– On all topics such as our children's' educations, marriages...

– Haven't we got along with each other on all topics up to now? Or, on almost all topics.

– If we had children, perhaps we couldn't do the same.

– Why are we speaking about children again now? Get out of the bed, have a bath and dress yourself. Otherwise, you will be late…

– Okay, I am getting out of the bed. Turn your back, and close your eyes until I go into the bathroom…

– Good heavens! You behave as if you weren't my wife for thirty years.

Üçgül stops controlling her ideas under shower; her ideas resemble passengers flying from pillar to post; she concentrates on Neşe who will come for fitting soon in the end. While dressing herself, she makes her final decision. She will talk with Ms. Handan.

– You are in fault, please change your mind! Think once again. If it isn't a serious relation, they will depart from each other soon. If it is serious, you can evaluate character of the boy. If you wish, you can also investigate him. Why will you oppose to their marriage, if he is also from a good family? Meanwhile, Neşe can also complete her school…

Kadriye Bakşi / Germany

She was born in İstanbul in 1955. She has been living in Germany since 1980. Her work life, which began as a factory worker, continued in a care home for the aged, and after training in adult education, she began to work as a social worker. She worked with women subjected to violence and harassment, with youth dependent on substances. She settled in Hannover in 2004. She worked in a project that prepares foreign women to work life in Braunschweig and kneaded the dough of her stories and poetry, mostly during the two hours that she spends on the train each day, between Hannover and Braunschweig.

Her story entitled *Variyola* won second prize in a contest for women's stories, organized by Petroleum Workers Union, in May 2007.

Her stroies entitled *Gece Vardiyası* and *Yağmurdaki* were published by Kül magazine in January and May 2008.

Ayla

Iris entered the kitchen, muttering "we're closing in two minutes and she gets into the shower now!" Manuella asked, "Is it Ayla again?" Yes, it was Ayla again who failed to obey the rules. It's forbidden to take a shower after 1.30 in the morning. The centre closes at 2.00. Five people are chosen by drawing lots, among those who have nowhere to sleep. Women who are fortunate may sleep in the hall until 7.00 a.m. The rest have to return to their places in the night and in the cold.

The centre for the addicted is located beside the central train station. It's now about ten days since I started to work here. The women who use the services of this centre range in age from thirteen to twenty five, who earn the money to buy drugs by selling their bodies. The city has thrown up its stepchildren away from view, as if they were unwholesome food. Especially the women using 'crack'(*) almost never leave this area during their short lives, since they can find everything they need in these streets to the north of the train station.

Drug sellers, who are mostly addict themselves, appear suddenly in the darkness, settled their affairs, and disappear all of a sudden. You see neither their arrival nor their departure. It's as if they walked through their own secret tunnels instead of the streets, and it's as if they had no faces under their baseball caps. Always the same tone heard while they bargain in a whisper – as if it's always the same person who speaks.

The men who come to buy the wounded, bruised, mortally ill bodies of the women also remain hidden in this thick darkness. Their nationalities, languages and age differences are hard to distinguish. Some go around in fancy cars, some on bicycles and some on foot. There are even those on wheel chairs. Because they are cruel, power-addicted, and

---

(*) Crack is a semi-synthetic drug made by boiling cocaine with ammonia. It resembles small pebbles, and is smoked in a special pipe. It causes mortal damage to lungs, heart and blood vessels. After the American continent, it is now spreading in Europe.

obsessive or extremely shy and lacking in self-confidence, these customers are at least as lonely as the women they hire. Also, for handicapped men who fail to meet the physical and intellectual standards of the society, the women here are often the only alternative to isolation.

On the dusty windows of hotel rooms that are rented out by the minute, and that are found to suit every pocketbook, strings of red lights go on and off. The hotel entrances are places where short, silent negotiations take place. The addicts wait at the doors, among blood stains, used syringes, and smells of decaying food, vomit, garbage and urine. Some stand around, some try to doze wherever they're sitting, and those who are really weary lie down. You never know if they're in pain. They never moan.

In basement bars, plump, blond women who once worked as prostitutes in this strict serve beer. They don't drink themselves. If they're not in a fight, they talk to their old customers whose eyes are glazed and fixed to the darkness, about the old days, and complain about the changes in the profession caused by the spread of drugs in the district.

The others who roam these streets are the missionaries holding pamphlets, and wearing smiles saying "you are also human; our sisters and brothers." They give out blankets or hot coffee to those who have enough patience to listen to their sermons.

And, there are the police. Here, in the midst of all the lawlessness, it's as if their real duty were to protect the view of the city. They limit their work to preventing the spread of the dirty commerce that takes place here, and that's accepted as if it were the fate of large cities, outside the boundaries of the district. The young officers who aren't yet hardened in their profession sometimes take the addicts they find in the streets to a hospital to save a life. But this isn't enough to improve the "bad image" that they have in the district.

And as for the work of our centre, it resembles digging a well with a pin. Tired women get a chance to rest at our centre. They take showers and do their laundry. If they're hungry, they can find a hot meal, and if they're cold, they find some clothes to put on. We also have a therapy program for those who want to get rid of the drug habit but there is not much demand for it. The room that's most in demand is the room where women who bring in their drugs from the outside may use them. There is usually a line up for that room. We give them clean syringes and tools, and we're there to intervene in cases of overdose. The truth is that we don't serve much of a purpose, except reduce contagious diseases and drug-related deaths.

Ayla is one of the women who come to our centre. I know her only from the complaints that I've heard ever since I've started to work here. I know from experience that if there are so many complaints about someone, it won't be long before she will be banned from entering the centre. Perhaps it's because something in me keeps refusing to work in the area of social work with interdictions, or perhaps it's because Ayla is from my own country of origin, I feel the need to get involved with the shower incident. "Does Ayla understand German?" I ask. "Perhaps she hasn't understood the rules." Yes she do understand German. In fact she doesn't know any other language. No one has ever heard her speak Turkish with the other women. For Ayla, speaking consisted of shouting and swearing, anyway. She is known as an aggressive, unpredictable girl.

"If you wish, I can go and try to talk to her," I say now. "Perhaps I can convince her to get out of the shower and to leave." Iris and Manuela are relieved, as if they were expecting me to make this offer. They warn me to be careful.

When I enter the section where the showers and toilets are located, I hear Ayla's grumbling and swearing, mixed with the sound of running water. It seems that she is mad at Iris for telling her to leave. Her voice rings like a scream. It's as if she is shouting, swearing and crying all at the same time. I open the shower curtain just a little and ask: "You are Ayla, aren't you?" In Turkish. At first, she is quiet. Now, all I hear is the sound of the water. Then she opens the curtain a little more, her brown eyes large and surprised, she watches me. I watch her, equally surprised. Her body, which she attempts to cover with her hands, consists of a heap of bones. She is taller than average but obviously no more than 35 kilos in weight. Her long hair that reaches her shoulders is pitch black. The red ribbon that holds some of her hair tied on top of her hair is wet, and is hanging over her forehead. Her toothless mouth is open. Her cheeks sunken. It's impossible to guess her age from her face or from her body that's a ruin full of bruises and wounds.

One thing is obvious: this woman is a 'crack' addict. It might be very difficult to establish normal communications with her. This substance that has a powerful effect turns the world into hell for the user when that effect is worn out. The addict, who feels as though she is falling into a bottomless pit, becomes aggressive. When she takes more of the substance, all connection with reality is destroyed anyway. Despite all of this, I decide to try my luck and attempt to communicate normally with her.

I notice her clothes thrown on the floor in front of the shower cabin. They're all dirty and wet. Her sneakers are full of bloodstains to the point that it's impossible to distinguish their original color, and they stink. It appears that Ayla has not taken them off for at least a week.

"I'll bring you clean clothes," I say. "I can look for shoes as well, what's your shoe size?" I'm still speaking in Turkish.

"Who are you?" she asks angrily, "You speak like my mother. Who are you?" She is speaking in German. As she speaks, her face and neck tense up as though she were suffering from palsy.

"I'm not your mother," I say, "my name is Nazan, I work here. As you know we close this centre at 2 o'clock. I think you should get dressed and leave." I've started to speak in German too. "Let me go get you some clothes. Would shoes sized 38 be alright?"

"Let me bring you clothes... let me bring you clothes..." she attempts to mock me, sticking her tongue out of her toothless mouth. Then she holds the showerhead towards me to get me wet. I react quickly and leave the bathroom. The floor gets wet. I go into the room where donated stuff is stored, to look for clothes. When I return to the bathroom with the clothes I have found, Ayla has disappeared. Manuella is mopping the floor. "How did you convince her to leave?" she asks. "Bravo, really. Iris and I were considering calling the police and banning her from the centre."

"Too bad," I say. "Has she left in her dirty clothes?"

"No," answers Iris. "She put on the clothes of one of the women who are asleep. Let's leave these things you've brought near her so she can wear them when she wakes up."

"You can leave," I tell them. "Your shift is long over. I'll deal with the rest."

That night when I first met Ayla was my first night shift at the centre. After tidying up and disinfecting the place, I slowly opened the door of the hall and looked at the women sleeping on couches. I approached to check their breaths one by one because we often encountered death from an overdose in sleep. I had to be careful. After this inspection, I withdrew into the office. I'm someone who is keen on my sleep at night. My first night shift was really not easy. I had to force myself not to fall into a deep sleep, because I had to control the women every two hours. In my fitful bouts of sleep, my mind kept turning around "the Lost Girl, Ayla."

Do you know her?

I think it was during the sixties. A little girl named Ayla was lost. For days, even months, the Turkish newspapers had carried news about her. At that time, I didn't even know how to read and write yet. I used to wait for my mother to return home from work in her high-heeled shoes and blue trench coat, to read news about this girl for me in the newspapers she would bring with her. Afterwards, I would fall asleep wondering what had happened to the little girl, where she might be, what she might have gone through. The next morning, I would wake up, hoping to run into her playing in our district.

Now, in strange dreams that took place neither in Germany nor in Turkey, and in which my childhood and my adulthood were mixed, and where people spoke both Turkish and German to understand each other, the "Lost Girl Ayla" appeared once again. I dreamed that I was telling my mother that I had found Ayla in the district of St. Georg.

Ayla did not appear at the centre for a while after the night when we met. Although my German colleagues said "too bad, just when we have a Turkish worker who could deal better with her, she has disappeared" they were secretly relieved because they were tired of trying to deal with her. I believed that Ayla had stopped coming because she was ashamed. My being Turkish had made her uneasy.

Perhaps it was a month before she returned. I saw her eating in the hall. After eating the broccoli, potatoes and meat that she mashed in her plate, she asked for another serving. It seemed obvious that she hadn't eaten anything for a long time. I was watching her from the corner of the hall where I was folding clean laundry. I thought she didn't see me. I was wrong. After her meal, she came up to me. "Is there any apple tea?" she asked. "Let me check," I answered. She whispered: "don't speak Turkish with me. I don't want it known that I'm Turkish." "Alright," I said. I asked our intern to prepare Ayla's tea. She sat in the hall the whole evening, watching TV. She gave her name for the draw to decide who could stay overnight. She lost. Her name wasn't drawn. As the closing time approached, Ayla began to act up. I reminded her of the rules. "Please leave at 2 o'clock," I said. "I'm cold," she answered. "I can't work much anyway because of the wounds on my feet. I can't spend the night outside." I reminded him that there's a Social Hotel that we call "Alex," at the station. I told her she could sleep there. "I don't have an ID," she said. "If they call the police, I'll be thrown out." No one would ask for an ID at the Social Hotel. I told her that the institution would know that homeless people don't have the means to keep Ida's and other such documents. Just last night Elke had slept there without an ID.

Ayla got angry. She began to cry and to hit around. She was shouting at me at the same time:

"Elke is German, you idiot! Elke is German..."

Two of my colleagues held her arms to take her downstairs and put her outside the door. Ayla kept shouting outside for some time. She rang the doorbell a few times. Then she left. We all stood silent for a while, our face bearing the traces of sadness and helplessness. "What if she is telling the truth?" I said. "What if she really cannot stay at the Social Hotel?"

"She is telling stories," said Manuella. "No one asks for an ID at the Alex."

Still, I decided to phone the "Alex" and find out for sure.

"The office of the Senator of Interior Affairs has increased precautions after September 11," said the colleague who answered the phone. She explained that now they had to take down the ID numbers of all the foreigners that stay there, to submit them to the office of the Senator. Yes, just as Ayla had said, Germans who didn't have ID's could stay there.

"So, how do you know whether someone without an ID is German or not?" I asked. My colleague laughed, "Don't you know?"

I was furious at the social worker on the phone and at myself for not having believed Ayla. "I cannot know people's identities from their appearances," I told the social worker. "I don't think it's possible to know that in that way. Goodnight to you."

"Goodnight." The voice on the phone seemed surprised at my anger.

I could not hold back my tears while telling my colleagues that Ayla could not have slept at the Alex. "We did not believe her," I said. "We made a big mistake."

"Nothing would have changed if we had believed her," said Manuella. "Ayla could not have slept here because she lost when we drew lots."

"Perhaps we could have found a solution," I insisted.

"Get that out of your mind," said Manuella. "Every night three thousand people in Hamburg sleep in the streets. Which one of them are you going to find a solution for?"

On my way home after my shift, I looked outside from the windows of the cab. I could not see Ayla. In one of those streets where I hardly found the courage to look at, she had probably crouched in a doorway. When I got home, it wasn't easy for me to fall asleep. I couldn't get Ayla out of my mind. I knew that my attitude was not professional. If I couldn't leave my workplace experiences at the workplace, I wouldn't last long in this job. Towards the morning, my strange dreams returned. My mother was holding her newspaper and saying, "That girl you saw at the St. Georg was probably not Ayla," pointing at the news story. "Look here, they're still looking for Ayla."

I had convinced myself that I would never find her. I had even forgotten her in the midst of my daily work, when I heard that she had been arrested. One of the women who came to the centre had heard the news when she had gone to visit a friend of hers, who was "inside." Ayla had no visitors. Her clothes were in tatters. She needed a lawyer to get her an ID and other papers. This was talked about at our weekly meeting at the centre. It was our job to pay attention to women who were in jail. No one wanted to visit Ayla. I took on the job.

I prepared a large package for Ayla. Perhaps partly because of the guilt I felt towards her, I wanted to take her everything I could think of. Apple tea, tobacco, sportswear, a nightgown, even a red ribbon. First I handed the package to the guardian. Then I started to wait for Ayla in a room where I was taken. I was somewhat uneasy with the guilt feeling that was lingering since our last meeting.

Since I didn't really know her, I had no idea what we would talk about. Actually, I had very rarely ever seen the faces of women who were drug addicts when they were sober. Even after they received their sentences, depending on the prison, they often found drugs illegally or the doctors prescribed medication to replace those drugs, in order to prevent suicides. But in detention, they have no chance to get anything. Ayla has been in detention for a long time because she has no papers - this means that for a long time she hasn't used drugs. I wonder what she is like now.

When the door opened, a well shaped, healthy and energetic young woman entered the room. It was hard to recognize her at first glance. She was not limping, and her face was not tensing up with ticks. She had an attractive face, free of pimples or bruises. We greeted each other. Without hiding her pleasure and her excitement, she said, "you've brought me such nice things. Thank you."

"I hope they'll fit you," I said.

"It doesn't make any difference," she answered. "Those that don't fit me, I can share with the other women."

After a pause, she continued: "I really had not expected anyone from the Centre to come to visit me. Thanks for coming." She had put on some of the clothes I had brought her, and tied the red ribbon on her hair.

"You look really good," I said. "You've gained a little weight."

Food is the easiest filler of the emptiness left by the absence of the addictive substance. "Inside," people usually gain weight. It's a joke of destiny. Detention saves some from certain death. For those whose health is in really bad shape, we secretly wish some time in jail, but we never say this out loud.

On my first visit, a large part of the time passed, talking about technical matters such as the missing papers, a lawyer, and a letter pleading poverty. Then Ayla described her situation inside. Apart from boredom, she was fine. She was eating to pass the time, and seeing a psychologist twice a week. No, these sessions served no other purpose than passing the time. The psychologist was a woman with a sense of humor - they were laughing a lot.

She was covering her toothless mouth with a handkerchief while she talked. Her clothes were clean; her hair had been recently washed. As she sat before me, she gave an impression of an intelligent, sensitive, gentle woman. She seemed a little vulnerable, but there was not a trace of aggression in her manner. At the end of my visit, she asked if I would come again.

The next day, I obtained the paper required for regular visits, and I visited Ayla regularly, every Wednesday during the four months until she was brought before the court and released.

On our third visit, I asked her if she had no relatives. I wanted to know if her family was visiting her. Ayla had run away from home many years ago, and didn't want a relationship with her family living near Köln. She was very afraid of her elder brothers. I asked nothing more about her family. Persisting on certain subjects out of curiosity could have disturbed her psychology, and seem disrespectful.

I think it was on our fifth visit that she spontaneously started to tell me the life story that had led her to addiction. She was the youngest of four children. Her sister who was the eldest had got married early and left the family. She lived in Köln as well. She had two elder brothers. When alcoholism came upon the psychological disturbance that was affecting their father more and more, the brothers stopped going home. They had moved in with their German girlfriends.

After starting school, when Ayla developed insomnia because she was scared of her father's nightly temper tantrums, her mother gave her some of her own sleeping pills. After age ten, Ayla began to take painkillers during daytime as well, to deal with her chronic migraine headaches. Eventually, she couldn't do without the medication. When her father committed suicide, and her doctor began to reduce the dose of her medication because he suspected her addiction, Ayla's life became very difficult. At age 14, at school, she met a youth who was a couple of years older than her. Stephan. Stephan was finding pills and bringing them to her. Ayla's mother forbade her to see this guy, and when Ayla did not obey her, the mother told Ayla's brothers about the situation. After the beating Ayla received from her brothers, she never went back home again. She was so afraid of her family that she ran away to Berlin with Stephan to cover her tracks. At the Youth Hostel they took refuge in Berlin, they were unable to obey the rules, so after a while, they were thrown out. To find money for the drug suppliers they found in Berlin, they were staying out through the night, and in the morning they were not going to school. One day, Stefan got caught stealing a car, and was taken to jail. Ayla fled to Hamburg. In Hamburg, she could not buy the expensive drugs she was using in Berlin. By herself, she couldn't steal. She began to use "crack" because it was cheap, and powerful. It wasn't important that it was deadly – anyway, she was living because she didn't know how to commit suicide.

I listened to Ayla for weeks.

Without comment. Without judgment. Without pity. I only tried to understand.

Ayla, whose 21st birthday we celebrated in jail, was actually still lost, and I had no idea how she might be found and made to return to life. Could Ayla still be found?

When her ID and her residence permit were ready, she would be brought to court. She would sign a document saying she would seek therapy, and then she would be released, under the law of "therapy instead of punishment." She would return to the St. Georg district. She has nowhere else to go. She would continue the misery from where she had left off. She had no other life. No hope. No purpose.

She told me the story of her life, as if it was the story of someone else's life. Without anger, without self-pity, without tears, dreams or pleasure. Without touching any emotion. As though she were reading a news report in a paper.

On one of our last visits, close to her court appearance, I came in a little late. It was almost noon when we were shown into the visiting room. That day for the first time, I realized the importance of my visits to Ayla. Her eyes were red. She was pale, and looked sad and pensive.

"I thought you weren't coming," she said without a trace of reproach in her eyes.

I apologized for being late. "What's wrong?" I asked. "Didn't you sleep well?"

"I couldn't get to sleep," she said. "Thoughts don't leave me alone. They hurt. I wake up slowly, like waking up from torture. All the feelings that I suppressed with drugs for years are now holding me to account."

"What are the thoughts that affect you so deeply?" I asked. "Wouldn't you like to speak with the psychologist?"

She did not answer. She looked at my face for a while, undecided. Then she took her head between her hands and leaned her face on the table. She cried silently for a while, with sobs that shook her whole body. Then she lifted her head. It was as if her look pierced me, and she whispered as though she were speaking to a ghost on the wall. "I can't get my daughter out of my mind," she said. "I want to see her in my mind's eye, but she is faceless. I can't recognize her. I couldn't anyway. She must have grown up by now. I'm so scared that she might be unhappy."

So she had a daughter around five-years-old. No, she was not seeing her. The last time she saw her, her daughter was a three-week-old baby. Her father was very likely Stefan. When she was born, the Youth Office had taken her away from Ayla and placed her with a wealthy, childless family. Ayla didn't know the family. She had lost their address.

For hours, she told me about the time of the child's birth, and her memories of motherhood. It's the first time that I'm seeing Ayla weep while sober. It's the first time that I hear speak of someone with love and with longing. I share the anxiety and sadness that she feels for her child. For the first time I begin to glimpse the hope that I might find Ayla somewhere, that she might return to life, somehow.

"If you wish we can look for your daughter," I say. "After your court appearance, we can arrange a meeting through the Youth Office."

"No," she says. "Not yet. I'm not ready. I don't want her to see me toothless like this. When I get outside, first I have to find money to get my teeth done."

•••

On August five of the year two thousand and three, Ayla had her court appearance. It was a Tuesday. I entered the hall during the short break before the sentence was given. Iris whispered, "Everything went very well. We said she would have therapy at our centre. It's very likely that she'll be released today."

Ayla was released that day.

After the decision of declared, she turned her head back, looking for me with her eyes. Our eyes met. I read more anxiety on her face than pleasure. I smiled at her eyes that seemed to be saying "what now?" She smiled back.

I thought I knew what would happen. She didn't yet. After everyone left the hall, she and the lawyer went into a chamber to complete the paperwork. I joined them and asked the lawyer for permission. First, I handed Ayla the address where she could get money to get her teeth done. Peter Hütte. The Priest of the Paulus Church. I had met him while I was working with youth. A good friend with a big heart. As soon as I told him about Ayla, he collected money for her. He even knew a good dentist.

"But it's only a loan," Ayla said. "I'll be sure to pay it back."

"Alright," I said. "That's up to you."

I handed her a second address, which I had jotted down behind a photograph. The photo was of a beautiful little girl with blonde hair up to her shoulders, and who smiled from the depth of her dark eyes. She was holding a doll whose dark hair was braided and who was wearing a red dress like her.

"Look," I said. "This is Yasemin. Her doll is named Ayla. She asked for your photo as well, so you should get your teeth done right away."

Ayla looked at the photo for a long time. Then she hugged me and stayed with her head buried on my shoulders for a while, to hide her tears.

That night, I dreamed of my dear mother again. Her newspaper had good news. "The lost girl Ayla was found, my dear," she said to me. "Don't worry. All lost children will be found some day."

Başak Devrim Andreutti / Germany

She was born in Bursa in 1974. After her secondary and high school education in İstanbul Italian Science High School, she was graduated from İstanbul University Communication Faculty in 1998. She is also closely interested with art in addition to literature. She held a personal art gallery in İstanbul in 2003. She has been living in Hamburg since 2004. She knows five languages.

Letters to My Aunt

July 20, 1991

My Dear Aunt,

I can again write to you, in fact only to you just as usual. You're my only friend and single family member. If you ask whether writing is better than talking, or not; I always fail to make myself understood by means of talking. A new country and language. Who could know that I would settle in a foreign country after marriage? When I was a child, nobody could even persuade me to imagine settling in a foreign country whose language is unknown to me. How many of a person's dreams become true in the entire life? Even if you know that it will become true, can you really be ready for that moment?

I came here four days ago. Fever of first day still continues. Although I try to keep my true thoughts and feelings to me, you will probably understand how I am. I can't succeed in hiding my fearfulness. I do always look around. I strive at memorising roads, trees and shops. I commend myself that knowing my own way makes me more confident. I look for some familiar things hoping that I may see or hear about an acquaintance. It seems everybody knows that I am a new-comer in this district. I feel as if everybody were looking at me. Houses are again houses, people are again people, but what is the reason for such a great difference?

Our house is next to the railway station, and located at a central point. It is a five storey, sharp roofed, blue building. I like its being close to the station, I feel as if I could arrive in my home country immediately by train. Despite its high roof and large windows, our flat is a small one. Our houseowner is living at upstairs. When I first saw her, I got scared a little bit. In my opinion, she seemed everready for shouting. My husband told later that people of this locality generally speak in such a styled manner. Let it be admitted that I can't reconcile myself to here. If somebody fails to undersand words told to him/herself, then he/she must listen by heart.

My husband was off duty this morning. We wanted to do something as early as possible. You must see his fascinating surprises to make me happy. Maybe, he always thinks that I am here because of him.

We had our breakfast, and went to a park close to our house. Whereas summer has already made itself evident in Turkey, it seems that spring has just started here. Eveywhere is very green and decorated with flowers. Green is somewhat different than we know. Think leaves resembling pistachios. And flowers resembling pictures. There is such a beatiful rose array that can't be told by words. Do you know the red rose having velvet leaves? Its face is even larger than an open palm. Who are growing such roses? Don't be jelous since they are more beautiful than your roses. Yours are unique. I am sure that you will also like here if you see one day. Here, parks aren't similar with the ones we generally know. They look like private gardens rather than public parks.

Ohh, my dear aunt, I know that I don't talk about my health in this letter. I'm sure that you are curious. I'm good, my dear aunt. I'm really good.

August 29, 1991

My Dear Aunt,

We are both residents of this country any more. We went to foreign office yesterday. We had a large file of papers with us. Strange to say, those pieces of papers are indicators of our lives. Besides, I couldn't understand anything about the written information. They also gave a small piece of paper to us. From now on, we will have carried that paper with us for five years in this country.

In fact, reception of that paper was an extremely demanding process. However, we didn't wait as long as we had waited with you in bank sequences once upon a time. When it was our turn, they called us. Our transactions didn't take even half a day. I considered but couldn't tell my husband that whether there was a foreign office in Turkey, or not. I wonder if there are any foreigners waiting in a line in Turkey. How many people get excited from the heart when it is their turn?

My husband told what they had talked after we went out of the office. They asked when I would learn their language and when I would commence working. If I had known that they asked questions about me, I would have certainly replied them. I feel really depressed since I can't understand people around me. Everybody is talking about you and you can't understand anything even when they are talking in your elbow. I can't withstand any more. I must find a way out.

I reminded your kitchen yesterday night and I wanted to try cooking similar things with yours. I considered that I might lessen my emotion of longing if my kitchen smelt just like yours. I baked pastries. I decided to give some of them to our house owner. You know, she is somewhat our neighbor and we are living under one roof. I knocked her door and poked pastries at her. She is a tall, grey haired and scowling woman who is almost fifty years old. First, she looked at me at length and stood still for a while as if she had been waiting for me to ask something to her. I was at a loss for words, and poked pastries at her once more. I wanted to say, this is customary in our country, but I became tongue-tied. I felt as if long hours had elapsed. Eventually, she took pastries from my hand and I cut loose from waiting. I thought that she whispered something. While assuming that she thanked to me, she closed the door at once.

Fortunately, my husband came home early in the evening so that I could talk with him. I told everything one by one. Even, I, myself, didn't notice that I was so bored. I probably spoke too much and he listened to me all night long. But what else can I do? In this huge city, I don't have any other friend with whom I can talk.

Do you think I'll manage to live in this city?

September 8, 1991

My Dear Aunt,

It's getting cold here rapidly. We have already started wearing our winter pullovers. However, it is just the beginning of September. If we were in our country, we didn't get into our house in these days. We could eat dinners in your grape garden, and drink coffee while listening to summery cicadas. Your neighbors didn't leave us alone. They came one after another. We could talk with each other cosily under shining stars until the midnight. Was I very young then, or am I too old now? Strange to say, I deplored by remembering the past.

No, my dear aunt, be sure of that it is not because of my moodiness.

Grape leaves aren't sold in this country. That's what I'm thinking about.

November 18, 1991

My Dear Aunt,

I have restarted school after eight years. I have a class again. A class where I can't smell chalks. I go out to the blackboard again. The only difference is that I don't wear school uniform any more. I am relearning alphabet. I repeat what I have already known. I learn a different language this time. Eventhough I have never heard these voices, I know their meaning.

I am not sure whether I can be successful, or not. I draw consolation in my classmates' not being better than me. There are some ladies who don't know even one foreign word although they have been living here for fifteen years. I ask how they have achieved to survive under these circumstances. Believe me, I also get amazed with their answers.

I can't live as they do. I can't put up with asking for help whenever I can't understand something. It is very difficult for me not to be able to understand people talking around me. It is also impossible to ask everything to my husband. He doesn't have to wait like a guardsman for my businesses. Nevertheless, there are some missing things, in fact there are always missing things.

To tell the truth, I am worried about something else, something which I can't tell anybody. While speaking with a friend in the class a short while ago, I forgot a Turkish word which I have already known. I tried my best, but I couldn't express myself. Besides, my husband notices that I often use inverted sentences nowadays. What if I forget Turkish?

My dear aunt, I hope I won't forget Turkish, will I? Do you think it is possible to forget a native language?

February 20, 1992

My Dear Aunt,

I can’t bear such a life any more. I can't write any letters to you for a long time. I am so confused. I can't accommodate myself to this country. Everything is alien to me. At first, I tried to ignore problems since I came to this country just a short while ago. I thought that "everything would be better" step by step. However, I can’t bear any more. I can neither understand what people say nor express myself. How can I look for a job under these circumstances?

I know that nobody can understand me. In the eye of public, my problems are groundless since I have a house and a husband. Besides, I also don't want anything other than a simple and happy life.

Then, why do I struggle for establishing order here? I forget my past knowledge while trying to improve myself. Is my mind so ungrateful, why can’t it keep my knowledge hitherto?

I might have started missing my country, our house, your small green garden, you… as of now. If you were here, could everything be different? Or, is it my fault to be here? If you had advised me, I could have managed everything better. I can’t decide even the first step…

If I say him that I want to return, does he come together with me? If he leaves his job and we return to our country, will it be a quick withdrawal? Isn’t it strange to resign myself when I'm so young? It may be strange, but it is certainly true. You can run out of patience and endurance at a certain moment in the life. A moment which cause you to accept that there is no other way. A moment that you think that you can’t do anything more.

Oh my dear aunt, how can a country be rainy everyday? Strange to say, I have been counting sunny days for a while. In the previous month, only three days weren't rainy. And, I had my eyes free of tears just on those three days.

But, please don’t disclose these things to anybody else.

April 27, 1992

My dear aunt,

I rise to the occasion this time. I achieve speaking the language. Maybe, I can't remind the first word I told in my life. Besides, I can't remind initial happiness of people who had brought me up at that moment. But, believe me, my present excitement and happiness due to being conceived by other people is not weaker than their feelings. May be I am not reborn, but I find myself again.

As an adult, I reexperience my emotion of victory when I first went to grocery to buy a bread as a seven years old girl. I felt as if I had carried out a very important task. I can also communicate with my house owner any more. Still, I can't completely understand her words. But, she smiles at me any more. Or, maybe this is what I assume.

Growing up is a really difficult task. When I was a child, everybody was talking in my language. Then, does everything become alien as we get older?

It is still cold in this city. It seems that spring term doesn't intend to start here. However, my soul gets warmer day by day. I don't feel as cold as in the past.

May 8, 1992

My Aunt,

I write this letter again to you. I feel different this time. There is somebody else who knows our correspondences any more. Somebody who explores the strong tie between us and who is so kind that he never tries to break off this tie.

I was rearranging cabinets yesterday night. My husband entered into the room so silently that I couldn't notice that he was behind me.

He caused me to jump by saying that "You are very lucky." He started laughing at me. I think this was because I looked at him as if I had been a child caught in the act.

He joyfully asked, "From whom do you receive so many letters?" I opened my mouth to reply, but couldn't speak. I stood still across him with envelopes in my hand. He came up to me, thrusted out his hand and took a letter from my hand slowly.

"But, this letter was written to your aunt, did you write it?" asked he. Of course, he is the person who is most familiar with my handwriting, so it's needless to reply. I kept quiet.

"And what about other letters?"

"They are also for my aunt."

All of a sudden, his face turned dark. He focused on letters. I said to myself that, he's thinking what to say. I didn't want to put him onto spot. Also I didn't want to sadden him. I dare say, he also thought the same for me and hence left letters onto the table and turned towards me. He covered my arms with his hands and looked at me in a consolatory manner as usual.

"As you also know, your aunt passed away four years ago," said he.

"I know..."

"How long have you been writing letters?"

"Since we came to this country."

We don't hide anything from each other. It is obvious that he is my single friend and confidant. I didn't want to cause him to be afflicted due to learning a hidden secret of me. However, it was certain that he was worried about something different.

"Believe me, I don't oppose to your writting letters. But, you may have a problem which causes you to write for such a long time. Why didn't you tell me this problem? You know that I always listen to you. I think there can be only one reason which makes you write these letters. This can be only because I can't support you sufficiently. I cause you to feel alone. Not having any other relative doesn't mean that you are lack of a family. We two constitute a family."

I also thought that these are the right words. We are all of one mind that he's right. But, letters that I had written to you were very different. They weren't paralel to talking with my husband.

I could easily explained my feelings to him. He also knew most of the things I had told you. My only desire was to feel myself closer to you and my country.

"Then, let's send these letters to Turkey," said he.

To Turkey... To the house. To your house having a small garden. Why not? Maybe, I always feel depressed because of this. Maybe, I get worried because my words don't arrive in their target. Here is also a wrong place for them.

Just like that my dear aunt... I'll post your letters tomarrow. Each of them will be delivered to your house.

I don't know how long it will take until accommodating myself to here. I also don't know how long it will take until recovering myself from bitter. Can a lifetime be enough? We will see.

I'm here, my dear aunt, but I am also just near you within a world created by my letters.

Havva Öztürk / Holland

She was born in Çorum in 1977. She was graduated from Marmara University, the Department of Communications and Public Relations. In 2002, she got married and moved to Holland. She is the mother of a 4-year-old girl. She works as the editor of the culture and art pages of two magazines that are published in Turkish and in Dutch throughout Holland.

The Figurine Queen Who Lived in a Cocoon

It had been years since she had completed the autumn of her life. Even the most remote leaves on her tree of life were now faded, decayed and mixed with the earth. Now, she was a living dead. Like all lonely Dutch women who were approximately ninety, she tasted the pleasures of life only in her dreams. Even the Dutch Government considered this generation that had witnessed to the Nazi genocide, as a burden. She and her peers were now an unproductive and useless mass, exploiting the retirement funds of the state.

Her body was now fully integrated with sleep. So what if she died? Her whole personality was being nourished with the crumbs of far away memories reflected in her dreams. She would be eighty seven in one week, but most people who knew her thought she was too senile to be aware of her age. As the oldest in the family, she was no longer disturbed by the attitude of family members. It was the time of selfish and cocky youngsters who worked like machines throughout the year, and who began to search an exotic country for their holidays as summer approached. Young people who were lack of moral values. They considered going to church stupid. Cooking at home is unnecessary. The strict rules that her generation adhered to, throughout life was only valid for these young people in work life now, to improve their careers. This generation, that was indifferent even to itself, seemed to be the genetic remains of the age of machinery. This group of people who had no values said they respected all beliefs, but she didn't find them sincere. It was this generation that had crucified Jesus.

She was suddenly startled by the chimes of the antique clock in the living room and decided to end her laziness in bed, and get up. She put on her house coat and went into the kitchen for breakfast. She was fortunate, compared to many ladies stuck in tiny kitchens, because although she was living alone, she had a spacious kitchen. Even though it was fifteen years since her husband had died, she was continuing to live in a spacious, three-bedroom apartment belonging to the municipality of Rotterdam.

Despite the fact that foreign families with many children were covering such large apartments, she was determined to stay in this huge place until her last breath. Other Dutch people, who were not as strong willed as her, had respectively left the district of Oranjeboom where they were born, and moved to new neighborhoods that were being established on the outskirts of the city. Actually, you couldn't call that as moving. It was more like taking refuge. Within ten years, the whole neighborhood was taken over by immigrants from Turkey, Morocco, Indonesia, Taiwan and Surinam. But she was determined not to leave this neighborhood which she considered her ancestral home. She was determined not to leave her house.

Throughout their history, the Dutch people had never been so alienated from their own country. Now, it seemed as if all the famous avenues, attractive shopping areas, known bars and neighborhood markets of the city were left to the foreigners. The Dutch who disliked these new guests had withdrawn from the city centre. She actually had no problems with the blacks from Surinam or West Africa, because at least those were former Dutch colonies so those blacks spoke Dutch fluently.

There were eight apartments in the building where Ms. Marianne Van Gent lived. Six of her neighbors were from Surinam, and one was Turkish. The Turkish family, who lived above her, on the third floor, had worn her out completely. She found no reason to complain about the families from Surinam because they had few children, and they were at work all day. But the family who lived one floor above had forced her to make numerous calls of complaint to the police. They were driving her crazy. She didn't know if she should react to the fact that they left their baby carriage at the building's entrance instead of taking it to the basement, or to the children of their guests who kept running around above her until midnight, of to the naughty grandchildren who were sure to drop something on her head when she got out on her balcony, or their little son who would go down the stairs jumping and making noise. All the police stations in Rotterdam knew her voice by now. Often, they would hang up on her, before she even got a chance to finish what she was saying. Many people of her generation suffered from the disease of "hunting down disobedient citizens" and of telling the police on them, but in her, the disease had reached extreme proportions.

As she was pouring her steeped tea into her cup, she was startled by the sound of laughter that came in through the open door of the balcony to fill the room. She slowly went towards the balcony to find the source of this gleeful laughter. There it was. The three rowing teams that were canoeing in the canal that passed in front of the apartment block. "My god," she mumbled to herself, "how young they are! How full of life..." Their lives weren't restricted by the walls of rooms like hers. Each of those young people was surrounded by a circle of people made up of flesh and blood and fresh spirits. Even the hungry gulls flying around the canoes that moved forward in the dark and dank waters of the canals that rarely received sunlight seemed to remain with the group. The primary school located to the left of her apartment block was also full of lively sounds, the playground at the end of the road before the school, filled with children. Even the canal across her house was receiving more guests than she had ever had, it was meeting people. For a moment, she had a feeling that she was the only person in the world, punished with such kind of loneliness.

The wind brought the ringing of a bell to her hears, announcing that the noon break was starting at the school, and that within ten minutes, the street would be filled with dozens of dark heads. Just fifteen years ago, this old school building did not house a single dark child. By now, it felt to her as if the school, that was once like a golden wheat field had burned down to ash, and left the space to children with black heads. School of the neighborhood was full of foreign families' children, it was impossible to meet a single Dutch child. This fact was almost officially recognized. The schools where the foreigners were in the majority were referred to as "black," and those where Dutch children were in the majority were called "white" schools. During the time when Marianne Van Gent's children were in school, this neighborhood school had not yet turned dark.

A little later, tiny hands began to ring persistently the doorbell of Sakine apartment. The three children at the door were Sakine grand-children. Sakine had two daughters, two sons and eight grandchildren whose parentage she was beginning to confuse. These three rambunctious children were among the regular guests upstairs. Since their parents worked, it was Sakine who was looking after them. When the children, who upset Ms. Gent many times every day finally managed to get inside, Ms. Gent chose to return to her breakfast. She bit into her soft-boiled egg, thinking about the way she had looked down on Sakine for nothing for all several years, because the home of that modestly dressed Turkish woman was never crushed by the heavy steps of silence and emptiness, like her own.

Ms. Marianne Van Gent, who fed hundreds of figurines in the living room of her spacious and empty house, was empress of a secret army. Her display case, the tops of coffee tables, the television stand, in short, all the furniture in the room were obliged to host a series of figurines.

From the Dutch peasants of the 1600's, to aristocrats, from the bourgeoisie women who went to the balls in 19th century, to the modern citizens of Holland, Dutch people from different backgrounds and identities and submitted to Ms. Gent's secret empire. These human figurines were the only witnesses of her painful and lonely life so she bestowed upon them an esteem that she would never bestow on the real people she knew.

Just when she had started to enjoy her breakfast, her doorbell rang.

"Good morning Etna, I had forgotten that you were coming today."

"That's surprising. You used to look forward to my days. Have you found someone else to pick on?"

"Come on Etna. When did I ever pick on you? All I want is that you do your job properly, and not in an haphazard manner."

"Oh Ms. Gent, if you were to search all of Holland, you would not find a cleaner who is more practical than I am."

"That's right. You are practical all right. You whip through your work."

"I'd better start with the living room as usual."

"Wait, wait! The living room is all clean. My figurines have taken a bath."

"Oh, that's true. The living room is clean and tidy. I wonder if you've found a second cleaning lady without telling me..."

"No, no. During the weekend, my daughter-in-law and my son Mark were here. Against all my objections, my daughter-in-law did some cleaning, and my figurines took part in her campaign."

"Oh, you really have a good daughter-in-law, don't you? Are there any such hard working young women around these days? The bakeries sell sliced bread because the women are too lazy to slice their own."

"It wasn't because she is hard working, really. She just wants to get on my good side. Until she gets a residence permit in Holland, she wants to ingratiate herself to me. As soon as they get that permit, the first thing they do is to throw their husbands out. That slut might have seduced my son but she can't fool me. Anyway, you might as well start with the balcony."

"All right, madam."

The weekly cleaning lady Etna who was sent to Ms. Gent by the state, had a hard time here. Marianne Van Gent would look over her shoulder, constantly ordering her to pay more attention as she dusted the endless figurines, thus driving Etna crazy. They had argued many times because of this. Ms. Gent had complained to the company that hired Etna many times, but hadn't been able to get rid of her. Perhaps the cleaning companies had grown insensitive towards Ms. Gent because this was the sixth woman that she was attempting to dismiss. This reaction of similar to the reaction of Ms. Gent's own children.

Ms. Gent was salting her sliced tomatoes, when she noticed that the potted flowers in her kitchen had dried up. As if to spite the living room that was crowded with figurines, the kitchen was filled with potted flowers. Hanging pots seemed to supplement the pots standing on the floor. This was more like a little garden than a kitchen.

"Etnaaa... Stop fooling around on the balcony, and come here to look after the flowers!"

"Ouff. This woman never lets you work in peace. Alright, I'm coming."

While she was sipping her tea, she began to think about her children. A week later, it would be her birthday. Yet none of the children had called yet. Ms. Gent's daughter who was married to a rich Belgian man was living in Anwers. Although she could drive down in two hours, she showed her face no more than once a year. Hanneke, who rushed to visit shopping centres as soon as she arrived in her mother's house, didn't even bother to phone between visits. As for her younger son Marten, who was a computer engineer, he had married the daughter of one of Holland's most ordinary families, and made that would be "Barbie doll," a member of her own family. With those mini skirts and exaggerated make up, Annet was immediately noticed by men wherever she went. She had exaggerated gestures and seductive eyes... Surely, she was not a daughter-in-law worthy of Ms. Gent's family. But the hardest blow to Ms. Gent was dealt by her eldest son Mark who six months earlier, married a foreign woman who did not even understand Dutch, and who, with her shyness and dowdiness, was completely different from Annet. This marriage had struck a real blow to the family ties that Ms. Gent had built on establishing through her entire life. So this was the reason why Ms. Gent did not even want to get out of bed for days, and why she was distracted these days: Mark's great betrayal of her only mother, and all she stood for.

•••

She was still doing her hair, and about to miss the last bust that could get her to school on time. Zühal, who checked her school bag once more before throwing herself on the stairs, was panting and sweating when she got on the bus. In the bus that was filled with students and with people rushing to work, she couldn't find a corner to squeeze herself in, so in despair, she made her way to the back of the bus. The Maas River that divided Rotterdam in two, was shaded by two bridges. The white bridge, as graceful as an enchanting swan, always seemed more appealing to her than the red bridge that was built in the classical style. While she was still living in Istanbul, the postcards that Mark who was her lover then (her husband how) had sent her, the silhouette of "Rotterdam with the white swan" that had charmed her the most.

Zühal, whose family lived in Eskişehir, had received an environmental engineering degree in Istanbul, and after graduating from university, she had found a job with the municipal government of Istanbul. She had met Mark during work on the tube crossing project that was expected to solve some of İstanbul's chronic traffic problems. At first, she had not at all liked Mark, who was smart, handsome and opinionated.

The bus began to empty its passengers, but soon filled up again at Blak. Zühal found a seat, and when she noticed that her classmate Leyla had just got on the bus, the waved to offer Leyla a seat beside her.

"Hey, good morning. Haven't you awakened yet? I had to work hard to attract your attention..."

"Ihh, of course, I have awakened long ago. I couldn't even sleep at night. There is so much that's troubling me. With all those knots tied inside, do you think I can get to sleep?"

"Why? What's troubling you?"

"You know, I used to think 'I'm getting married and going to Europe. I'll have more rights and freedoms. It turned out to be the reverse. Things are worse for me than ever. Just five years ago, I used to think that Sinop was not up to fulfilling my dreams. Now, I'm constantly dreaming about Sinop."

"It sounds like you've become an archaeologist of memories. The more you dig, the more precious memories you unearth.."

"It's easy for you. You can joke. Your husband is a Dutch man. You don't have a mother-in-law like mine who sticks her nose into everything you do. Your husband doesn't try to prevent you from going shopping alone. The major activity in your life is not this language course... It's only six months since you've arrived, yet you started the course right away. Look at me, I wouldn't even have been at the language course, if it hadn't been compulsory by law. Ah, if only I had started sooner, I would have learned this language fluently..."

"Perhaps I have problems too. As long as your complaints keep going, I can't get a word in edgewise... You want to be able to live as you wish, and to be free to go anywhere you like. I, on the other hand, am tired of being alone and not having a friend whose door I might ring. I think you're lucky to have people who welcome you."

"But your husband belongs to here! His ancestors going back seven generations must be buried here. As for us - even our dead are immigrant. All the rosy dreams I had when I was looking at the turbulent waters of Black Sea at Sinop have drowned in the dark waters of Rotterdam."

"You say that, but god will provide, don't worry. My own father is such a traditional and obstinate man that he has denied me for marrying Mark. Actually if he hadn't what would have changed? He never expressed any affection for me, yet he took away my right to a father which I never really enjoyed anyway - just because I married a Christian. My step mother benefited from the ice between us. Here, I have no job. No one. And don't worry, it's not only the Turks that produce intolerable mothers-in-law. I know, they try the force on their daughters-in-law, the conditions that they experienced themselves forty years earlier, but the Dutch are no different. My mother-in-law doesn't take me seriously enough to force anything on me."

"Oh, c'mon. The Dutch are progressive people. They're not ignorant like our people who are suddenly exposed to a modern culture which they are wholly strange to."

"They're progressive towards their own kind. But Mark's mother is someone that's so difficult to communicate with. Although she normally speaks really slowly, when I'm around she deliberately speaks Dutch very fast, to make sure I won't understand. When I visit her, I offer to help her with the housework but she doesn't want me to touch anything."

"How odd. Mine wants me to work constantly. She complains that I was lazy at my mother's home, and that I came to her place, not knowing aything. She blames my mother for my incompetence. She says it would look bad to the neighbors if she were to clean the windows, when she has a daughter-in-law. When I was a young girl, I used to take my time to go to the table when my mother called me for dinner. Now, I cook so many varieties of dishes, but I can't please anybody..."

"My mother-in-law doesn't let me touch anything in her kitchen full of plants, so I don't have the luxury of cooking. Never mind cooking. If we ever visit her unannounced, and the table is set of a meal, she doesn't even invite us to join."

"Really. Cenap used to say 'the Dutch never invited someone who arrives without an appointment to their table' so it's true!"

"Yes, it is. On one occasion, I decided to drop by my mother-in-law's place because Mark would be working late. Of course I didn't know at that time that the notion of 'Guest sent by God' isn't a concept valid for the Dutch. That day, she had invited some people from the church choir for dinner. I was starving. The table was full of a dozen dishes, but no one invited me to join in because I had dropped in without a prior notification."

"Hmmm. I eat all the food at my mother-in-law's place as I wish. Does yours have any other strange habits?"

"Well, they consider it very rude for someone to ask where a gift was purchased or how much it cost. Two months ago, my sister-in-law Annet had bought a food processor for my mother-in-law. There were some other guests there as well, and I asked Annet where she had bought the food processor and how much she had paid for it. Everyone giggled uncomfortably. I felt like a worm that day."

"So what? Mine want to be remembered but if I ever buy a gift, they reproach me for spending their son's money..."

"Oh, that's the way Turkish women ask for attention. My mother was like that, too. She expected a gift but she didn't want any spending."

"How do you get along with the rest of your husband's Dutch family?"

"My sister-in-law, Hanneke is very rich and pretentious. My other sister-in-law Annet wants to think about nothing other than getting herself dolled up. My brother-in-law, Marten is conservative and xenophobic like his mother."

"You must have a tough time, really."

"In a week, it'll be my mother-in-law's birthday. I would like to do something to make her happy but I have no idea what... I don't know..."

"Don't get her one of those typical gifts whose value has to be kept secret. Find something that's warm enough for the Turks and unusual enough for the Dutch."

"Yes but what? I couldn't find something like that in forty years... Mark doesn't care about his mother's birthday, because these days he is deep in his projects. And even if I were to find a wonderful gift, the iceberg between my mother-in-law and myself would prevent her from seeing my gift."

"Don't be so sure... Let things evolve..."

"I am letting things evolve ever since I got here. Oh, look, we've been chatting away and passed our bus stop. Let's get off. We'll be late to class."

•••

This was Marianne Van Gent's birthday, and she knew that it might be the last. Although it was six o'clock in the evening, no one had contacted her. Neither her friends in the church choir, nor the old family friends who were still alive, and nor her own ungrateful children. It was Mark's indifference that upset her the most. Among her children, it was always Mark – before his marriage to Zühal and after – who paid more attention to her. This meant that the Turkish girl had won the on-going battle between Ms. Van Gent and her daughter-in-law. Now, Ms. Van Gent had two rivals, including Annet. Who had any use for an eighty-seven-year old woman anyway? Her advice was no longer valid because she was behind the age. She was no good to listen to people's cares because her memory had lost its rhythm. "What's the difference between me and these figurines?" she muttered. She felt bitter about her fate, and about the fact that she was still alive.

The sharp scream of the doorbell rang, while she was on her way to the bedroom. She opened the door and saw Mark.

"Mark! I knew you would come to seem me today. Don't stand there, come in."

"No, mom, I'm not coming in. Just the opposite: I'm going to take you out. Come on, change your clothes."

"By my son, it's almost seven o'clock. Most places have closed. Where can we go at this time of the day? Where is Zühal?"

"That's a surprise. Come on, hurry up and get ready."

Marianne Van Gent chose one of the best dresses in her wardrobe and got dressed with an agility that no one would have expected from her age.

When she returned to Mark, he commented: "Mom, you're still as young and beautiful as you were when I was a child..."

When Marianne Van Gent and her son went downstairs, a small boat was awaiting them in the canal, before the apartment building. One of the canals that crossed the entire city before spilling into the Maas River, passed before her building. They travelled about ten minutes on the water that seemed to have absorbed the calm of the evening. Mark drew the boat to a yacht that seemed to be wrapped in the mystery of the night.

"Mark, are you thinking of getting me in this yacht?"

"Yes, mother. Now, be very careful, hold my hand so we'll climb the stair slowly. Alright, I'm holding on to your hand. That's fine..."

"Mark, you haven't said why you brought me to this empty yacht where there is no one..."

Marianne Van Gent was suddenly confronted by fireworks and hundreds of balloons let to fly in the sky. Guests who had been hiding formed a human flood around her and shouted all at once: "Surprise! Happy Birthday!"

Good God! Everyone I know is here! Marten, Annet, my cousin Jan Teen, Hanneke, my grandchildren John, Henry... Etna! What are you doing here?

"Many happy returns, Ms. Gent!"

Even Sakine and her children! The residents of the whole apartment block are here! I can't believe it. The golden girls of the church choir have come as well...

"Mark, my sensitive, gentleman son. I thank you for this gesture. I knew you wouldn't forget me, but I didn't expect this!"

"Unfortunately, mother, this wonderful birthday present was not my idea. This was Zühal's idea and she is the one who organized all the details."

"Happy birthday mother Marianne! This is hardly worthy of you but it's my birthday present to you."

"It was the greatest present anyone could give me, to make me feel alive, once again. This is the most wonderful birthday I've ever had. Now I know why Mark chose you."

Işıl Ertören David / Switzerland

She was born in Samsun in 1965. She was graduated from Ankara University, Language and History Geography Faculty, Psychology Department. She has been living in Geneva since 1998. She is married and has a child.

Foreign Bride

Sarıkamış was a village located in a retired spot of Anatolia, and was composed of fifteen-twenty houses. Sneezing of somebody living in a house situated at one corner of the village could be easilyheard by people living at the other corner. These people had soon gone to visit for wishing for a quick recuperation. The same was also true for that day. When Fadime of Pazaroğulları, who finished the phone call with her son which always caused her to cry, the great news had already spread over the village. Having heard the news, all her neighbors immediately visited her for congrulating her. Fadime, who couldn't get over her astonishment yet, was exposed to various questions of her neigbours.

– I'm very happy, Ms. Fadime, congrulations. When will they come?

– You well be happy, we can't see even our children in Turkey. On the other hand, yours are coming from too distant places. By the way, how long will they stay here?

– Oh, Fadime, lucky woman; you won't die with a desire left unsatisfied. They'll come all together, won't they?

In fact, for the people of this small village in which a monotone life was dominant, these news were really great. Mesut of Pazaroğulları had departed from the village years ago for the sake of sea which he had only seen in newspapers, books and which he had only heard in songs and ballads. When he had decided to work as crew in large transport ships, he had been fairly young. At first, he had sent messages stating that he had been fine and had missed his family very much. These messages had been written on beautiful cards posted from various places of the world, which were hardly known by villagers. Afterwards, they started receiving greater news about Mesut. That hawk-eyed, naughty, frisky, dark and weak son of Pazaroğulları had settled in America. Villagers got very excited by these news. They had heard about Germany, but that was the first time they had heard about America. Then, children who attended school in the neigbour village, stepped forward and told whatever they knew about America boastfully. In the end, villagers could only learn that America was a greater and more distant country than Germany. After comprehending what kind of a country America was, and where it was located; they started investigation.

– If so, how can Mesut achieve to stay there?

– Why did he settle in America instead of Germany which is much more approximate?

– Will he come back from such a distant country one day for visiting his parents and sisters?

Villagers who scarcely adapted themselves to the fact that Mesut had settled in America; got shocked once more when they learned that he had got married with a foreign woman! Serhat who was the adolescent son of Pazaroğulları Family's neighbors; ran up to her mother as soon as he heard these news, and said insistently that:

– Mum, mum, I also want to marry with a foreign woman just as my elder brother, Mesut.

Poor mother of Serhat couldn't find a way to persuade him for long days.

Young girls of village got really depressed about these news. Why did Mesut of Pazaroğulları get married with a foreign woman as if there weren't any beautiful girls in the village?

The old women were sure that he would never return to his home village any more.

And the old men of the village still tried to learn answers of their questions: Did Mesut's wife become a Muslim before marriage?

Poor mother and sisters of Mesut, were entirely busy with answering curious questions of neighbors. Besides, they didn't know anything more than their neighbors, but their neighbors were so curious that they had to use their imagination for satisfying their neighbors' great curiosity. In the end, marriage of Mesut with a foreign woman also turned into a narrative as below: Wife of Mesut was a beautiful and slim brunette. Mesut had fallen in love with her as soon as he had seen her. And the same was true also for his wife. Foreign bride verbally obeyed instructions of Mesut who she was passionately in love with. That's why, the bride changed her religion at once when Mesut wanted her to be Muslim as a precondition for marriage. Mesut had also given her a new Muslim name; Ayşe.

In the village, everybody had concentrated on that imaginatory Ayşe, each person added a further detail to the narrative which had gotten more interesting day by day. Besides, they believed these narratives so passionately that when Mesut called her mother by phone (meanwhile, technology had also arrived in their village, and hence electricity, water and telephone services were provided. Thus, Mesut started calling his mother from time to time instead of writing letters to her.) and told that they would have a baby; all the villagers got really shocked; "They have already had a baby, haven't they?" People who got confused when following up this narrative, expressed their happiness when they learned that the American bride had born a daughter. "It is very good, they have already had a son, and now they also have a daughter," said the villagers. Furthermore, villagers who visited Mesut's family for congrulating them, said that "Wonderful, really wonderful! Foreign bride is really fast, she had born two children at one go." Therefore, even Mesut's family got suspicious about how many children Mesut had.

After a certain time period occupied by gossips and chats about Mesut, villagers returned to their usual silent lives since they had received no further information regarding him and his life. However, the latest news were really shocking. Was it really true that Mesut and his family would visit their village which hadn't been considered even by the state until recent times? This was the greatest of news items they had ever received about Mesut.

You can hardly imagine the fever of villagers after these news. All of the women cleaned their houses as if they would be visited. Clothes and coverlets which had been kept in large chests for long years were taken out, washed and ironed. Afterwards, they had been mantled onto ottomans, armchairs and jacktables dilligently.

Young girls of the village applied henna to their hair and hands, outlined their eyes with kohl, and prepared their most beautiful dresses to be worn while welcoming the visitors. It seemed that they couldn't accommodate themselves to the fact that Mesut had chosen a foreign girl to get married with.

One day before the visit of eagerly-waited guests, the women had cooked the most difficult, but the most delicious desserts, pastries, and pancakes. The men were also busy Mesut and his family's visit. They were discussing in the coffee house of village so as to determine the most appropriate way of welcoming Mesut and his family. Each of them came up with a different idea. Some offered to "sacrifice an animal", some proposed to "fire shots for the honour of their visit", and some other suggested to "welcome their visitors by playing drums and clarions."

The village headman was the only person who didn't participate in this heated discussions, he kept silent until discusions weakened and then interfered suddenly, "Friends, please calm down. Our visitors are neither prime minister, nor minister, nor governor. A ceremony is meaningless. Visitors are very familiar to us; Mesut of Pazaroğulları and his family." However, he couldn't even complete his sentences which were interrupted at once. "How can it be without ceremony," said they to the villageman. "Maybe, a ceremony is needles if our only visitor is Mesut. But a foreigner will also come. That's the time to show our hospitality. Otherwise, what will the foreign bride tell about us in her distant country? What if our village gets a bad reputition there? We don't want to be ashamed against foreigners." The headman got bored of such discussions, and understood that a ceremony was inevitable. So he put an end to discussions by saying that "All right, let's arrange a ceremony. But I can't permit you to sacrifice an animal, or to fire shots. I will welcome them in the name of all village, and drums and clairons will be played."

On the day when Mesut and his family would arrive in the village, the headman put on his cleanest and newest clothes and started waiting in front of the house of Pazaroğulları. He was accompanied by a drum and a clarion player. In the end, when the automobile of visitors appeared, all the village was immediately informed about their arrival. All women, men and children of the village ran towards the house of Pazaroğulları, formed into rank behind the headman, and constituted a large welcoming committee. When a black car stopped in front of Pazaroğulları Family's house where a crowd of people were waiting; everybody stood still and stared at the car. Meanwhile, drum and clarion players who had been waiting together with the headman in front of the house for a long while started playing their instruments even before the instruction of headman.

At first, Mesut got out of the car. He was carrying a smart-eyed girl. His mother, father and sisters who had remembered him as in the past, hardly recognized him. That dark haired, dark browed, slim Mesut in their memories had sharply changed. The man who got out of the car was over weight, his hair was partly black and partly blonde, he had goatee and eyeglass. If he didn't go up to her mother and embrace her by saying "my dear mother", nobody could be sure that he was Mesut. When Mesut immediately embraced and kissed all of his family members, the headman was also convinced that he was Mesut, and welcomed him in the name of all villagers at once.

Now, it was Mesut's turn to get astonished. Why did villagers welcome him by such a great ceremony including drums and clarions. While he was trying to understand this, the real guest got out of the car. Ayşe, the foreign bride about whom villagers had created various narratives and who was expected to be very beautiful stood still beside the car. She was also looking at the crowd in deep waters. The same was true for the crowd.

Everywhere was covered with a deep silence, it seemed that villagers try to find similarities between the imaginatory Ayşe and the real Ayşe. In fact, the problem was that. There wasn't any direct or indirect similarities. This blonde woman was over weight, blue eyed, and so to say she was as tall as a jellyfish. Mesut's family and the crowd were looking at her amazingly, on the other hand views of Mesut's wife was not less amazing than theirs. If Mesut didn't come on the scene and introduce his wife to his family, silence and amazement could have continued for a very long time.

For Mesut's family, getting acquainted with foreign bride was really a difficult task. Mother, sisters and even father of Mesut were too short compared to her. They could only embrace and kiss each other if foreign bride bent down towards Mesut's family. But this was also impossible because foreign bride couldn't bend down due to her overweight. In the end, they were contented with shaking their hands.

After Mesut and his family entered into the house hastily, silence and amazement were replaced with gossips of the crowd. Beautiful girls of the village, who had been extremly jealous of foreign bride due to narratives during her, were walking on air. It was needless for them to tell anything; they looked at young boys of the village and laughed as if making fun of them. Didn't many of them imagine marrying to a foreign bride when they had first learnt Mesut's marriage? However, they were really dissapointed at that very moment, and got really afraid of her bulkiness. In fact, they had nothing to say. Just the old women and men were whispering among the crowd:

– Do you think our Mesut had lost his foresight while marrying with this foreign bride?

– Oh, my God! This foreign bride can skin Mesut of Pazaroğulları alive!

– Oh, my friend! This foreign bride must have grown up at fertile lands.

– Praise be! She is as stalwart as a calf. But, be fair my dear neighbor, isn't her face beutiful?

– Foreign bride eventually assimilated Mesut to herself. He doesn't look like Mesut who was a slim and dark boy once upon a time. It seems that he had been removed by the new Mesut who is appropriate with the foreign bride.

And, what about Mesut's own family? On the first day, they weren't so much interested with bulkiness, age, beuty or ugliness of the foreign bride because they were highly pleased with coming together with their son and grand daughter after long years. By the time their longing and fever came to an end, they started to examine their bride. They even asked her name for the first time. "Name of your bride is Sally, my dear mother," said Mesut. "I can't address her with such a name. Can't we call her as Ayşe here?" his mother replied. His son told this request to his wife shyly. Foreign bride didn't object to this request. Thus, Sally turned into Ayşe all of a sudden.

Ayşe, the foreign bride wasn't an ill disposed person. She always greeted welcomers debonairly. Besides, she expressed her satisfaction with eating various delicious desserts, pancakes and pastries made by neighbors elaborately. "Good, good, very good", "oh my god, this is wonderful!" she said frequently. Family members and neighbors always expected Mesut to translate her sentences in an one-to-one manner. Mesut got really exhausted but he had no other way. Each person to whom foreign bride told a thankful word, was in seventh heaven. The one who was praised by the foreign bride, immediately return to her home and endeavored to present new delicious feed to her. As a result, it became needless for Mesut's family cook anything in the house. Furthermore, they had other tasks: Foreign bride got exhausted from the heat, and hence wanted to have a bath. Hot water should be prepared for her. Foreign bride couldn't deal with her child properly due to her over weight. So, Mesut's sisters were also obliged to undertake this duty. Although foreign bride is a good and royal person, she was very lazy as well. Even, she neither made up the bed after waking up in the morning, nor fixed her night dress and put into the cabinet. She always expected people to serve her. "Mesuut, darliing, can you give another cup of coffee to me?" said she; and Mesut immediately brought coffee for her. When she ordered water from him, Mesut again fulfilled her instruction at once.

All family followed Mesut's services for his wife, his mother and sisters who accepted serving the men as a duty couldn't give any meaning to Mesut's attitudes. On the other hand, Mesut was content with his sitiuation and undertook such responsibilities in a highly satisfied manner. Mesut's father took umbrage at her son's showing strong interest in his wife, and often said his wife that "Oh dear wife! How can a man behave like this? Manhood has got lost!" He wanted to talk with his son in private on this topic, but he couldn't be deaf to his wife's appeals. Mother of Mesut often warned her husband by saying that, "Leave them in peace, they're happy with their mode of life. They are here as our guests for just a few days. Then they will return. Please don't tell anything to him."

Neigbours who almost never got out of Pazaroğulları's house, couldn't understand Mesut's attitude towards his wife, and especially the women tried to find a solution in their mind. On the other hand, the men complained about Mesut, and said "He caused our manhood humiliated by the women." Men of the village refered to Mesut as "Girl Mesut" while chatting in the coffee house.

When foreign bride got out of the house, all villagers watched her attentively. Most well-built women, and even bulky men of the village were too slim and weak compared to her. If the bride hadn't been so tall, she might have seemed less bulky, and might have not resembled a rolling ball.

Another topic which villager talked about was weight and length of foreign bride. They tried to venture guesses. The men even betted on this topic. They hadn't known how to learn exact weight and length of foreign bride yet. Nevertheless, they didn't give up betting. Their only aim was to obtain a new source of excitement.

Both foreign bride and villagers took each other by surprise. She tried to conceive how the women could be so energetic that they could take care of their children, clean their houses, wash clothes, cook meals; and further to go to arable field, and further she wondered how the men could always sit in the place, so-called coffee house under such an smoky atmosphere and why they never got bored of such a life while the women worked so hard. She asked the questions in her mind to her husband after they got into their bedroom at nights. "Here is a sharply different country from yours. This is a cultural fact peculiar to here,"

Days had rapidly elapsed while villagers and foreign bride were trying to understand each other. It was departure time for the quests. Again, in front of Pazaroğulları's house was crammed with people. Villagers who had been talking about their foreign sister for days, started considering her as a member of their own family. They stongly wished farewelling her and reinviting her to their village. Women of the village prepared lots of feed as if their quests had been going to a different city in their own country.

When it was the exact time for departure, Sally-Ayşe, the foreign bride candidly pressed hands of her parents-in-law and sisters of Mesut and all other farewellers. She also said "Allahaısmarladık"(*) to them. In fact, she felt really sorry about departure, since she had been showed great hospitality in this village, ate most delicious feed; and hand-made tableclothes and carpets were presented to her as gifts. She was treated debanoirly by everybody. By the time they got into car for going to the airport; both she and woman peasants failed to keep themselves from crying.

Many days and weeks had elapsed after foreign bride's departure, but villagers still went on speaking about her. Permanent quests of

(*) A cultural and religious way of saying "good-bye".

coffee house were sad, because they couldn't learn the true weight and length of her. So the winner of their bet couldn't be determined. The women and girls of the village also reminded her while cooking a food which the foreign bride liked very much. It seemed that foreign bride left something to each house and corner of village in order to be remembered by villagers.

Meanwhile, they had almost forgot Mesut. He had already become "Girl Mesut", so it was needless to talk about him. Any more, villagers would ask questions to Pazaroğulları family about the foreign bride only. They wanted them to transmit their greetings to her while speaking by phone. Villagers who wondered how Mesut had gone to America, settled in that distant country, and found foreign bride for long years, and who created narratives on this topic; hadn't tried to learn the real story while quests had been in the village. They entirely concentrated on the foreign bride any more. Who knows, how long they would talk about foreign bride, and what they would tell about her for giving a novel touch to their lives.

Yüksel Önaçan / Germany

He was born in Emirdağ, Afyon in 1945. He was graduated from the Academy of Trade and Economy at Eskişehir. He had worked as a teacher and school principal in Afyon, Ağrı, Germany and Eskişehir. He was retired in Eskişehir in 1995. He lives in Bielefeld, Germany.

Seher

As the roosters of the village began to compete with each other, beating their wings and crowing, the sun was slowly rising behind Emir Mountains, as if watching the slopes pitilessly razed for firewood, and greeting the smoke rising from hearths lit for breakfast.

The elders, whose legs ached with rheumatism even in their Turkmen beds, were up early, squatting against a wall, and waiting for their breakfasts consisting of cereal and milk. They were prodding chickens with their walking sticks, to chase them away. The chickens stared at the elders with vacant eyes, as if to ask "what have we done to you?" then let out angry chirps before walking away.

As soon as the sun touched its lips on the slopes made barren by erosion, the village van took its place in the village square, its muffler spewing out black smoke. Today was the kind of day when the guy from Bolvadin would say "I regret missing the Emirdağ market more than the death of my wife", a day when the workers in Europe were home for leave. The village van would make several trips to Emirdağ, to take passengers to the market, and to bring them back.

•••

Seher, while taking her tins of cheese and bowls of yogurt that she had made through the week, also woke up her 14-year-old daughter Hasret(*). They had to catch the village van for the first trip to Emirdağ, in order to open two stalls at the market. While Hasret sat up in bed and stretched, Seher turned her eyes away from her daughters developed breasts, and looked at the mirror behind her. She wrapped a scarf around her hastily combed black hair, and tied it up with a red cotton kerchief.

(*) The name means "longing."

Below her curly eye-lashes, her eyelids were droopy after a night of insufficient sleep. On both sides of her full lips below rosy cheeks, there were premature lines. While the nostrils of her well-shaped nose quivered as if to say something to an invisible being in the mirror, with her middle fingers, she wiped tears off her cheeks. It was as if this abrupt gesture of her fingers also expressed an indecision – whether to wipe away her past as well.

The village van filled up with its first group of passengers, made its way towards the marketplace, on the asphalt road, paved as a pre-election gift. Nanny Havva emerged from her garden surrounded with large stones. It was unclear whether her walking stick was supporting her, or she was supporting her walking stick. Her hunchback seemed to hold the secret memories of eighty years.

She pushed open the garden gate three houses down from hers. The weeds and thorns that had taken over the garden could not hide the red car glistening in the sun, and Rıza and his wife Dudu, who were about to get into the car. They didn't particularly wish to be hidden anyway.

The Nanny Havva began to call out in a hoarse voice: "Dudu girl... Where are you going over your aunt's body? Have you become haughty since you've been in Belgium?" Her left hand hanging near her waist was shaking.

Against the morning chill, Dudu slipped on the right sleeve of her sweater, thus displaying the row of shiny gold bracelets, which glinted in the sun.

"Ah my aunt," said Dudu. "Forgive my distractedness. I didn't see you. We are rushing to get to the market at Emirdağ. We were planning to come to see you this evening." She kissed her aunt's hand and touched it to her forehead.

Nanny Havva was licking her thin lips behind which her toothless mouth was visible.

"I won't get in your way then, "she said." But there's a favour I would like to ask of you. We're thinking of marrying off my grandson Osman and sending him to Europe to work. I hear you get along well with Sürmeli Elif. If you see her at the market, would you ask her if she might consider marrying her daughter off this month?"

"Bride price has increased to fifteen thousand Euros," answered Havva. "If you pay up this money, you can get the girl."

"Who do you think we are, girl? How could we ever put together that much money?"

"Look, my aunt. These days, Europeans who have daughters are rubbing their hands with glee. While I was shopping with Sürmeli at Kaufhof, the other day, Hatce of Karacalar approached us and asked Sürmeli for her daughter. You should have seen Sürmeli's rage. She put Hatce to shame by saying that "Sons are known to be fierce; if you give your daughter to them, you will get more exhausted than her." And she added that, those folks in Europe may have reputations but their teeth are full of holes. Be it young men or young girls, the folks who go to Europe to work are never happy. If your grandson sold vegetables at Emirdağ, he would be happier. Believe me, Europe doesn't offer anyone what it once did..."

"Never you mind. You see Sürmeli and you speak to her. You know well that women have to do this. He who stands in the shade casts no shadow. You spread the word a little..."

"Alright, I will but you shouldn't have high expectations."

Nanny Havva sensed that Dudu had changed and grown away from herself. She glanced at Dudu's bare legs shown off by a pair of open-toed shoes.

"Since she has found work in Belgium, her heels have turned into cigarette paper," she thought.

The population of Emirdağ and its villages would shrink during eleven months of the year because their residents were seeking jobs and fortunes within Turkey and Europe. In many villages, the migration to Europe had led to the closure of schools. When the seventh month of the year, often called "the month of the foreigners " arrived, and the workers of Europe returned home for their vacations, the returnees were eager to marry their children, to spend money, and to show off their cars or the gold bracelets jingling on their arms to each other. The merchants of the town counted on this month, to balance their accounts...

This Tuesday, the cars were parked haphazardly on the roads of Emirdağ, and the drivers had spread out in the marketplace to do their shopping. But there is something different than the usual. There were more cars with local licence plates than cars with foreign licence plates. These belonged to workers and bosses who had returned from Europe for their vacations. Since the break-up of Yugoslavia, many of the workers were flying back and forth instead of coming to Turkey by car. They were buying automobiles in Turkey, driving them during their vacations, and when the time came to leave for Europe, they were locking up their cars and leaving them in garages.

While the hot July sun scorched the melon grinds tossed away to a street corner, people were chatting with their acquaintances on the street or at the coffee shop. European workers were light-hearted and happy as if a load weighing on their shoulders had been left at the airport in Istanbul, or at the Kapikule border crossing.

Seher awaited customers beside a counter on which she had spread out her bowls of yogurt. She was sighing from time to time as she watched the women who worked in Europe, and squeezing her lips to prevent a defiant cry that might escape from her mouth. She couldn't get over the fact that she had accepted to divorce her husband to enable him to marry a Belgian woman for the sake of citizenship... Why hadn't he contacted her or their daughter in the last nine years after finding work in Belgium? With a strange longing in her heart, Seher remembered that night when he promised her that he would remarry her and take her to Belgium as soon as he would find work. Pain and rage filled her heart. Should she not have asked for some kind of assurance before granting him the divorce? What assurance could have been stronger than love?

– What do you want for this *helke*(*)?

Seher was startled. She blinked several times to conceal her tears. Her village mate Dudu was standing before her. Ever since their girlhood, they had never got along with each other. She blurted out the first figure that came to her mind:

– Four million...

– Go away! So much for helke that would hardly fill up my palm...

– I squat under the cows while flies get into my nose. This yogurt comes to you, all prepared, and yet you squabble...

(*) Pail, bucket.

– Go away! Do you think that money grows in the streets of Europe? You make me regret I ever asked you for the price. Go pour this out in front of a dog...

– I had to go into the fields months ago when the grass began to sprout, unlike you who were lounging in your warm room.

– Hah! When the workers of Europe leave, there'll be no one left to even look at you. Don't get such a swollen head. Tomorrow, not even a dog will eat that yogurt.

– A dog's guts can't digest butter. Go! You're giving me a headache!

– You with the crooked ass and dirty hair! Who do you think you're telling off!

– Bitch! What do you want the yogurt for anyway?

– It's because you're crazy that a Belgian has stolen your husband! Go die of shame, may an ill wind take you away.

When Dudu hurled these words at Seher, she had dealt a real blow to Seher, who was shedding tears of regret for having permitted her husband to marry a Belgian woman, even if it was only a formality. All the insults she was preparing to hurl back at Dudu got stuck in her throat. All she could do was give Dudu a look as if to say "may what happened to me also happen to you..." Dudu was crushed by this quiet but piercing look. She melted away into the crowd. An elderly woman who had heard the exchange muttered behind Dudu:

– Your airs break the stones, your stones crack the skulls...

The unexpected support from the elderly woman did nothing to stop the flow of hot tears from Seher's defeated eyes.

About twenty steps away, the calls of the fruit and vegetable sellers did not prevent the slumber of the pigeons that had taken shelder from the heat, in the shade of chimneys.

– Tomatoes! One buck for three kilos...

– Peaches from Bursa!...

– Don't buy these without tasting them!...

Later, when the sun began to dwarf all shadows, Hasret joined her mother with her empty yogurt tins. She turned a tin upside down and sat on it. "I sold it all, mother," she said, as she took out a bunch of money out of the pocket of her faded shirt. "Now, we can buy that green dress that I like so much."

Seher stuffed the money in her own pockets in a haphazard way, and hissed "No way."

Upon hearing this, Hasret became ill tempered.

– I might as well hang myself and die.

– You should hang on a windy day, hissed back Seher who was already smarting from the morning's quarrel with Dudu. "What are you waiting for? Get on with it so we can have your funeral during the afternoon prayers."

Hasret had never known her mother talk so pitilessly. When she lifted her eyes, she noticed that her mother's face had taken on a greenish colour. Suddenly, Hasret was so scared that she forgot about the green dress.

When the crowds became saturated with the pleasure of shopping and began to leave the market place, leaving behind a lot of litter, Seher and Hasret got on the village van, to get back home. Seher's heart had softened after some reasoning that her brain had carried on – although in most similar situations, the reasoning would be done by others – and she had bought her daughter the green dress that she had been coveting. Now, Hasret was holding the dress gingerly on her knees, to make sure it would not get wrinkled.

The young driver turned on the radio that was attached above the rear-view mirror. The music, suddenly filled the passengers' ears and made them shut their mouths. The lines on their faces, that had deepened by the cares and anxieties of the day, suddenly softened. There were smiles on some faces, and some were singing along with the music:

"There's a road in front of their house leading to the police station,
Well-rounded bride, I beg of you, come and fill up your pitcher at our place,
My rosy Fadime, my honey Fadime, my Fadime with roses on her cheeks,
Wake up, wake up my Fadime. It's morning. Say your prayers..."

This was a regional ballad that had even spread to foreign countries. Whenever the people of Emirdağ heard this ballad from someone, they realized that they were from the same region.

Watching the mother and the daughter on the rear-view mirror, the driver was thinking: "Good for Seher. She is healthy, attractive, and throughout these nine years she has protected her reputation, while most women's reputations are destroyed three months after their husbands go to do their military service. Hasret is turning out to be a beautiful girl. I might as well send her a message to steal her heart before her eyes are opened... It's not for nothing that our fathers have said 'to buy cloth, check out its edges, to take a girl, check out her mother'..."

Meanwhile, Seher was also thinking about her daughter. "She is growing, and becoming more beautiful each day. Ever since we've been receiving more of those TV channels, even I can't distinguish truth from falsity. 'Birds with chicks do what they see.' The likes of Hasret have their minds way above their heads. I wish someone were to show up and ask for her hand before she gets it into her head to imitate the characters on TV, and makes a mistake. If a decent suitor were to show up, I could marry her off..."

"My rosy Fadime, are you Georgian, are you the tower of the hillside?
I can die for you yellow bride, are you a match for someone who is no good?"

...

And the minibus speeded towards the village, mindless of disturbing the sheep grazing on the roadside...

Yesterday's forest village, today's mountain village, sat between two valleys and looked weary as though it was the one who had travelled to the marketplace at Emirdağ and back. The herd of cows, which the herdsman had brought from the valley below the village, had scattered in the village roads, and then each cow had found its way to its place in a barn, waiting to be milked by the hands of a woman or a girl. The sun, having seen all it needed to see, had disappeared beyond the region of Adacali.

Hasret was sensing her mother's mood and making joke after joke, to break Seher's silence, while trying on the new green dress before the mirror. Yet Seher had milked the cow, boiled the milk and set the yogurt, without opening her mouth even once.

In her bed lit by the moon, while Hasret imagined herself in her green dress at the centre of a wedding procession, she heard her mother who was laying beside her make some moaning sounds that she had never heard before. The arms that were stretched towards the ceiling, and then brought down, the legs that were being pulled up towards the loins and then throwing off the bedcovers, scared her. She thought her mother was having a nightmare.

"Mother, mother..." she shook Seher by the shoulder. Her mother, still moaning, gave her a push with her elbow. Hasret got up and turned on the light. She panicked when she saw her mother's body tensing up, her eyes rolling in their sockets under open lids. "Mother, mother!" she shouted once again. Then she noticed her mother's hands in tight fists, and rushed outside, without even thinking of taking something to cover her white nightgown.

The white nightgown hardly covered Hasret's breasts, large like quinces, from the gaze of the moon. Seher was thrashing about in the grips of an attack...

Rıza was thankful to be driving along these village roads in a brand new car, when the memory of riding a donkey here was fresh in his memory. He was also pleased to have come to the rescue of a villager in difficulty, while he drove towards the village, with Hasret in the front seat, and Seher and Rıza's wife Dudu settled in the back. He offered chocolates to his passengers, before sliding a tape into the car's music set.

If the oaks are budding, let them bud,
Tell that bad-tempered one to come without delay,
To die by hanging rather than taking an evil wife,
Evil can destroy any life...

Seher's body had relaxed with the injection that the doctor in duty at the hospital had given her, and with the medication that she had swallowed. Her brain seemed to have stopped its constant activity of taking life too seriously.

When the two women first saw each other, they had averted their eyes. But a moment later, their tears had mixed with each other's, a telltale sign that the ice between them was melting. Neither of them knew why that ice had formed anyway...

Now, Seher had let herself go, under Dudu's care, and was enjoying having her face, cheeks and chest being wiped with lemon flower cologne by Dudu.

Dudu was crushed by guilt from the moment when Hasret had burst into their room shouting "My mother is very ill! She has to be taken to the doctor." The fact that, on the way to the hospital, Seher unconsciously kept muttering "I didn't let him be grabbed by the foreign woman. It was his own doing," was breaking Dudu's heart. She sought refuge in words, in an attempt to win forgiveness.

– Don't be so hard on your husband. Europe leaves people in so many unpredictable situations. Who knows, maybe he couldn't find a job. Maybe he got involved with drug dealers. Maybe he got sick. Maybe he couldn't put together three pennies, and didn't have the face to get in touch with you. In Europe, money is between the jaws of a lion. It's so hard to save. Don't be deceived by our showing off with a car. Our child gets loans from the bank and we labour throughout the year to pay them off. I'm sure your husband would have contacted you if he could. But don't worry. When we get back to Europe, we'll find him, won't we Rıza?

She wanted her husband to confirm her good intentions.

Rıza, addressing the silhouette of the two women in the backseat from his rear-view mirror didn't hesitate to give hope to Seher and Hasret,

– May my blood flow out of my body, if the first thing upon our return to Europe won't be to find your husband," he said. "We already have a lead, don't we girl? People have seen in France, really."

"It's as if we determined the lines of our future when we named our daughter Hasret (longing) said Seher, her voice drowning with the song spilling from the cassette player.

"Just because you pass through Emirdağ once, don't think that you've found the road...
When gold falls on the ground, it doesn't break into pieces.
Just sleeping with a beautiful woman for one night,
She may lose her reputation but doesn't become a widow..."

The headlights of the car climbing uphill were stretching into the distance, while Seher's hopes were also reaching way into the distance. The stars in the dark blue sky seemed to be blinking as if they knew that the only bread that available to helpless folks endlessly, was the bread of hope.

Zehra Gologu Süer / Canada

She was born in 1950 in İstanbul, she was graduated from Hacettepe University Department of Psychology. After completing the Science Mastership Program in 1979, she went to North America. She has been living in Toronto since 1985. She still works as one of the few minority psychologists who are registered to College of Psychologists of Ontario. She is married and has a son.

Canadian Citizenship

She had such huge black eyes… And her wavy pupils of eyes are covered by a little fluster, a little shyness, and a little fear. She didn't sit the seat properly; she merely perched on the edge of it instead. She was tucking her wool scarf that she wrapped up tightly and her hand gloves into a bag in a hurry. Upon raising her hand, her auburn hair dropped to her shoulders. Her rich, thick, and straight hair covered her face reaching to the salient cheek bones. Holding them between her short and chunky fingers, she tried to warm up her cheeks that turned red with the cold weather. The winter of Toronto was merciless; when it stroke, you could feel the minus 20 degrees cold in your lungs. Though January and February were peek of the cold weather, the life was going on in its regular pace. There was a saying in Canada: "There is no such thing as bad weather; there is only bad clothing." You must have good clothing and go on running!

Looking above his eye-glasses, Mike took a glance at the waiting room. There were rows of people on rows of seats. They were interviewing the people one by one in the three rooms that were separated from each other with huge glass windows. "It is crowded again today," he thought. In recent times, it was always as busy as that day. They had enlarged the waiting room, and recruited two new officers. The number of the new immigrants increased more and more, and applications for citizenship soared enormously.

Mike had been working at this job for years. He interviewed several types of people every day at the office. People from all ages, from all nations… The place where Mike was born and grew up was a small town. The population of Greenwood was not more than ten thousand The districts would be composed of single flat houses away from the town center and scattered around the roads bending among the dark pine tree forests. The town center comprised merely of a main street and a couple of bystreets intersecting with it. Since there were not many people on the streets, you might think that the population was less than it really was. There were small and neat shops lined on both sides of the main street. There was a boutique in the middle, a dry cleaner next to it, then a restaurant, a café, a bank, and the others... They were all lined up next to each other. On summer days, the colorful flowers were jiggling in the big flower pots in front of the shops. In winter, the same road was decorated with Christmas lights. The roads were so clean, and also so empty and isolated. This Greenwood was livened up with the people coming in winter for skiing to the hill and, with the owners of the boats coming to the marina at the lake side in summer. At other times, it was so silent that you could even hear the sound of the footsteps. The shops closed at 5 pm, and the town became deserted by 7 pm. Just as all the people of the town, Mike's family also got up early in the morning. Every member went to its own business, and they came together for dinner at half past five in the evening. The entire household went to sleep at half past nine.

His dad was a tough farmer, but used to work a lot indeed. He welcomed the dawn drinking a coffee, and saw off the sun drinking his beer in the evening. He didn't talk much. Actually, they used to talk only about the necessary issues at Mike's home. Although not very often, when he drunk too much beer, his father's strong and furious voice was heard from all rooms of the house. In those evenings, Mike tried not to confront his father. He knew very well that his father would smite all of them with a tree branch standing in the corner. Four children... Isn't it easy, is it?

His mother was a religious Christian; they didn't even mention about abortion at home. They used to go to the church every Sunday regularly. He had a brother and two sisters. Although he was two years younger than Mike, his brother seemed elder than him. With his long height, thickset body, and tattooed arms, he was exactly 14 years old when he grasped his father's arm with the rod in the air. "Never use that again on any of us," said he to his father. Mike had never seen his eyes burning as such before. His arm was firm just like a steel hanging in the air while holding his father's arm. "Never," he repeated. Mike could remember very well that he left the house a week later. Afterwards, his two sisters got married one after another.

Mike continued to go to the church every Sunday. It was not true that he liked it, but he never objected it though. Having graduated from high school, he moved to Toronto which was three hours far from there so as to go to university. He did not only apply to the scholarship that the state gave with a small interest rate, but also began to work.

The school years were far from being easy, but he was accustomed to work hard. He finished school while working part time on school term, and full time on summer holidays. When he was graduated, there was a great deal of debt that he had to pay to the state. He also first met with his wife in Toronto; Mary was a teacher. After graduation, they rented a house, and lived together sharing the expenses for a while. Having found out that Mary was pregnant, they married and had two children.

At the weekends Mike took his children to hockey, ice skating and music courses, and for the rest of the time he scarcely had enough time to do the repair works of the house that they bought recently. He didn't go to the church any more.

It had been quite a long time since had started to work at the immigration bureau, and he was good at that job indeed. His colleagues loved Mike; he was a calm, consistent and serious man. He used to get up at six in every morning, read the newspaper while mixing his cereal with milk, leave the house at half past seven, and he used to be at his desk at eight sharp. This pace never changed; just as his father trained. Two years ago, he was appointed to the position of evaluating the applications of the people who wanted to get citizenship, and applying their exams.

In the recent years, people from countries which are completely unknown to Mike, has moved to Canada. The most difficult ones were the refugees' applications. Appearing at the border gates unexpectedly, these people asked for seeking asylum on the grounds that their lives were in danger. Refugee applicants were investigated, registered for legal protection, and further they were given a little money enough to live on every month. Until the trial was concluded and it was decided that the story they had told was logical or not...

A number of Turkish people coming by a plane that landed in Montreal in mid 1980s were also sought asylum in Canada in this way.

Canada Immigration Bureau was really surprised. Until then, Canada hadn't even asked for a visa from people who came from Turkey. At that time, Mike had just started to work at immigration bureau. Actually, he found out the presence of a country called Turkey and its location during that occasion.

Mike looked above his eye-glasses to see whether the following applicant to come was ready or not. 'Number 14' was shining in red in the electronic table out of his door. Upon seeing the number 14, Fatma jumped to her feet in a flurry. When she entered the room, she also brought her hurry along with her. Mike pointed the chair on the other side of the desk with his hand, and told her to close the door.

"Thank God, I haven't had a mistake yet," thought Fatma, and she perched on the edge of the chair he pointed. Mike was reading the application form before him. Age: 29, educational status: High school, came to Canada 8 years ago. After the listed questions such as your name, your surname...

It was an exam that was carried out on the people who were entitled to apply for citizenship upon living in Canada as an immigrant for three years. It could be regarded as a kind of perfunctory. However, Mike was an officer who took his job seriously, and he always chose his questions carefully. He believed that the citizens needed to know at least a few basic things about Canada in order to be a citizen.

– What is the population of Canada?

Fatma had studied that question last evening from the booklet that was prepared for the exam.

– Where is the capital city?

She remembered it too. She felt relieved.

– Who is the prime minister?

Oh, who was that man with a crooked mouth? What was his name? Nothing came to her mind.

Mike asked that question on purpose, thinking that it would be easy to answer. Indeed, he got a little bit angry as she couldn't answer it.

– Who is the minister of finance?

Fatma thought that it was a hopeless question. But, she really knew the man with the crooked mouth asked in the former question. Darn him, why didn't his name come to her mind?

Actually, Mike didn't expect such failure from that woman whose eyes were as fresh as paint, and who was not different from any other young person with her clothing. He got angry in such cases. "They still attempt to become a citizen, though. How much do they know about Canada in order to be a citizen, and to enjoy the same rights as me?" he always thinks inevitably.

Fatma had applied henna on her dark brown hair last night too. Her rich hair shined in a red-brown manner. Her friend found the imitation of that newest fashion perfume; she also bought it. She prepared herself for a long time. She didn't even sleep properly the whole night due to the nervousness of this exam.

"Her English is not bad. She has a strong accent, but all of them have. They don't take this seriously, I think. They would like to be a citizen of this country, but it seems as though they do not even have an idea about whose citizen they are going to be. No, no; they do not have respect." They just had to read a small booklet, but they didn't even read that. Mike went on reading the questions from the booklet in front of him calmly and with a stable tone of voice. The situation was not bright. He took off his eye-glasses slowly, and said "Get prepared well for the following exam."

Fatma's black eyes wide opened, and fixed at the pupils of Mike's eyes. They were not moving at all. It was the second time that she took that exam, and she wasn't able to pass it again. It was the only exam that she took after she had left the school. Her fixed eyes were not still moving, but they were gradually filled with tears. What would she tell to his son now?

– You failed again, mum? Her son would say sarcastically.

The daughter is still small; she doesn't understand, thank God. Her husband would grumble "You didn't even manage it, anyway. Now we can't get a passport for you and so, you can't even go to Turkey to visit your family."

Fatma married her husband in their country, and she sent him off to Canada soon after the wedding. Living with his husband's brothers, she waited him for four years. Those long four years… Her brother-in-laws were old; she met all their needs at home. Two years together with two snuff and ungrateful old men. At last, since he couldn't resist her complaints any more, her husband took him to Canada as a refugee. However, his trial also hadn't been concluded yet. Anyway, the ones coming as political refugees either came without any official letter and say "I hardly saved my own head with a lot of suffering. The state didn't give me permit for exit," or they made up another type of story. In the event that the person who took refuge in Canada left the country before his or her situation was clarified, he or she would not be allowed to enter the country again. "Now that you can enter and go out of your country, what is your problem then? You have to wait. Just take your Canada passport, and get your feet firm on the ground," said her husband.

Of course he said that. He would say everything. "Do you know how much money I gave to the brokers so as to bring you here?" he used to say, and whenever she intended to complain about something, he would say "I brought you here, but you still make a noise."

"I wish you hadn't brought me! What's good of it! I sat alone speechless for a year in a house with a single room. There were a mass of man in the apartment who looked like black beetles. There was always a terrible stench in the halls. How could I know that it was because of the stuff that they put in their meals? Oh, I am scared of the Arabs. I didn't even put my nose out of the door for a month. I don't know whether I should tell you 'God damn you' or 'God bless you', but you just laughed at me. I wonder, what's good of your bringing me! I can't even see your face."

Her black eyes were filled with tears so much.

Mike closed the file and sat up in his chair.

So, the exam was over.

Fatma made an attempt:

"I didn't learn English; I had never had enough time to do so. I didn't go to a course. Anyway, I can't even read and write properly in Turkish. I left the primary school when I was at the fifth grade. But what can you expect from the fifth grade in a village? I just learned a few words. But I muddle along somehow. How can I read and understand that booklet? Are you crazy? Besides, I do not have time for it. Do you think that I read newspapers and watch television? It must have been at least a month since I last sat and watched TV. And that was the time when we watched a Turkish movie from videotape in a neighbor's house. How can I know those names? I clean two houses everyday. I have two children and also take care of them. Have a heart! Does it matter whether I know the things you asked or not? What I want is just a passport. I want to go and see my parents. I even collect money in those four years. My milk sibling is going to marry; I want to attend his wedding. I want to smell the fragrance of lime trees. I missed them; nay I missed them so much," she wanted to say.

However, when all the words she didn't say turned into tears and streamed from her eyes, she already came to the stop that would take her home.

Oya Efe Özüdoğru / Holland

She was born in Gölcük, Kocaeli in 1963. She was graduated from İzmir Trade High school. In 1993, she got married and moved to Holland. She lost her entire family, except her elder brother, in the earthquake of Gölcük in 1999. Her daughter, who was diagnosed with leukaemia in 1998, got well. She is planning to turn the journal that she kept during her daughter's illness, into a book and to donate the proceeds to the foundation for children with leukaemia. She spends time reading, writing and painting. Lives in Roosendaal, and is the mother of two children.

The Wife of Ahmet the Blind

Many years ago, while we were planting seedlings in the strawberry fields, with Melahat she sighed, "ah, for a Mercedes." "What?" I said, "Did a flower pot fall on your head?" She repeated as if she hadn't heard me, "I can't get a Mercedes out of my mind," she said. Melahat was obsessed with the Mercedes.

One day, while we were still planting strawberry seedlings, Melahat said, "girls, if you have a car, it should be a Mercedes."

"Melahat ," we said, "what is that?"

"Girls, you are totally ignorant," she said. "Everyone knows, even in Turkey. It's just you who don't..." She had laughed at Ayten and myself. Actually we were laughing at her.

- We don't know what it is... Why don't you tell us?

- It's a particular kind of car. It's used by rich people. There is a star in front of it.

- Really? All right, it's a car. But what good is the star? we asked, giggling.

- The star is the symbol of wealth, girls," she said, and she added: "You live in Europe but you're really ignorant."

- All it is a car with four wheels. What difference does it make that it's a Mercedes or another brand?

- It makes a lot of difference. When you go back to Turkey, you can show off with a Mercedes..." she started to lecture us.

She began to sound like a minister of State for the Economy. Ayten asked her:

-Where did you get this interest in a Mercedes, Melahat ?

Melahat started to pour her heart out, as if someone had touched a wound in her.

"Ah girls," she said, "it was many years ago. Ahmet the Blind left my four babies and me with my parents, and went to foreign lands to work. In the beginning, we were receiving his letters regularly. On one occasion, I had written to him "when are you going to send for me?" He has answered, "Why do you want to be here? This is no place for you." I wrote back "If it's no place for the likes of us, what are you doing there?" but he did not answer me. Of course I made as if I had believed him, because he was more literate than I was. I hadn't even completed the third year of primary school. If I didn't take his word, whose word would I have taken?"

"After a while, the letters begin to peter out. One day, Osman Çavuş from our village, returned from Holland to our village for a holiday. While chatting, I blurted out: 'Say, what's our Ahmet the Blind doing there?' Ah, girls... I wish I hadn't. Osman Çavuş looked right, looked left, not knowing what to say. When I insisted, he sighed deeply,

"He is alright," he said. "What can I say? I don't want you to hear it from me. He is going around with blonde Dutch women."

"How can that be? He is a married man and a father! Haven't you ever asked him about his wife and children waiting for him at home?"

"Yeah, I did but he didn't really listen to me. I didn't get remarried here, what more can anyone want? He said. Our religion permits up to four wives."

"May God create a man out of you Ahmet the Blind," I said. And I fainted. When I came to, there were people around me, each one saying something different. Osman Çavuş was saying "Be quiet, be calm!" but nobody cared him. My mother walked up to him like a roaring lioness, "If we don't wail, who do you think should wail?" she asked. "Look at the catastrophe that has descended upon us," she said, wailing. My parents had trusted their one and only son-in-law. They had valued me less that they valued him. And look what happened. Did it snow on the mountain they had trusted so? Osman Çavuş said, "There is only one solution to this... Melahat and the children will go to Holland."

So I wrote a letter saying either you take me where you are, or I'll divorce you. It was only twenty-five days after I sent that letter that a speedy reply came from him. "My Melahat, don't ever divorce me. I promise, I'll bring you here, but I don't want you to say 'why did you ever bring me here?' in the future." He added in the letter that the paperwork would take some time. That was fine. Even if they would take two or three years instead of months, I knew how I would deal with him once I got to Holland."

Melahat would have continued to tell her story, if only the noon break had not interrupted her. Her story was absorbing us totally; we were listening with great interest when the train siren and the loud shrieking of Ayten rose together.

"Ayten, why are you screaming as if an ass has kicked you?"

"What more do you want? These foreigners have drunk all the fruit juice and left us the sediment in the bottom again. You'd think they expected a dog to drink it."

"It's always like that. Why are you screaming as if it's the first time you've noticed it?"

"I'm going to complain. They try to instruct application of human rights to other countries ! Indeed, they intend human rights for them, but not for us. They don't value us half as much as they value their pets. Ah, our Turkish traditions..."

"What do you think will change if you were to complain? You'll receive the same response: you continue to work here if you wish. If not, quit and go home. There are many who want to be in your places. If one Turk goes, another comes immediately..."

One day, I never forget, it was in the depth of winter. We were wearing heavy coats, scarves, thick socks and gloves. We were working in an unheated, icy place that looked like an aircraft shed. Most of the workers in there were Turkish. We were cold, and made the mistake of asking the assistant foreman: "Would you turn on those radiators?" Well, we sure had it coming. "If you don't like the environment, go home. You want to warm up so you can get lazy..." We had received our answer.

During the noon break, while we huddled around boxes to eat the lunches that we had brought home, we were also listening to Melahat, who continued to rattle on like a speeding car. No one could hold her back anymore. She was just rattling on and on. Who would have guessed how full her heart was?

So, the paperwork for Melahat took not three or four months but an entire year. In the end, Ahmet the Blind who got the news that everything was ready had showed up in the village.

"Come on, get ready," he said to Melahat , "I don't have much time. I could get only one week of leave from the foreigners. Next week we're going to Holland. In the end, you'll be European as well." So, Melahat who had never even gone down to the city from the village was on her way to Europe with her four children.

"The trip took three-and-a-half hours. We got home at midnight. The children had fallen asleep in the bus but I was too nervous to sleep. After we put the children to bed, mine looked at me with a grin, "come, let's go to bed too. I've really missed you, girl. There are things I want to tell you, come morning."

"Ahmet, I'm not sleepy. Let's talk now."

"No is no. Don't interfere with my way of doing things. I don't need a woman's advice. Come to bed so I'll make sure you get sleepy. It has been so long. Didn't you miss your husband, girl?"

"So I went to bed unwillingly. I was impatient for the morning. I was feeling as if I were in the home of a stranger. I kept turning this way and that way in bed. He fell into a deep sleep after getting what he wanted. He didn't even wonder: does Melahat want it or not?"

We laughed at this comment because we had heard similar complaints from many Turkish women.

"In the morning, we put together everything my mother had sent along for our trip and sat down to breakfast with the children. It had been a long time since we had eaten all together as a family. We enjoyed our meal – the Dutch cheese was tasty too. Then Ahmet said, "come on Ali, take your brothers and sisters and go outside to play."

"Come here Melahat. You'll clear the table later. I have to go to the coffee house, so let me say what I have to say.

I stopped what I was doing and sat beside my man.

"Here is Holland," he said. "You are no longer in your village. Here, you'll have to obey my rules, or else you'll get into trouble. Let this be the first and the last time that I tell you this."

"I would go along with anything you say, my dear Ahmet."

"Good. Then listen well: First, you are not going to go outside without my permission. If necessary I'll lock you inside. Second: the Dutch say hello to everyone even if they don't know the person.

Sometimes they even kiss people. You shall never respond to them, you'll push them away."

"Really? Wow!"

"The third thing: if we're going to go somewhere, we'll all go together. If you think you'll get bored, then you can stay at home, do the housework, look after the children, cook and clean."

"Fine, my Ahmet, as you wish."

I had just arrived from the village. I didn't know the language; I didn't know how to get around. I thought he was right. During those first days, I was filled with the shock of arrival in a foreign country. I didn't even understand how the days passed. But a little later, I began to feel bored. Do the dishes, clean the house, iron clothes, and cook, try to please your husband every evening… The same routine every day! I had been outside no more than three or four times since my arrival, and that was to go food shopping at the supermarket. I was beginning to rebel. I realized that I had been freer in the village back home. Yet it was I who had said, 'come and get me.' I was to blame for my situation."

"After finishing my housework, I used to secretly look outside from the window. Many women were taking their children to school. Why shouldn't I? I thought, and decided to talk to Ahmet about this that evening. I cooked the dishes that Ahmet enjoyed the most to humour him. After the meal, I made him some of the Turkish coffee that we had brought along with us from the village, and I sat beside him.

"If you permit me, I would like to say something..."

"Say it. What is it?"

"Everyone takes her child to school..." Before I could finish my sentence, he cut me off.

"What is it to you, what everyone else does? Don't get me in a bad mood..."

"Well, if you will let me, I also want to take our children to school. You leave in the morning and come back home in the evening. I get bored alone all day. No neighbor, no relative. Let me take the children to school, my Ahmet. They want it too."

First he scratched his head as if he had fleas. Then he called out to the children.

"Kids, do you want that?"

"Whatever you say, father," said the children, reluctantly. My eldest son hadn't even replied.

"Alright," said Ahmet, "but I have a condition. You don't wait even for a short while either here or at school. You'll leave the children to school and you'll return home right away."

That was enough for me. For about a month, I went back and forth to the school with the children, but after that time, the children didn't want me to go with them. When I asked them why, they hemmed and hawed, and when I pressed them, my eldest son gave me an answer that shocked me. "The mothers of all the other children are dressed in a modern way, while you look like someone from the middle ages. You tie a yemeni, cotton scarf, around your head. Instead of stockings, you wear some loose pants like a shalvar under your skirt. Mom, we aren't living in the village any more. Look around you. We're embarrassed to be seen with you.

It would have been better for me to die, than to hear those words. If it had been Ahmet who had said those things, perhaps I would not have been so upset. But to know that my own children whom I had raised myself; thought in that way about me, hurt me terribly. I cried for hours, I thought about what he had said. My son was right. On the way to school, people were looking at me - I had noticed that. Some of the other Turkish women were dressed in a modern way and their heads were open, some others were wearing headscarves but they no longer had *shalvars* they were wearing stockings under their skirts. No one was looking at them like they were looking at me.

It was partly because of my family, and partly because of Ahmet's attitudes. I wanted to go to school; they didn't let me. "What's the point of sending a girl to school?" they asked. "She'll get married as soon as she comes of age." They took me out of school and sent me to a Koranic course. If I attempted to open my head, they said "Sinful!" They scared us off with religion all the time.

After that day, I decided to become modern. This is how I felt inside. Just because we are women, don't we have a right to live? First, I took off the shalvar under my skirt and put on thin stockings instead. I had not taken off my headscarf yet. I had started to change my appearance but I still had a long way to go. I needed to change what was inside my head as well.

One day, on my way to school with the children, I met Sema. Her children were attending the same school as mine. After some greetings, Sema invited me to her place. How could I go? I couldn't say "my husband won't let me" and I really wanted to go. I knew I had to find a way. Selma would become the wind that would blow change in my direction. I was feeling this – sensing that Selma could help me. What could I do to get permission? I should talk before Ahmet headed to the coffee shop."

"What happened next Melahat ?"

"Oh, girls, look it's getting late. This is enough for today. I'll tell you the rest of the story tomorrow. My mouth is more tired than my hands."

I don't know about Ayten, but I didn't sleep at all that night. My family was not like Melahat 's family. They had wanted me to go to school. "If you attend school, you can become administrators even in Holland and no one can get in your way," they were saying. I was living in Europe; I had every opportunity. Why shouldn't I succeed? I was studying and working at the same time.

The next morning, Ayten and I had started work but Melahat was nowhere to be seen. Just as we were beginning to speculate that she hadn't been able to get up because she was too tired from yesterday, the foreman came up to us. "Today it'll be just the two of you working," he said. "Melahat is sick. You Turks get sick so often..." He left muttering irritably.

For a whole week, we worked without Melahat. We kept wondering who the hero of her story would be, and how the story would end. We produced many stories through that week. In the end, our hero started work but she looked weak and tired. The family doctor had sent her to a hospital for tests. "I gave some blood," she said. "I had a tummy ache for a long time now. I kept expecting it to go away so I didn't go to see a doctor. Finally when I saw blood, I did go. Don't worry girls; I'm solid like a rock! I got over so many things. Come on, let's get to work to avoid any comments from the foreman. If he sees us talking, he'll rush to our side. Well, where were we?"

We giggled, and then settled down away from the foreman, and while our hands worked, our ears listened to our heroine.

"So girls, one evening, when I was serving Ahmet his coffee, I broached the subject. I was ready for anything. 'What are you going to tell me girl?' Ahmet asked, "Are you going to suggest having another baby?"

"Ahmet, I met a woman named Selma. As you know, I don't go anywhere other than the school. I have not met anyone since my arrival. I met Selma on the way to school. She invited me to her place. If you give me permission, I would like to visit her."

He exploded like a bomb: "Stay where you are! You've really gotten carried away lately. You took off your *shalvars,* I looked the other way. And now you're eager to hang around with city women?"

Before I had a chance to reply, he slapped me, and left the house, banging the door behind him.

"That slap was like a powerful earthquake that shook my brain up inside my skull. This was the first time that he had raised his hand against me. I knew I hadn't deserved it. It wasn't right to beat even an animal.

When he roared like thunder, even the children had scattered away. Was this why I had come to this foreign country? I had neither mother nor father. A husband who existed in my life only in name. He used to come home when he felt like it – sometimes at midnight, and sometimes he would arrive drunk and say to me: "Get up, fix me a meal." If there was nothing he liked, he would say "Get us, make me a pastry. Amuse me!" What dreams I had dreamt when I left my village... I had imagined my life would change for the better here – yet I was being condemned to live in the Middle Ages. Even my children were ashamed of me. As a woman, I existed only in name, yet our Atatürk had given us women all the rights, even before the European women could win them.

"First there was the oppression of a father. A girl does not need an education. Stay home! After that, pressure from a brother; don't look out of the windows! Don't talk to anyone. And then I got married to face the oppression of a husband. I had to break these chains. I knew that I had the strength to break them."

After that night, he began to stay out even later. Some nights he wasn't coming home at all. This situation suited me. After that slap, parts of my brain that had been numb had started to work. First I went to Selma's place. Her house was like a library. I looked through them with astonishment. "Did you read all of these?" I asked her. "Books exist to be read," she answered. "Reading is not a hobby for me, it's a way of life. As you read, your horizons grow wider; the cells in your brain become active. Believe me, I couldn't live without reading. Yes, I have read all these books you see here. I hope you read too... Do you?" What would I tell her now? Yes Selma. I go through two or three books a day... Or should I tell her the truth? Faced with her enlightenment, I felt like a tomato growing in a hot house. In embarrassment, I said, "Selma, I studied until grade three at the village. You know how village life is. They don't let girls stay at school. Until it's time to marry off a girl, the family prefers to have her work in the fields or do housework..."

"That's alright, Melahat. If you wish, you can start everything over again. Learning to read has no age. I see this light in you. I hope you have been attending courses to learn Dutch."

"What are you talking about? I wasn't even allowed to go outside. Even when I went to see a doctor, or went shopping – everywhere, Ahmet was hanging around me like baggage."

"That's alright too. You cannot change the past, but the future is in your palms. You can shape it as you wish. You have to learn to stand on your own two feet. As a woman you have many rights. You should know them – this is nothing to be ashamed of. Those who prevented you from knowing should be ashamed. All you need is the will. When you begin to learn things, you'll be happier and you'll have a much more rewarding relationship with your family, your children and the people around you."

"Selma, would you help me?"

"If you really want to learn, I will. You have to prepare for hardships."

"I'm willing to take on any hardship. All I ask is that you be my guide."

"You will erase from your mind, words such as "I'm tired, I'm discouraged, I can't do it. Instead, you'll use the word "I'll succeed."

"May I borrow books from you?"

"You don't even have to ask for permission. 'My library is available to anyone who wants to read."

"As I began to read, I felt like hitting my head against a rock. How ignorant I was left! It was hard to believe. Later, I registered for a Dutch language course. I was going three times a week, and would you believe it girls, I felt as if I had a new lease on life... I was doing everything for myself. I could hardly recognize myself. This is what had to be done. It was as if a little candle inside my mind had grown to become a light bulb of 75 watts!"

"Well Melahat, what happened to Ahmet?"

"Ah, the winds of change were necessary for him too. But where's that kind of good luck?"

When he left for work and the children left for school, I was studying Dutch. After doing my homework, I would set out on a voyage among books. Ahmet was different now. It was as if he had forgotten the way to our place. If I ever asked him why he hadn't come home, he would say, "am I going to answer to you?"

Now, I knew some people so I began to hear things. I even heard that Ahmet was living with a Dutch woman. If it had been in the old days, this would have upset me, but by then, there was neither love nor respect between us. He wasn't worth any pain. When he came home, I didn't even see him. He just got himself some clean clothes or ate something and left again, without my asking, "where are you going?" He didn't even care about the children any more. We all lived our separate lives.

"I was happy with my life but I had financial difficulties. I had improved my Dutch, gained confidence, began to make friends with my neighbors. I had to improve my financial situation. I decided to work. I felt that I should tell Ahmet about my decision, just because he was the father of my children. So I did. I was expecting him to shout and rage, but he was surprisingly indifferent. Then he spoke slowly; I'll let you work with one condition. We'll buy a Mercedes. You'll give me money for it.

"What's a Mercedes?"

"What do you think girl? It's a starry car like a young girl. I'm tired of going to our village in an old, beat-up car. In a Mercedes, you settle down royally, you show of on Dutch roads and in the village..."

"Well, our car is new too..." I said, but he insisted. "I'm tired of people at home saying 'what kind of Foreign workers are you? You don't even own a Mercedes." I found myself agreeing with him. The last time we visited our village on vacation. People had said things about us. Especially Ahmet's family just went on and on about this."

The next day, I went to the employment office. The woman there told me that they had garden work available. That was fine; I was ready to work at any job. My work started at six in the morning and lasted until four in the afternoon. The children were now old enough, so it was no problem. For many years, I planted seedlings outside in summer, and worked in mouldy smelling places in winter. Later, I began to do cleaning at work places, and I even picked apples and pears.

"In three years, I had saved enough money for a Mercedes and handed it over to Ahmet. I had become a contemporary Turkish woman who was contributing to her home and to the education of her children. Now, I also had a bookcase in my home. I would take my book along to read during the lunch break at my workplace. Dutch women did this as well. They were reading in trains, in buses. You would see the rare passenger without a book.

Years followed years, and our lives flowed like running water. One evening, while I was reading, the doorbell rang. Who could it be at that time? Ahmet was no longer coming home. Sometimes, he just saw the children outside and left. Before opening the door, I asked nervously: "Who is it?"

"It's the police. Please open the door!"

I opened, my heart beating furiously in fear.

"Madame, your husband has had an accident. He is in hospital. We've come to take you there. Please get ready to go."

Before I fully understood what was going on, I found myself in the police car. Finally, I managed to ask, "What happened to Ahmet?"

"His lady friend has spilt acid on his face. One of his eyes is blinded. He can see thirty per cent with the other eye. This is the information we have. At the hospital you may learn more."

"His nickname at the village was always "blind" because he was clumsy. Now his situation matched his nickname. I didn't know whether I should laugh or cry. I was very upset, because he was, after all, my children's father. I had come all this way because of him. If I had stayed in the village, I would not have been any different from the Ayşes and Fatmas there. Here, I had transformed myself to the Melahat of my dreams. My daughter was a teacher, one of my sons was a police officer, one an engineer and the third one was a computer technician. They all spoke three or four languages.

While I thought these things, we had entered Ahmet's room. He was just gaining consciousness. He was looking at me as if to say, "I was wrong, forgive me."

"Melahat, you are such a solid woman. I had thought you wouldn't come to see me, you would have been right not to come. For so many years, I made you suffer. You never gave up. You kept struggling. I should have known how to value you. That woman got mad at me and threw acid on my face, when I had abandoned you and my children for her sake. Look at me. Am I any different from a dead man? Do you think we can forget the past and start all over again? What do you say?

"What can I say? All of this will pass. Get well first, we'll talk later."

Ahmet could no longer leave the house. He couldn't drive the car with the star. One day he said to me: "You will drive this. Today I registered you for driving lessons. You start tomorrow." I wouldn't have believed this even in my dreams! I had become the head of our house."

After that day, Melahat was unable to come to work for close to a month.

Knowing she was ill, we were anxiously awaiting her from day to day. One day we called her home. Her daughter answered and told us that Melahat was in hospital with cervical cancer. I dropped the receiver. She was an extraordinary woman!

Ayten and I rushed to the hospital. We found her reading a book in her room. "Come in girls," she said. "I couldn't tell you when the doctor rushed to get me in the hospital. It turned out to be a good thing because I hadn't had a vacation in a long time. This has turned out to be a vacation..." Melahat was making fun of her illness. Instead of us comforting her, she was comforting us. Every once in a while, she seemed to get serious and would mumble to herself, "I lost my womb for the sake of a car... Ah Mercedes, I didn't know what you would cost..."

Throughout her illness, it was Ahmet who looked after her. Now, they were friends, allies, in a way that they never had been before. What they had lived together had taught them a great deal. Whenever we visited them, we found them reading together, or talking to each other. Once, Melahat told us, "Girls, I can't recognize Ahmet anymore. If things continue like this, I may end up falling in love with him all over again..."

Now, I was reading too. My aim was to finish school and to become a good psychologist. I would defend women's rights and spread the word around me.

As for Ayten... She was made to marry her uncle's son, when she was eighteen. After this marriage, which she had not wanted at all, she had become one of the oppressed women in Holland. Finally, she could not stand it, and took refuge in a women's shelter with her children. Now, she is living on her own with her children. We see each other from time to time, to talk about the old times.

Years later, I did finish my studies and began to work at an organization that supports women. I work as a counsellor to women who have experienced family violence. The women who use are services are mostly of Turkish, Arabic and African origins. On each of their faces, I see Melahat 's face. They look at me as if they were saying, "we are going to become another Melahat."

Betül Özgül Odabaşı / Germany

She was born in Ankara in 1962, and started to school when she was only five years old since she had learned to read and write herself beforehand. She was interested in folk culture. Therefore, she performed folk dances at Folk-Tur, and she took courses on Turkish folk music. She practiced on Tahir Alangu and Pertev Naili Boratav's works during that period. She graduated from Hacettepe University Department of Psychology in 1984. She worked at a number of different jobs both in her country and abroad.

She utters the names of Füruzan, Sevgi Soysal, Adalet Ağağolu, Sait Faik Abasıyanık, Cevat Şakir Kabaağaçlı, Fakir Baykurt, Necati Cumalı, Dostoyevski, Çehov, Hamsun and O'Henry as the writers who influenced and inspired her in her teens.

Still living in Frankfurt, she is married and has two children.

Immigrant I am, Immigrant You are, Immigrant S/he is

She was in a country, the language of which she didn't speak, and the people of which she didn't know. She left her family, her friends, her job and her whole past behind. There were a lot of reasons that forced her to take this decision, but the most important one was her child's growing up away from her father. Until his departure, their daughter became grumpier and more fragile. She didn't enjoy the meals any more. She had trouble in sleeping. And how about her interest in brunet and eye-glassed men! The men resembling her father indeed...

She didn't think thoroughly about what she would take with her while leaving her country. Except the bedside books and letters... She left her clothes to her best friend, put up her furniture and goods for sale, and she suddenly found herself in a different continent and in a different climate.

Vural welcomed them at the airport on a Sunday. It was as though the great longing of the years came to an end suddenly. The father and daughter hugged each other tightly; the time stopped, the world stopped. Long afterwards, having pulled back her arms around her father, Özlem touched his upper lips with her finger. His black thick moustache was cut! Besides, he tied back his hair. All of a sudden, she ran to her mother. She pierced her father through and through once more from that distance.

Vural came closer and this time, he hugged his wife. Tülay also hugged him in return. "Come here, let's go to get an ice cream for you, my daughter," said Vural.

– Where are we, daddy?

– In Duirsburg, my girl. From now on, we are going to live together here.

– Always?

– Always.

Vural noticed that Tülay stole a glance at him.

– Where will you buy ice cream daddy?

– From here.

They chose a table with a sunshade over it, and sat there. Vural turned to his wife and asked:

– Let's drink coffee Tülay, would you like it?

Vural, in German, ordered coffees and ice cream. Then she turned to his daughter and said:

– You were not afraid of the plane my girl, did you?

– No, but I became a little bit sick. The eye-glassed brunet man took my hand. Then it was gone!

Vural made a wry face.

– How are you Tülay? You look a little bit tired.

– It is because of the travel. I will be fine when I rest.

The house that Vural rented was not so far. Besides, Tülay's luggage consisted merely of a couple of suitcases. She looked for people in the street, but it was useless.

– Where are the people?

– You can't see anyone outside on Sundays! Everybody lapses into a deep silence after a crazy Saturday night. Wearing their neat and clean clothes, religious people do their Sunday praying in the church early in the morning, and then they rest at their homes for long hours.

Tülay was fed up with that silence. She stared at the greenness of the park ahead of them. A drunk was sleeping under the tree at the corner. There were empty bottles around him. Two teenagers were sprawling on the grass; they didn't seem to care about anything. After having passed the park, Tülay asked:

– Are we going to walk more?

– If you are tired, let's use the tramway, said Vural. He looked at the time table when they arrived at the stop.

– It is going to come in a minute.

Tülay laughed at him when he said that.

– You sound so sure when you say that, said she with a mocking tone.

– Do not even think that here is like Turkey. Everything is precise here.

As soon as Vural finished his words, the horn of the tramway was heard. They put the luggage to the entry of the door. They chose a seat for four people, but the tramway was completely empty anyway.

It could be seen from her face that Tülay was really tired. It was weariness of the last three months. She wanted to be got sent to Germany for work in order not to give up her job as a teacher since she loved it very much. She sought help from everybody to this end. But it was useless! She didn't know anyone of high authority from Ministry of Education. It was all over with a petition letter. Having left her family, colleagues, students, and a warm and sunny country, as well as her dreams, she just came there! Now, she was in Germany on a hot day of July.

While the tramway was getting close to a hospital, all of a sudden Vural took one of the suitcases. "We are getting off here," he said, holding Özlem with his other hand. At that moment, the whole area was filled with the sound of the bells rang from a big church. Özlem looked for the place that the sound came from.

The building resembled a church rather than a hospital, though it was written "hospital" on the door. The house was just on the corner of the back street, on the ground floor. Its little windows with white curtains had a scene of the street. Vural said with pride:

– Here is your new house. His hands were shaking while opening the door.

– Daddy, which one is my room? asked Özlem impatiently.

– Look, here it is.

As she was accustomed to sleeping with her mother, she asked curiously:

– But, there are only two beds here. Are you going to sleep with us?

Tülay was petrified with astonishment in the middle of the room. The house consisted merely of a living room and a bedroom: the worktop and kitchen cupboards right in front of a two-seat sofa, a mini refrigerator on the right side, a mini TV next to the window looking at the back garden, a petite bathroom facing the street door, a shower cabinet, the bedroom next to the bathroom, two beds facing each other, a small square table before the window and recently picked up white daisies on it, and a zipped movable wardrobe on the right of the table.

The little girl had already started to play with the plush toys on the bed. Tülay said "I brought something for breakfast. I will unpack them while you are preparing the tea."

Happy that the silence was broken, Vural put the tea pot on the stove. Then, he watched his wife. Tülay put the things she had brought to the worktop: half a kilo of full-fat cheese and tulum cheese from Erzincan, law-salt olives and cracked green olives from Gemlik in packages of one kilos, two ring bolognas, halvah with cocoa, two liters of extra virgin olive oil, fresh long green peppers, two cans of homemade jam, and spices. She took a package full of sesame bagels out of her bag and she put it on the worktop too.

Vural was lost in thought. Boiled water was ready. Tülay brewed the tea, and he put some food into the plates. The small room was filled with the excellent smell of *simits*(*). Özlem was so silent. Her father looked inside the room to look at her. She had fallen asleep hugging a yellow duck. He blanketed her body, and put a chair and a pillow beside the bed. Closing the door slowly, he went to the living room. The table was prepared and teas were poured into the cups. He took a small piece from the hot bagel and smelled it. Then he took a piece of cheese using the tip of the bagel. He was still the same; in the past, he wasn't accustomed to using a fork unless he had to. "How are you?" said Tülay.

Despite knowing that this question would be asked sooner or later, Vural gulped.

– I don't really know how I'm. I feel weird. I can't even know who I am. I thought about it over and over, about why I am here. I was so lonely. I couldn't sleep for days and nights. I had pain in every part of my body. I even tried alcohol so as to sleep. It made me feel worse.

– You have tried that way before…

– Yes, you are right… Bu I was desperate. Then I went to a doctor; to the hospital beside that very house. Turks go there!

– Well, what did he say?

(*) Bagels.

– He said that everyone experiences the things you go through, it will be over when you get used to here. In addition, he gave me a book too. It is in the back room, you can take a look at it later.

– Is that all?

– Yes.

Tülay got angry:

– Is that so? It will be over when you get used to here, huh? Who awards them with diplomas? If this profession is that much easy, then let everyone be a doctor!

– It is not that so. I had little money left. Although I told him that, he still prepared a bill for me. However, I had found out that Directorate of Social Affairs pays the bills of people who are in the same situation as me. He got one hundred Deutsch Marks from me.

Tülay hold her head with her hands. She was so angry that she wanted to smash and break something. But the only thing she could do was to say "I hope we will meet with that doctor again."

Watching the light of the street lamp, Tülay fell asleep. However, soon after she woke up due to being startled by a dream in which she saw one of those beautiful days that she had with her grandfather. It was still dark. The father and daughter were in sound sleep. She turned her face to the grey-like sky, and said "Ohh my God, what am I doing in this country? Here will be my reality from know on, those places will remain as dreams."

She put some water to boil so as to make tea, but she was so far off in thoughts that the water nearly finished since it boiled for such a long time. There were the sounds of motorbikes outside. Then she heard the horn of tramway. Even though it was still night, the people already started the day. She looked for slim tea glasses to pour her tea. But she didn't find any; there were only tea cups in the cupboard. She chose one of them randomly, and poured her tea. She thought about Vural "How can he live here, how can a man spend his time alone within these walls?"

She opened the refrigerator; there was no egg, no fresh bread either! Putting on her clothes, she went out to buy something to eat. She took a deep breath upon entering the Turkish Supermarket which was a little far away from home. It was as though she was in Turkey! While taking bread and eggs, she saw the irresistible freshness of lettuces, green onions, parsleys, dills, and mints. At breakfast, Vural liked to eat green vegetables and tomatoes which are added oil and salt, and a little bit lemon. She chose the vegetables one by one. Then she thought about making burghul salad for Özlem towards the end of the afternoon. And there would be icy cold ayran with it..!

For the first time in her life she had seen a cucumber as big as an arm. What's more, it was in a nylon cover. She didn't buy it. She came into the queue so as to pay for the food. The young woman at the cash register was wearing a chiffon headscarf and a white apron dress. She put the things she bought in a line on the belt conveyer on the cash register. It seemed bizarre to her to do the payment in Deutsch Mark.

Having gone out from the supermarket with bags in her hands, she noticed the gardens extending along on her right. They were separated from the pavement with iron fences. There were small pools, fruit trees, and swings. Flags were fluttering on the top of cottages -flags in yellow, red, and black colors. She was not in her country anymore!

She slid into the house in haste. The front window was open. Hearing the sound of the keys, Özlem jumped from the sofa and went to the door. "Where have you been mum? Didn't you tell that we would always be together?" said she, and clung to her mother's legs. She had woken up when her father went to bathroom to take a shower, and seeing nobody around, she began to cry. Having put the bags to the floor, Tülay hugged her daughter and said "You were sleeping honey. So, I went out and bought some of your favorite foods. I didn't mean to upset you, I am sorry. "What did you buy, let me see them too," said Özlem while carrying the bags to worktop in the kitchen. Her mother put some cherries into a plate and gave it to her. Özlem made earrings form cherry bunches, and wore them immediately. Then she ran to the dressing mirror in the back room and watched herself for a while.

At that time, having shaved and smelling excellent, Vural went out of the bathroom. "Good morning" he said, looking at his wife. "Good morning" answered Tülay, carrying the dishes to the table. Then he hugged his daughter. Özlem passed her fingers on her father's soft cheeks. She completely forgot about the cherry earrings!

They had gone to bed half hungry the night before. This time, they filled their plates with food and enjoyed their breakfast. Vural felt himself like a newborn that morning. His eyes were fixed at his wife's ring finger while supping his tea. That shiny piece of metal, the meaning of which he didn't know when he was young, now meant a lot to him. How much the people changed as the years passed!

"Where is Özlem? She became so silent again" he said. Having learned that she was in the garden, he watched her from the window. She seemed happy. Tülay wanted to clear the table, but Vural stopped her. "We will clear it together" said he, and pulled her close to his side. He hadn't seen her for a long time; he missed her scent. At that very moment, everything stopped. The world stopped. The magic that they thought lost was coming forth from obscurity again with each touch. Now they were in an unknown land, and apart from themselves, nobody knew the way to there…

Tülay sank into a deep sleep. Having taken a pillow and a blanket, Vural came in. He covered her body with blanket and relieved her head with the pillow. Then taking her daughter with him, he went out. He took her to the children's playground in front of the hospital. Özlem first jumped into the sand pool, and then to the slide. She stopped as she came in front of the semi-conical shaped big swing in that was made of straw. A blue-eyed child who had golden hair streaming in the air was swinging there. "I want to swing too," she said to her father. Vural stopped the swing. She put Özlem in it and told her to hold the ropes tightly. Özlem was screaming cheerfully as the swing gained speed; she was so excited as if she was in a hot air balloon. After the German kid got out of the swing, she waved her hand and said "Tschüss." Özlem waved back and said "Goodbye!" in Turkish.

They left the playground and walked parallel to the tramway line. That street was a busy and active street. There were shops on both sides; a doner shop, a patisserie, a perfumery, a greengrocer, and banks… You could find there whatever you want. There were also laundry homes the windows of which were made of glass form top to the bottom. They entered the "Halay Bake House" together. People from Erzincan opened that place. They ordered two buns with cheese filling. The place was so full with customs that the staff had trouble in dealing with all of them. Turning to the man at the cash register, he asked:

– How is it going? Can you make enough to live off?

– There is pretty good money in this job. But it would be hard to make the both ends meet if the staff were not my relatives.

Tülay woke up with a pain in her stomach. "It must be because of hunger," she thought. She got up to take a glass of water. She went to the bathroom and washed her face. It seemed that the woman in the mirror was not herself. She could neither sleep, nor eat well. Then she noticed that Özlem and Vural were not in the back garden. Seeing them nowhere, she looked around. There was not any note on the coffee table.

"They will come soon. No need to worry," she said to relieve herself. She turned on the television in order to hear just a voice. They were broadcasting the news in a language that she didn't understand. "Ohh my God, what a rough language it is! How will I get used to it?" She zapped the channels one by one. There was not even a single channel suitable for her. She began to get bored. "At least they should have informed me about where they are. They are really think-headed!"

"How can I express my concern if I call the police, or the nearest hospital? I do not know anyone in order that I call and ask for help!"

She felt that pain in her stomach again. Her heart began to beat hard.

Then it occurred to her: "I am in Europe. Definitely there must be someone here who knows English," she said and thought of calling the police again. She lifted the phone receiver; there was no line!

She didn't even notice that the phone cable was pulled out... She felt too bad to be able to stand on her legs. There was nothing she could do. She became sick and rushed to the bathroom.

Then... The sound of a key was heard at the door. Unconsciously, she turned the bathroom lock at the same time. She froze up, and knelt down behind the door. Despite not knowing that what she waited for, she began to wait. Afterwards, she recognized that someone was talking to her: "Tülay, are you there? Why don't you come out? Has anything bad happened? Say something, Tülay!"

Semra Kalkan / Canada

She was born in 1964 in Konya. She was graduated from the Department of City Planning, The University of Dokuz Eylül in İzmir. She had worked at various municipalities and in the private sector as a city planner. She spent the year 1991 in England as a childcare worker. She travelled to Japan, Thailand, Cambodia, and Greece. She has been living in Canada since 2005.

Immigration Diary

It was a luminous summer night, when the exuberance of the city seemed to rise towards the sky. I had emerged from the dull confinement of the Subway station, and walking unhurried and distracted, towards my home. I was passing indifferently through the treed, orderly roads and in front of silent houses in a calm and clean neighborhood near Lake Ontario.

Just as I often do in the troublesome moments, I lifted my face to the sky, which has always fascinated me, as though it might offer me a way out. Tonight, the sky was not black, but deep blue. My eyes turned towards the light that had turned the blackness of the sky to deep blue. The night was lit not only by the city lights, but also by nature. As soon as I saw it, I sensed the blood in my veins flowing into my heart. I had found the colour of life that I had lost since leaving my country. Suddenly, I felt the beauty of the trees, and the charm of the night. It was as if a moment ago, all was still in a lifeless image, but everything had now come to life. Now I could run. I was ready to embrace the exuberance of the city. For some moment, I stood there, looking in wonder.

It was as if I had run into one of my dear friends whom I could see infrequently, and who could understand me without a word, or even a look. How satisfactory it was to stand still before a friend who knew my entire past and who accepted and loved me exactly as I was. I said nothing because that friend would understand me without words. She was covering me without paying attention to the mistakes I had made in the past. I wanted to embrace her back. I had to share with her the experiences of the longest months of my life. I realized that I would meet her at least once a month, and rejoiced. What's more, she could see me, and everyone I loved, at the same time. My loved ones could see her, too.

I had discovered this little game when I had left home for university at the age of 17, as a consolation of my longing for home. That's why there had always been a special bond between the sky and me. This immensity that covers all of us, without discrimination, and that takes me away at each glance... Tonight, the full moon had arrived to light it up with joy. I had taught this game to my boyfriend as well. Now, I could guess that he had also encountered the full moon, and was filled with the same emotions as me.

Across continents, I thought, longings had grown more intense, even though the technological means of communication are so extensive. There was no special reason why my longing should be so sharp because I had no special worries or sadness. It was not because of war or poverty that I had come to this distant land. It was out of my own desire. I knew that I could go back home whenever I wanted, and would be greeted with love. So why was I missing what I had left behind so much? Had I not prepared myself to this separation for months?

The wisdom of centuries reaches us through some pure words, and many of us assume that we understand and know those words. If necessary, we can write a couple of pages of essays on some of them. Yet, the only words we truly understand are those that confirm our own lived experiences. The others refer to the lives of other people. We may know them but we cannot feel them. Many of us assume that we do not have much to learn as we grow older. I sometimes assumed that as well. But Canada is teaching me all that I never knew about life and most of all, about myself.

If it had been so easy to understand, own up to and apply the experiences of ages, many of us would take wings from happiness because we would not make any mistakes. Yet each one of us rediscovers our own truths, through our own lived experiences. We learn from our mistakes. Some mistakes have to be made, or else some things will always remain missing. Many of our mistakes are crucial in turning us towards the good. They form the thick, bitter and instructive lines of our lives. They are even reflected on the lines of our faces and on our gestures.

My arrival in Canada was the result of such a mistake. When I look back at the process, it seems like a conscious, well-planned one. Yet, I find that it was built on a foundation of a simple mistake: that mistake was to under-estimate immigration! In other words, the mistake was to just arrive here one day, taking the many-dimensioned difficulties of immigration lightly. But without this mistake, my story of immigration would not have existed. I would not have pursued my curiosities, and come here. If I had had any idea how tough the process would be, I would probably have lost my courage, and I would have changed my mind. That would not have been the end of life – but I would have lived on with a sense of loss.

Actually, there is probably a mistake somewhere in all stories of immigration. Those who immigrate set out on their endless journeys, perhaps because of that mistake, or false assessment. They can take on that tough experience only because they do not fully know what they are taking on. Dreams never include the ugly nakedness of the truth. They are often formed as a defence against the unbearable pressure of reality. Dreams are the colours that our brains add to the monotony, pain and ugliness of reality. They are born in us, as an expression of our commitment to life. We even feel strong and determined enough to actualize some of them. But as soon as dreams begin to be transformed into reality, they loose some of their charm and we feel the difficulties that they entail. That is exactly moment when new dreams may begin. What was once a dream has become the reality, and this can be unbearably boring. While I was describing to a friend, the difficulties I faced when I first arrived here, my friend who knows me well said: "You are making your dreams come true." Yes, I was. Should I not have been filled with happiness? But making a dream come true may not be so exciting, precisely because it's no longer a dream but a reality.

When I look back at those first weeks after my arrival, it seems to me that the period, which most resembles my inner state at that time, is the period after the catastrophic earthquake in the Marmara region, in 1999. Although it was only on television that I witnessed the details of the event, and although I was experiencing great pain, I had rapidly accepted reality – as if I were a saint – and I was carrying on my daily life as if everything was normal. That was a strange inner state. I had seen people walking hand in hand near buildings whose five floors had collapsed into each other, to get to the beach. Or people whose vacant and frozen eyes were frighteningly calm, and who looked nowhere in particular. These things made me think of the greatness of the shock people had experienced. Yes, an ordinary person could not deal with such a catastrophic event in a short time. What happened was that the brains were stopping when confronted with reality? We were all experiencing shock in different ways.

I had not experienced great pain in my life. That earthquake was the greatest. I joined one of the relief teams to go to the earthquake region for a week, and went through another earthquake with the people who lived there. These continuing earthquakes were forcing people to re-live their fears and their pain at unexpected moments. Something got entrenched in my mind then: nothing could be understood without being experienced. Even if you could understand, your feelings could not match those of people who go through the event – without actually experiencing the event; your feelings would remain false. Although I had suffered the losses of the earthquake survivors, I would not truly understand their feelings, because I had not suffered their losses.

Now, I was experiencing the shock of an earthquake that I had created in myself, with my own decision. Of course I was experiencing the relief of having survived an earthquake, but the shock was not something simple. My brain and my body were so far away from their ordinary functions that during the first month and a half, I couldn't even apply for a job. I wasn't myself. I think the shock of my own earthquake was lasting longer than the earthquake that took place in nature. There were some friends who appeared from nowhere, who understood me, and who helped. Without them, my story might have ended differently. I was glad of their support, but could not understand why they were supporting me. One day, Peter said: "When I arrived here, I received the support of people whose name I didn't even know. This is my way of thanking them."

In the end, I decided to start to look for a job in Canada, at a place where I had a strong likelihood of succeeding. The reason why I was unable to get around to applying for jobs was the high number of applicants brought about by the high volume of immigrants. It was a simple mathematical fact that many of the people in this mass would be filtered out and it would take a very long time for them to find jobs to be able to make a living. I sat down and thought: why did it matter where I went? What was tying me down to Toronto? The answers to these questions determined my choice: it was the job I would be doing that was important, and not the place where I would go. I had understood that I would not be able to sustain the telemarketing job that I had been doing for two and a half weeks. My first job had been a house-cleaning assignment that lasted a day-and-a half. Then it was the telephoning. After two weeks and a half, I realized that I would lose my spiritual health, expecting these jobs to do me any good.

Even though I had arrived in this country, thinking I could do anything, I was now seeing that I was not prepared for this. I had to stop looking for temporary jobs. I had received no responses to the eight job applications that I had made, to find work in my own profession. Everyone around me was saying: "if you can't find what you are looking for, you have to take what you find." Especially that young Turkish woman whose house I had cleaned... I could not forget her words: "You do not know how to appreciate the job that you have found. It's a good job," she had said for the telemarketing job. Either I had completely lost my emotional balance, or the point of view of the people who said such things was completely different from mine, because they were living in Canada.

It was time to leave. It had been more than two months, and for the first time in my life, I was beginning to feel my age. Each time I looked into the mirror, I was surprised by my own image because my hair was greying rapidly. I was psychologically tired. I no longer had the energy to start anything. That day, I went to work, mulling about in my mind, the idea of quitting. I wondered if there might be a response to one of those eight applications... At moments when I was along, I found only crumbs of my previous hopes in my heart.

After a couple of hours of working uninterestedly, I ran to the phone. Normally, I would check for messages upon my return home, but today I was impatient. It was the voice of a woman who spoke very fast. What I managed to make out in the midst of my tremendous excitement was that I was being invited to an interview. I listened to the same message several times, trying to calm myself down. I was not mistaken. This was a response to one of those eight applications I had made. I wished the interview could take place there, at that very moment. Then, I called right away, and said I would go to for the interview. A couple of days later, another message arrived. They gave me an appointment for ten days later. Now, I knew the date and the dime. People say, "Time is relative." How true! Those ten days seemed like years. How would I managed to get to sleep, how would I have lived through those ten days?

I could neither work properly nor sleep properly. It was as if life had stopped that afternoon of August 12 when the message had arrived. I could not think of anything else. My pacing in my room at night got to such a point that even my normally patient landlord was getting impatient. But I did not even care. Whether I might be thrown out of my place, whether I might lose my current job, the exuberant weekends and starry nights. None of those things brought even a little flutter of anxiety or excitement to my heart. All my feelings had focused on one point only. I gathered pages of information. I memorized facts about that work place. I was determined to go to that interview ready for the best possible performance.

Finally that day, which I thought would never come, arrived. Nothing existed for me, except for the telephone, my desk and the papers on my desk. Oh yes, there were the people at the other end of the phone, who would be asking me questions. It was my birthday. Two years earlier, at my fortieth birthday, I had found myself flying to a new continent, and thought: "God must be telling me something." Perhaps now, God had new things to tell me. I will never be able to calculate how many years of my life were spent in those ten days when I prepared for that telephone interview. All I knew was that it was not an ordinary day.

The phone interview was over. Thankfully, I had to wait for only three days for the results. Those three days seemed easier to bear than the previous ten days had been. This time, I was being invited to a personal interview. For many days and nights, I gave thought to what I would wear, what I would take along with me, and what I would say at the interview.

I no longer had the energy to continue the telemarketing job. Even if I failed to get the job for which I was being interviewed, I would no longer do telemarketing. But I would never forget that place where new immigrants who had different professions were repeating five memorized paragraphs, fifty times a day, without conviction, to make sales and remain alive.

After the personal interview, another fortnight passed while the paperwork for my employment was being done. I started to think that waiting without doing anything else – focussing only on one thing, was a different way of dying. That's what I was doing during those fifteen days. Neither my brain nor my body was in an ordinary state. After days of aching anxiety, the final outcome was announced by a phone call. I was hired.

It was now time to leave Toronto. My belongings were half assembled, some ready to be sent to Turkey, and others to the new location where my job was taking me. This was an extraordinary relief. Yet, as I thought about things, I realized that I had grown to love this city. So, perhaps it was life experience that added value to the moment and to a place. In this city, I had life experience that amounted to three months and three weeks. It was a period of bearing witness to the immigration stories of millions of people. I thanked that city for giving me shelter during that time, and for sharing my trials.

I have always had great respect for experiences. But the most valuable experience in the world was my own, because I had made my own decisions, and I had lived with the consequences of my mistakes. My experiences had allowed me to cover the distance of a tiny grain, on the road leading to the fulfilment of my dreams. There could not be anyone happier than I was because I was living for my hopes. Even though I could not attain all of them, hope was shedding light to my life, and most important: there were people who loved and trusted me, and who were by my side on this road – even if some of them lived half way around the world. It was not the bread I ate or the water I drank that kept me alive, it was their love and trust. Before that great force, mountains and oceans were insignificant.

Now, it was time to set out. I had not come to this country to end my travels, but to continue on my way. The only difference between this and my other trips was that this was a little longer. I set out from the coast of Lake Ontario where I had endured like dervishes, towards the southwest, to land of winter where I would nurture new hopes.

Ferda Aydın / Holland

She was born in Şereflikoçhisar, Ankara in 1971. She emigrated to Holland in 1991. She was educated there on children education and has worked in Holland for six years. She was married and has two children.

White Passion of the Steppe: Education

Here is steppe where colors are lack of blue and green and soil is extremely dry. All tones of yellow are scattered to fields which are as if painted by an artist. Hereabouts, white appears following different tones of yellow; Tuz (salt) Lake resembles pearls creeping towards the steppe plain; and it is as straight as a line. But it is also worn, exhausted and ruined because of dry soil; it is passionately in love with wind and water just as people of steppes. Its heart is covered by the lover who has never come despite its long lasting and passionate love. It has sung soulful songs for this dreamy lover for centuries. Salt Lake has hid various loves and separations within hillsides surrounding it and resembling pieces of crystal. In its each part, there is a different story just like young Nuran's passion of education.

That day, it was extremely sunny and scorching as usual in steppes. After long months without rain, fractured soil was in deep hunger for a single raindrop just as dry lips. Plain was decorated with yellow wheatears which were shaking against warm wind and which looked like a new bride. Resisting sweaty weather with hooks in their hands, one or two persons per each field were reaping ears with their hearts and souls. They had no other way... Each of them hoped something different. Some would get married to a girl with red scarf, some would find solutions to their problems, and some would have food for winter.

These golden ears meant one-year food for Uncle İsa, who had callous hands, fractured lips, bent waist due to heavy working conditions lasting for years, and for his family. After hard and violent years just as colorless and pale steppes, hair of Uncle İsa had also become pale and lost its shine. His olive black hair appeared as if covered by snow. Of course, it wasn't easy to struggle against dry soil. Besides, he also had various painful and hopeless periods in his life. He participated in Turkish War of Independence. He honorably fought in the war for the independence of his country. His exhausted body met up with enemies when he was just a 14-year old boy who hadn't got married with a girl with red scarf yet. They triumphed in the war under the leadership of Mustafa Kemal. Enemies were dropped into sea. Uncle İsa was also awarded an Independence Medal just as the other brave children of country. He always felt honored since Atatürk, himself, had presented his medal, and told what a great commander Atatürk was in an enthusiastic manner. Moreover, he didn't take of his medal even while he was sleeping despite opposition of his wife. "Don't grumble too much, this medal was entrusted by Atatürk to my safekeeping, I can't breach his trust. I must protect this medal," said he to his wife.

Uncle İsa had two daughters and two sons. He always paid great attention to his children since he had been a parentless child. That's why his daughters got married to men from neighbor villages upon his request. "I always yearned for my parents in my childhood, and now I can't bear yearning for my children, too."

Ali, his elder son, got married to a rich girl who he had met during his military service and he was living with his wife's family now. He had never liked the village. He hated pale and colorless soils, and got bored of his home village. He wanted to be surrounded by smell of roses. However, the only dominant color was yellow hereabouts, and it was impossible to smell anything other than burnt steppes. Therefore, he had benefited from the opportunity he had taken. After Ali's departure from village, Uncle İsa got very depressed, yet he continued begging for him after each prayer and expected him to be happy. Maybe he was undutiful, but it was impossible to ignore his own child.

He was only supported by Dursun who was the apple of his eye. "They will certainly take care of me when I get old," said him to himself. Firdevs, Dursun's wife, was also very respectful and softhearted. Everybody envied them in the village.

The only point which Uncle İsa couldn't feel was that Dursun wasn't satisfied with his life, too. Even if he didn't express himself, he was also fed up with eating cracked wheat rice everyday, wearing patched clothes, and dry soils. He also had dreams, infinite dreams. There were colors of rainbow which was so close that seemed easy to touch and which disappeared as he got closer. He wanted to be surrounded by these colors in his whole life.

Germany commenced labor recruitment after 1960 and some of their villagers also went to Germany. People, who had gone to that country with rawhide sandals and patched clothes, returned from there as the owner of most beautiful cars and brand-new clothes. Germany embellished dreams of Dursun. Was Germany also drought as here? Did people pray for rain? When did they smile and cry? Were there rainbow colors of his dreams in Germany, or was it also pale just as hereabouts?

His father always refused his going to Germany. And he didn't want to afflict his father. His brother had also departed from their village and caused their father to be hurt. If he also departed, his father's old heard couldn't bear up against this yearning. Dursun heard his father's devotions after each prayer. He always prayed for Dursun. How could he do such a thing? He was struggling against himself helplessly. He couldn't keep his emotions and ideas under control.

In steppe, living conditions were getting more challenging day by day. Firdevs, his wife, was pregnant again; fifth children would be born soon. It was required to bring them up and provide their survival. Dursun had hardly completed primary school due to poverty. That's why; he wanted to make it possible for them to be educated. "I must go to Germany to prevent their becoming ignorant just as us, and withering away just as steppe," said he. He would take his courage in both hands and discuss this matter with his father once again that night. "I must do this," said he, "I must achieve to provide a healthy future for my children."

Dursun and his father who had worked under a scorching weather all day went to the house barely. They sat at table after washing their faces and hands. While eating his meal in an appetite manner, Uncle İsa was fairly happy. "I hope we can complete our job within a few days," said he. Seeing that his father was really happy; Dursun thought "It is just the right time, and I must tell my father that I'll be registered for going to Germany." "Father," said he slowly. Then he gulped and kept silent. He chewed his morsel and said "Father" once more.

– Why don't you tell what you want, why do you act as if a baby who learn speaking just a short while ago? Tell what you want, and don't annoy me.

– Father, if we take facts into consideration, we are unable to earn our living by a few fields.

– What do you mean?

– Are these fields enough for supporting all of us? We pick up a scantly livelihood. My great God didn't grant even a little rain onto soil this year, how we can get sacksful wheat. We will run out of grains until mid-winter at the latest. All animals will perish before spring period. Please, don't be insistent any more; let me registered for working in Germany. God willing, I can return after working a few years. We can purchase property by means of our savings, and it is also better for you, isn't it?

Uncle İsa turned pale and got out of spirits all of a sudden. His face, which had blushed due to working under extremely sunny weather, turned into snow white. He started breathing as deeply as a raging bull. He put the spool onto the table and sat backwards. "Please, bring a glass of tea, my daughter," said he to his daughter-in-law.

Dursun continued speaking by the help of his father's silence.

– Look Dirty Hasan went to Germany and became rich. It is said that he purchased properties in the city. And he didn't return to village.

– Do you think he had followed the right way? He caused all his family to be stricken by poverty. Then, he indulged himself having a life of pleasure. May God forgive us... Don't cause me to sin... Don't you know what I talk about Nanny Fatma had lost her life day by day due to waiting for him in front of the fountain day and night. She dropped dead by the side of fountain. He, the unfilial son, didn't even come to her funeral. He had taken her for a ride by promising to return in a few years. Do you also want to do the same? If so, put all the cards on the table.

– No, my dear father, may God grant you a long life. I intent to say that you will also live more graciously from now on.

– Thankfully, I have already had a gracious living. Put a sock in it, and go up about your own business. Fortunately, these fields can support both of us. Who has provided your food until now?

"No way it can feed us," Dursun said himself. "How can it be possible that the fields which can't even feed the grizzly cow will feed us? We were run out of feed last winter and the animals in the stable ran to waste. Children could not eat anything other than cracked wheat. We are fed up with that. And isn't there anything else important other than feeding our stomach? Who will feed my soul, my dreams? They are just like horses wandering untended. Who will curb them? Will I grow old in this way? Will my children, my innocent children, be in the same boat living the same fate? Who gives this right to my father? Moral laws?"

The people living in this territory have grown used to conceal their love. They experience their joy and grief within themselves. They think love and crying are something to be ashamed of. The tears dropping form the eyes do not touch the earth. Otherwise it will be a sign of weakness or infirmity because nobody has mercy on the people of this moor. They always have to meet their fate alone and to struggle with the harsh territory, and meanwhile, they feel the acrid moisture of the salt in their lungs. But they have never complained about it. Thus, they do not feel any compassion for the ones showing a sign of weakness.

Dursun was a man loving his children very much but he couldn't show it in order to abide by the wrong traditions. Before he had the chance of loving, kissing and hugging his children as much as he desired, the time passed so quickly that they came to school age. As their ages were close to each other; Fadime, Nuran, Sezai and Salih started school respectively. Uncle İsa, who objected the girls' going to school at the beginning, was actually proud that the girls were more successful at school than the boys. Now he could better realize that he made a really good decision by allowing Dursun who insisted on girls' starting school. Especially Nuran's success deeply affected him.

Nuran, the second child of the family, was born in a spring day two months premature. That's why she was a physically delicate girl. As it is said, she was like a leaf in the wind. However, she was a very smart and beautiful girl. It seemed as if there were flames burning in her eyes. She was so petite and poky, but so sweet and pretty as well. Her teacher also liked her and used to call her as "my little bird." She was the most hardworking girl of the class; she used to finish the homework before everybody and she tied to her teacher's apron strings. She was the first student who learned how to read and write. Her teacher was hopeful of her success and said "Nuran will be a sample of pride for the women in this village."

Turkish nation, who had completed Independence War successfully thanks to great genius Mustafa Kemal Atatürk's leadership, has made progress in the light of Atatürk and his reforms. However, there are still a lot of things to do, a lot of obstacles to overcome despite the long years that has passed after the war. The most important obstacle is to provide education services even in the remotest regions of the country, and especially to educate girls so that they can contribute to the economy and future of the country. It is a strong taboo to send girls to school in steppes, just as in the other rural regions. It is believed that they were born merely to work and give birth to children. Nuran's teacher also knew that situation but she wouldn't give up her plans about Nuran. "Didn't I went to school to fight for educating the women?", "Didn't we take an oath to bring our country on an equal footing with modern civilizations?" said she. Although she didn't know him well, she felt that Nuran's father was different than the other men of the village. She saw the desperation and rebelliousness in his eyes. However, since she thought that it would be too early to talk this issue with him, she waited till Nuran's last year at primary school.

Nuran used to take top grades at school every year. Dursun was so proud of his daughter that he used to secretly hug her in affection. During her summer holidays, Nuran used to take food to the fields for his father everyday with his brothers and sisters, and she used to play with water in the fountain. Only cold water can help reduce the effects of the burning sun. There wasn't any sea, thus it was impossible to dream about a sea image in this vicinity. Nuran saw the sea in her school books and she was fascinated by the view of it. She asked her teacher excitedly:

– How did such a great amount of water come together, teacher? There is not even a small stream in our village. There is Salt Lake, but it has only salt in it, not any water! Besides, it is not even blue like the sea, it is plain white.

After the humdrum repetitious years, Nuran began her last year at primary school. However, she was still a squat; she didn't grow even an inch. Her teacher made fun of her by saying "Oh my little bird, don't you eat just a little bit? You can't even reach the board." One day, when the summer holiday was at hand, the teacher entered the classroom with files in her arms. The students began to make predictions with curious eyes about what those files could be. The teacher said:

– Sit down your desks and stop talking, please. Do you know what is there in these files in my hands?

– No teacher.

– These files comprise your future. These are the exam papers. Those who will be successful at this exam will be entitled to go to teachers training boarding schools of state. If you successfully complete your education there, you will become a teacher as me, and you will serve as a teacher in various parts of the country. You will teach the principles of Atatürk that I have taught you to the next generations. I trust you very much.

Listening to the teacher with all her ears, Nuran was filled with joy and happiness. At last, her dreams would come true. She filled the exam paper carefully, and then she checked her answers one by one. She didn't want to jeopardize her future by mistake. At the same time, there were prayers between her small lips; she was saying "My dear God, please help me."

In that evening, Nuran told her father what her teacher said, without skipping any detail. "Where will you go to school if you are to be successful at exam?" asked her father.

– There is a teacher's training school in Hasanoğlan Village of Ankara, our teacher said.

– But my daughter, what about your grandfather? Do you think he will allow you to go that much far?

Nuran looked at his father with wet eyes; she said gulping:

– Grandfather is not my father, you are my father!

Hearing those words, Dursun's eyes were filled with tears. He wiped his eyes so as not to show his tears to his daughter. It would be difficult to make her understand the conservative traditions, customs, and the sorrow of the steppes. "But is it going to continue like this?" he asked himself, "Who will response to these appeals?"

– Oh my little bird! There are lots of things that you don't know of. Life is hard here. I wish everything would be as easy as you think.

– You can make it easier. Do that, father. Pleeeease!

Hugging his daughter with affection, Dursun said:

– I promise, my girl. If you win the exam, I will send you to the school. No matter what other people say, I don't care any more; I will break this chain.

Finally, the time for the expected summer holiday came. The village was filled with children who were as chirpy as cricket. While the women were preparing dried cow dung to use it as a fuel in cold winter days, the men were working hard in the fields of steppes under the vigorous sun. Uncle İsa was also in the fields with his son. Sitting under the shadows of a tree for lunch break, he was enjoying the buttermilk that his daughter-in-law had prepared.

– Well son, happy for you!

– What for, father? Anything happened that I don't know of?

– What can it be, my silly son! Thank God, the girls finished school. Now they can help their mother with work. She was doing everything herself. Now my daughter-in-law can rest a little bit.

Looking at his father with sturdy eyes, Dursun said:

– I am not sure about Fadime, but I think Nuran should continue her education, father. What do you think?

– Rubbish! Who inspires you with those advices, I wonder. Have you asked for my opinion? Where will they go to school, they are jut girls. If there were a school in the village, wouldn't we allow them to go there, huh?

– We can send them to Ankara, father.

– With what money will you send them? We can't have enough money even to feed ourselves, let alone sending the girls to Ankara! Nay, have you ever seen that the girls are sent to other regions for school? By jingo, the villagers will stone us. We will be so disgraced that we can't even look at their face.

Dursun answered roughly;

– Let them stone us then, I don't care!!! I want to send Nuran to school, that's it!

Realizing Dursun's determination, Uncle İsa said with a soft voice:

– My dear son! Let's send the boys to school, there is only one year left for them to finish school. I mean we can't send both Nuran and the boys to school. We can't afford it.

– If you had not been too obstinate to allow me to go to Germany for work, I would send all of them to school.

– Oh my! That story of Germany again!

Then Dursun saw Nuran running from the village to the field. Out of breath, she was waving a white envelope in her hand.

– Hope nothing is wrong! Isn't it Nuran coming? What can be the matter? Can it be some bad news?

– No, father! Heaven forbid!

– Son, don't you see, there is an envelope in her hand. Who can send us a letter other than the government? Though I am an old person, I have never received good news from government, not even once.

"My Daddy," said Nuran while hugging his father happily. Disturbed by the reaction of his father, Dursun pushed his daughter away from himself, and said:

– Easy girl, take a breath. What is the reason of your excitement?

– Daddy, I won the teacher's training exam! What's more, I ranked first!

– Good then, way to go!

In fact, he wanted to hug his daughter tightly, and to share her happiness and joy. However, he couldn't do that.

Uncle İsa said angrily:

– Didn't I tell you that I would not receive good news from the state?

– What happened to you, father? Why did you get so much angry?

– We live from hand to mouth, and now you think of sending the girl to school.

Upon hearing her grandfather's words, Nuran began to sob. She said:

– But grandfather, I want to be a teacher.

– Stop that silly crying!

Dursun looked at her crying daughter, and he felt something bleeding in his heart. He felt overwhelmed by the pressure of suppression, quietness, and the words that were on the tip of his tongue but he never dare utter over the long years. At that very moment, he felt himself more desperate and smaller than Nuran. "Darn these traditions," he said himself. Then he thought; "If I behave just like my father, my own children will also experience this grief. The steppes must turn green form now on. Our children must be ahead of us, this chain must be broken."

– Now, listen to me, father. I have never cried out against you. I did whatever you told me to do, thinking that you are my father, you are my elder. You told me not to go to Germany, and I obeyed. You even chose my wife yourself. But it is high time for me to father my own children. You or the villagers, I don't give a rap to whatever you say. My daughter is going to go to school and she will be a teacher. Besides, do you know what Atatürk said? He said "Educate the girls. Our women will be scientists as well. They will be educated on an equal footing with men."

Uncle İsa was so bewildered by his son's words that he was like a bird that got a stone to the head from a sling shot. "What on earth was he talking about?" He was breaking the moral laws by objecting his father. However, looking at his son's eyes and listening to his words, he already realized that he was resolved. If he insisted on, he would have to face the failure. He couldn't take the plunge of losing both his son and his granddaughter. After a few minutes of dismay, he said:

– Alright son, let Nuran go to school. Let her be a teacher, and let the other children go to school too. It was out of my ignorance to object you till today. We are uneducated; we learned nothing other than holding the plough. If the Great Commander said so, it won't be appropriate for us to voice an opposite opinion. If he said it, it must really mean something.

After saying that, he hugged his granddaughter and his son tightly. In this hug, there was the feeling of longing for mother, father and education. There was hunger for water, there was love, there was resentment of the years passed.

Then, tree bodies hugging each other in plains walked under the sun happily towards the school that was at the slope of the village.

Kemal Yalçın / Germany

He was born in Honaz in Denizli in 1952. He had studied at Isparta Gönen primary school. He was graduated from İstanbul Çapa Teacher Training College and the Department of Philosophy at İstanbul University. Between the years 1973-78, he worked as a philosophy teacher at Kırşehir and İstanbul. He went to Germany in 1982, and carried out research at the Department of Philosophy of the University of Bremen, on the subject of "Sheikh Bedreddin and the Development of Philosophical Thought in Turkey." In 1996-97, he taught at the Department of Turkish Instruction of the University of Essen. He has been living in Bochum since 1989, and teaching Turkish as a mother tongue. He has published novels, stories, poems, academic texts and children's books, some of which have been translated into various languages.

Emine Işık

Emine Işık was the Turkish student who wrote the highest number of poems and stories at Heinrigh-Böll-Gesamtschule. I had been her teacher for four years. She started writing poems from the time when she was in 7th grade. Her Turkish was among the best in the class. She would sit in the front of the class, directly across from the teacher's desk, her desk almost touching mine. One day, she gave me a small piece of paper. "Teacher, don't read it here," she said, shyly. "Read it later." I quietly took a glance: it was a poem.

Flowers and People
People are just like flowers
If you water flowers, they grow and bloom
People smile if you love them
If you care for flowers, they get more beautiful
If you care for people they get more beautiful as well
If you place flowers well, they grow fast
People grow fast if they are where they want to be
People are just like flowers.

Emine Işık, 19.12.'93

"What a beautiful poem! Let me read it out loud."

"Teacher, they'll laugh at me..."

"Class, let no one laugh. I would like to read out loud a poem that Emine has written."

I read it out loud.

"Did you write this beautiful poem all by yourself?"

"Yes, teacher."

"Let us applaud Emine Işık who is the writer of this poem!"

That's how Emine began to shed light around her. Every week, every month she was bringing a new poem or a new story that she had written. Two days after "Flowers and People," she quietly put "Strange World" on my desk.

I find this world very strange
People don't say sweet things to each other
They hurt people whom they hate
They don't love children as they would like to
They don't love animals
I find this world very strange.

"Emine, this is a marvellous poem! Class, we are applauding Emine. Emine, ask me for a reward..."

"Thank you teacher. I just write because I feel like it."

The year was 1994. The first Turkish class after Christmas and New Year. She looked straight into my eyes and gave me the following poem that she had written during the last days of 1993. I read it without a word.

Have you seen?
Have you ever seen the sunrise?
People's joyful days
The light of peace in children's eyes
Have you seen these at least once?

Have you ever seen the sunset?
Have you seen people crying for bread?
The fears of children at war time
Have you seen these at least once?

Emine Işık, 28.12.1993

"Emine, this is extremely good! Emine, you'll be a poet if you continue like this!"

"Don't make fun of me, teacher."

A child can not be more unpretentious, more modest.

"Oh please, Emine. Would I ever make fun of your poetry? Your poems make me happy. I see you as a poet."

She completed 7th grade, with a gilded "excellent" grade. At 8th grade, she fell in love with the pop singer Tarkan! She began to write

"Tarkan" on the board, in her notebooks, and on her desk. Then her poems started to flow again. An untitled poem:

Life is sometimes so pitiless
It will burn your heart one day
When it burns the heart, everyone understands
The kind of world this is
......
Sometimes I want to cry
But then I think about the world
I think about the reasons for evil
But I can never find answers.

Emine Işık, 11.12.'94

"Emine, write as much as you can... As you write both you and your poems will get more beautiful. If you permit me, I would like to send your poems to the literary magazine, *Kalem*.

"Oh, teacher, who would ever publish my poems?"

"You keep writing. Someone will surely read them."

I began to send Emine's and other students' pieces to Kalem.

She handed me the first poem of 1995, at the school's dining room. "Teacher, please read this."

If possible, I would bring peace to the world
I want to see people in all countries
Live like brothers and sisters
Most people have such pain in this world
The number of dead is increasing
Now I understand
We should love everyone
People think only of themselves
That's why there is more torture
I'm indignant to pitiless people
No one can make me accept them.

Emine Işık, 17.2.'95

I read it. The poem had some spelling and wording errors.

"Emine, have you eaten?"

"Yes, I have."

"I haven't. If you have time, please sit down. Take something to drink while I eat, and let's talk about this poem."

"Don't you like it, teacher?"

"It could have been better. I think you wrote it a little carelessly."

I ordered a Fanta for Emine. While I ate and she drank, we corrected the mistakes in her poem. I returned her poem.

"Please revise it and bring it back to me. Poetry is not like anything else. It's a serious task. A single letter or comma is important."

"Thank you, teacher."

Two days later, she placed the poem on my desk, silently. With her eyes, she was saying "I've made the corrections, teacher." With my eyes, I answered, "Very good. Good for you!"

In 1995, Emine started to write stories, and left poetry for a while. During summer vacation, she had gone back to Turkey, and the air and sunshine of her country had done her good.

"Teacher, I wrote a story," she smiled. The title: "Foreignness." Two full pages.

"Good, Emine, so you have started to write stories. I'll read it after class."

She had told the story of an anecdote from her trip to Turkey. She had written down her name and the date on top of the page.

Emine Işık, 17.9.'95

"Despite the fact that I was born and grew up in Germany, I'm a stranger, wherever I go in Germany." This is how the story started. She had expressed her sadness at being perceived as a "foreigner" in Germany. The text ended with the following words: *"Tears flowed down my cheeks. If I am a stranger in Turkey too, where am I not a stranger?"* I felt great admiration before my student who had expressed her thoughts and feelings in writing. "This girl will become a writer," I thought.

A week later, she gave me another, four-page-long story. "Yes, this girl will become a writer..." Three months later, another story of five pages. The ability of an 8th grade student born in Germany to write such a story filled me with admiration.

One day, she said "Teacher, I wrote another story. I would like you to put this at the top of the book called *Wild Rose* that we are publishing as the Literature Working Group, or I shall withdraw all my poems and stories in the collection.

"Wait, Emine. Let's be calm. Let's read your story and understand it first, we can then decide where we'll place it."

The students on the Wild Rose committee were all excited to support Emine.

"We read this story, teacher. It's very good."

"... It describes our situation, teacher."

"Let's put it first in the collection, teacher."

"Wait, children. Let me read it please."

"Read it out loud, teacher, please!"

"Alright. Listen now."

Title: "Mother, I only want my Freedom." Date: 30.11.'95

The group of students listened to the three-page-story, without a sound. Emine was crying and Lale was quietly stroking Emine's head.

Hediye asked: "What do you think, teacher? It's very good, isn't it?"

Lale: "Teacher, it is very good! So sad!"

Aynur: "Yes, I think it's very good."

"Teacher, we all agree. Let's place it at the top of the list."

"Wait children. Alright, we may. But we have to be careful. There might be people who don't like this story so much. First, we should change all the names in it. And find a pseudonym for Emine."

Aynur:

"Why, teacher? What's wrong with the story. She is describing us. Why should anyone be upset with it?"

Emine: "No, teacher. I won't change my name. If you insist, we won't publish it."

Hediye: "Teacher, you had said we could write about anything we wanted, freely..."

"Yes, you are right. You can write about anything you wish but I wouldn't want anyone to make any comments that might be hurtful to you..."

Aynur:

"Why, Why? I don't understand."

"Aynur, I want you to be reasonable. This may not cause you any harm but people whose names are mentioned in the story could get upset."

That day, I could not make the group accept that the writer's name and the names of the people in the story should be changed. As the publication committee, we did decide to place the story first in our volume, *Wild Rose.* Two weeks passed. I went back to the subject. "Children, I beg of you, please let's take out some sentences from this story and change some names." The publication committee was adamant: "We might be able to change some names, but not a single sentence can be taken out."

"Alright, children. As you wish."

Mother, I only want my Freedom

On a Sunday, I was about to take my younger brother outside for a walk. As we put on our coats and walked into the hall, I heard a voice. It was Merve's voice: "Mother, don't!" I hated Merve's mother, because just like my own mother, she was making it impossible for Merve to live freely. After walking with my brother, I returned home. Merve's mother Aunty Emine and my mother were commiserating together. Well, it seemed that Merve and I were trying to be like German girls. The truth was that all we wanted was to be able to visit our friends from time to time. Anyway, Aunty Emine said Merve wanted to see me, so my mother sent me to Merve's place. I rang the doorbell, but no one opened the door. Suddenly I was afraid. Merve could have done something crazy. But, five minutes later, my fear abated because Merve opened the door. "Oh, it's you," she said. "I thought it might be someone else so I washed up." She had washed up to wipe the traces of her tears. She said her mother had beaten her. The reason was that Merve had not kneaded the bread dough well!

Our problems were similar. We were both fourteen. We were known at school. Everyone spoke behind our backs. Even in class, we were unable to open our mouths for fear. We both felt unable to find a solution to our problems.

The next day, we were distracted at school. The problem in our heads seemed very bid. After class, our teacher wanted to see us, he asked us why we seemed in such a strange mood. We told him everything. Our teacher suggested us to talk with our families. Merve and I both knew that talking would not help. Merve said "I cannot." I decided to face a talk.

When I got home, my mom and dad were sitting together. I told them everything. As usual, they were interrupting me. I was full of anger towards them. I felt as if I hated them more day by day. My mother was humiliating me before others, by saying "My daughter wants to be like German girls." One day, when she did that, I answered back: "Mother, I'm not trying to be like German girls, but I admire their parents. They allow their children to live as they with. They don't oppress their children, as you do." My mother fell silent.

Two years passed. My parents did not change. We had a bird in the house. My parents never allowed it to leave its cage, just as they never let me leave the house. The bird and I were sad for each other. One day, my little brother had left the cage door open, by mistake, and the bird had flown out to find liberty. After this event, I spoke to my mother again. She seemed to understand a little better, but still, she did not let me get out.

In time, I understood my mother. She was imposing on me the same restrictions that had been imposed on her. Perhaps it was because she was ignorant, or because she was frightened. One evening, she spoke with me: "Look, my daughter. You are sixteen-years-old. Now, you know what's right and what's wrong. After this, you deserve to live more freely, but I'm afraid of one thing. What if, just like that bird we used to have, you never return home?" She embraced me and cried. I hugged her and kissed her. I had tears too. I told my mother she had made many mistakes."

Merve had run away from home. I was happy, not because I was finally offered some freedom, but because I had succeeded in obtaining what I wanted, without bitterness. After that day, my mom, dad and I got along well with each other, but the memory of my pain remains in me. If I ever have a daughter one day, I swear not to restrict her freedom."

Emine Işık, 20.11. 1995

9th year student.

The volume of *Wild Rose* was almost ready for publication. We placed Emine's text on the page after the introduction. Emine's roses were blooming! The Publication Committee was very happy to have placed the story on top...

We printed five hundred copies of *Wild Rose* with the money that the parent-teacher association had collected. We organized a meeting for our book at the conference hall of the Heinrich-Böll Gesamtschule, on Wednesday, June 6, 1996 at 7 o'clock in the evening. The forty students whose poems and stories were in *Wild Rose* were sitting at tables covered with white tablecloth, facing the three hundred guests and parents. One by one, they stepped on the stage to read their own poems and stories.

Fakir Baykurt gave a speech after the readings. He honoured the Publication Committee of *Wild Rose*, by referring to them as "the writers of the future." Since Emine had the highest number of writings in the book, she was the one who presented me a bouquet of flowers in the name of the Publication Committee. She approached the microphone. When she started speaking, her voice was quivering. "I thank our teacher in the name of the Working Group on Turkish Literature, for the time and effort he has contributed to our work." I received the flowers and kissed Emine on both cheeks, with joy and affection.

On this happy day, some family members or relatives of all the writers featured in *Wild Rose* had come to the meeting. My eyes searched for the parents of Emine who had contributed the most, but no one from her family was in the hall! Emine was subdued. Her eyes were not smiling. Clouds of sadness seemed to pass across her face. I tried not to leave her along. Fakir Baykurt said "Bring Emine Işık to me, let me see this jewel of a talent." I introduced them to each other. He honoured Emine, "I really like your poems and stories published in *Kalem,*" he said. Continue to write. A new writer is being born. I congratulate you!"

At the Heinrich Böll School that evening, the *Wild Rose* perfumed the air. At the entrance of the hall, there was a photograph of Heinrich Böll, taken when he received the Nobel Prize for Literature. As I was leaving the room, my eyes met his. It seemed to me that he was pleased with the accomplishments of the writers in *Wild Rose.* It seemed to me that he was smiling. I was so elated that evening that it took me a very long time to get to sleep. It had been no easy task to successfully complete a project that spanned four years. I fell asleep towards morning.

I jumped out of bed with the bitter ring of the telephone. Is this good news or bad news at this time of the morning? "Hello?"

No greeting or introduction. The angry voice of a man was shouting: "What kind of a book is this? What is *Wild Rose?* This is a book exposing family problems! We argued the whole night about it. There are two crazy girls in this book; one of them is mine! What kind of a teacher are you? Did you not read this thing before publishing it?"

A woman started shouting in the background:

"*Wild Rose* huh? May their rose wilt away. This book isn't worth anything. It's a book about family problems..."

Then a familiar voice, Emine's:

"Mom, stop. Don't shout! Mom, don't hit me. Stop!"

The angry father asks me:

"You, the teacher or whatever... Why did you put this text in the book?"

"Good morning. Please don't shout. Who are you? What is happening there? This book is made up of the stories of students..."

"They are not stories! They are true! Look at the title of this one: *Mother, I only want my Freedom.* It reveals our family secrets to the world!"

"Sir, this is a story!"

"Are you going to teach me what a story is? Who is this Aunty Emine, huh? She is revealing our family secrets!"

"Sir, please don't keep shouting. Listen. This book contains stories and poems by the chil..."

"What story? Everything is stated clearly. How will I ever hold my head up now? How will I ever go outside again and face people? I am not sending my daughter to your school anymore. I'll take her to Turkey and leave her there. Look at this. She hates us, does she?"

"Dad, that's not what I said..."

"Shut up. Are you going to teach me something?"

"Sir, please calm down. Why don't you put on some tea. I'll get dressed and come over so we can talk."

"No, don't come here. Don't! What is left to talk about? A proper teacher would not publish every text he reads. He would ask me, as a father, for permission. You publish only if I give you permission. Why did you not phone me to say "your daughter has written something like this?"

"Sir, this is only a story..."

"I'll begin with your story now..."

He slammed the receiver down.

Oh my little writer Emine! Do you see now how things have turned out? Now try to straighten things out if you can... My little Emine is now trapped. It isn't an evil witch or a wicked giant who has cornered her, it's her own parents. Try, if you can, to free her hands to hold a pencil again... We need magic to do that.

My house seemed to close in on me. The street seemed suffocating. I got dressed in a hurry and rushed to school without breakfast. None of the teachers had arrived. The school director, the classroom teacher, the department head – no one. Ah my student whose pencil is flowered and whose hands are capable. Ah my hopes, my labour, and the light of my eyes. Oh my little writer...

When the time flows slowly, it flows slowly...

But the time that flows slowly, finally flowed on. The teachers began to arrive one by one. Each one would ask me: "What's wrong with you?" "Are you ill?" Finally the class teacher arrived, and I told him the whole story. His face changed colour. "Let's wait a little while," he said. "Let the lessons start."

One hour.

Two hours.

My child did not arrive. Obviously she was in trouble.

We phoned her home. No answer.

The classroom teacher explained the situation to the department head, and the department head explained it to the school director. It was a Thursday. No news through the day. That evening I call. No answer. The next morning, I call. No answer. On Friday, at noon, finally it was answered.

"Don't worry teacher, I'll come to school on Monday!"

Through her voice, I could almost see her sad face at the other end of the line. What would you do if you were in my place? Would you have waited for Monday? Or would you have headed straight to her house?

I could not. The damage was done, anyway. I awaited the Monday. Like I said, when you want the time to pass, it does not. Those two days seemed like two years. First thing Monday morning, I have a lesson with Emine's class. I entered. Emine is sitting at her desk. Her head is down. She is not looking at anyone's face. The classroom is icy cold – a damning atmosphere. The students look at me. I look at Emine. Emine looks at the floor. Dark circles under her eyes. Not a sound in the classroom. The room is closing in on us. It seems dark. I'm going to explode. I opened the window.

"Welcome Emine. How are you?"

"......"

"Look at this photo. I had taken it while you were reading on the stage!"

"...."

Emine tore up the photograph, tore it in small pieces and threw it before me!

She covered her face with her hands that used to hold a pencil. She began to sob in the classroom. Emine did not speak at all during that lesson. I did not either. The class did not either. Emine did not speak at all with me during that week. I spoke. But I couldn't say "Emine, speak!" to her.

I waited and waited but she never silently left a poem on my desk again.

I waited for a long time, but she never placed a story on my desk again.

Emine was going to be a writer.

Emine's pen never flowered again. They had turned off Emine's light before the dawn of day.

•••

Ten years passed. One day, Arnold Street Primary School would be testing the level of German children who were about to start grade one. The children had gathered in front of the school with their parents. One of the mothers approached me with a smile.

"Hello teacher. Do you recognize me?"

I looked at her face, at her eyes carefully. With one hand, she was holding the hand of a smiling, dark haired girl.

"Emine, is it you?"

"Yes, teacher. This is my daughter. She'll be your student next year!"

"What is the name of this beautiful girl?"

"Sevgi"(*)

"What a lovely child!"

I stroked Sevgi's head. She was shy. She snuggled up to her mother.

"Emine, tell me. What have you been doing since I last saw you?"

"After completing my basic education, I had occupational training to work at a child-care center. I got married. My husband is an engineer. Thank God, he is an understanding person. We have one child. For two years now, I have been working at a neighborhood where there are many Turkish people."

"I'm so happy to see you again. What else do you do? Do you still write poems and stories?"

(*) Love.

"Teacher, after the beating that night, I never took a pencil in my hand again. I was very angry with my father. After I started working at the child-care center, I re-considered what I had experienced, and I forgave my father and my mother. I became more tolerant towards the world and other people. I don't want my daughter to go through what I had to go through.

"When will you write about what you went through?"

"I'm not ready to write about myself yet. But one day, I'm sure I will."

"I can make the revisions for you."

"I promise, teacher. I'll write!"

Aynur Sommer / Germany

She was born in Bafra, Samsun in 1969. She was graduated from Gazi University, Department of Radio and Television in 1994. Her immigration started when she went to Stuttgart in 1995 and she has been living in Berlin since 1996. She completed her graduate education with thesis on Ancient History in 2005. She writes short stories in Turkish and German for preschool children. She makes music for children. She is married and has two children.

Children of the Clovered House

Our home was very close to the school. It was the first house on the left, across the school. It was yellow whitewashed with no window at the front side. But it had a wooden entrance door large enough to be noticed. As its front side was used as an advertisement wall, it didn't look like a house at all. The four-leaf clover, emblem of a bank, was so suitable with the yellow paint that, anyone who passed by in a minibus, a horse-drawn vehicle, rarely in a tractor or in a truck would certainly have a look at our house. We were even regarded as the children of the clovered house among people. The green paint of our clover would become crisp and crumble in small patches under the sun shining at the front side of our house all day long. It took years before this advertisement, which certainly achieved its aim, disappeared. Although now young girls and boys would go in and out of the house instead of those small children, the nickname the children of the clovered house would pass from one generation to another without any change.

I was the smallest child of the clovered house. When I passed through the barred gate of the school, just thirty footsteps away from the house, with my red thick stripped blue packsack; I was greeted by Nurgül, my best friend. Among the tall and thin, dense silver leafed trees of the school, the children were running about, calling at each other and screaming in their black school uniforms and white collars. A group of girl students were playing hopscotch and similar games. Uncle Mecit, our school's attendant was trying to pass through them and reach stairs of the school. There would always be a cigarette in the mouth of spindly Uncle Mecit. As its smoke would always blow around his face, we didn't know quite well how his laugh or glance was. He was going to ring the bell in five or ten minutes, I should hurry up, I should ask Nurgül how to make multiplication and I should take mine out to show her.

– The papers of my notebook look so beautiful now. Mum used red strand. Which color did yours use to embroider?

Nurgül was gazing at me in astonishment, trying to make sense of my words:

– What did she embroider? What do you mean by strand and color?

Probably Nurgül didn't make her homework or she did it in a different way. The bells would ring soon and the homework would be controlled. I had been all keyed up since the homework was given yesterday; my excitement was increasing gradually, my hands were shaking and my face was growing pale. I was talking about the mathematics homework; we would prepare a paper of multiplication. What was so complicated about it, why was Nurgül so surprised?

– Show me, what these red stranded multiplication operations are!

I took my red stripped blue backpack down from my back, laid it onto my knees and opened it by pushing its buttons which shined like car headlights in the darkness. How could I know that the buttons would shine so, I had never gone out with this backpack in the evening! But I had heard it from dad, these buttons worked like reflectors so the drivers noticed the children in the darkness and the accidents were prevented. But was it also true for here? No of course, in a beautiful, fabulous town with pavements, traffic lights and a broad avenue upon which the cars continuously passed by; in the town of Heike, Thomas and Wolfgang; in that pleasant place with markets smelling of candy, chocolate and chewing gum, in that distant town where there were nicely-dressed dolls in the shop windows.

My red stripped blue bag had given the clue at the very first day; everyone had understood that I had been to that distant town. Maybe dad had taken this bag from that town where he was earning money for us. But no, although it had been three months since the school started I had just showed up. On the first day, when the children realized that I didn't know where to go, they gathered around me and took me to the second class. As I didn't have a desk I was left on foot until the teacher arrived.

How much time I had before Uncle Mecit rang the bell, two or three minutes? With my chest up-and-down because of the rapid beating of my heart; with my shaking hands and knees; with my pale lips, what would I go through today? I took my notebook, right lower corner of which was involute, out of my bag. I was gradually getting closer to the red stranded page; I took my fingertips to my lips so that I could lay the last page back easily. Here was my beautiful page filled with red stranded crosses.

– Here, how does it look like? My mother is good at canvas embroidery. Look, all of them are in the same line. In fact she would even fill another page with yellow strand but I said it was enough. And yours?

Of course my mother had said "The others never wanted me to do something like this, to embroider on a notebook page! You might have misunderstood your teacher." But I had started to put press on her when she got up from the bed. I had slipped needle and thread to her hands saying, "Hurry up; I need to get to the school!" She had also asked my opinion about the color choice "We can embroider with the color you like," she said. As mum lined up the crosses on the paper swishing, she had started to enjoy the work. She even cheered over to me saying "How beautiful the notebook of my little baby became!"

For god's sake! What kind of laugh it was! How could a small girl manage to laugh so loudly? Nurgül had said "Oh, you got it wrong!" and then burst into laughter. She just couldn't stop laughing and also couldn't realize that I was in great panic.

What was the multiplication? I had learnt adding and subtracting in the first class. I was one of the two most successful students. I had learnt to read fluently in a very short time. One day after I read a story in front of the blackboard snuffling, my loving Hatice Teacher filleted a red ribbon on my collar. While I was walking back to my desk blowing my nose with the handkerchief I had taken out of my pocket, I couldn't understand why the ribbon was filleted. After I sat on my desk, I remembered mum watching the children going around with red ribbons on their collars enviously and then I understood that it was a good thing. This year what caused me to misunderstand the multiplication? Why did the multiplication remind me of mum's canvas embroidery?

There was another mathematical operation mentioned in the class: division. While I was enjoying crashing cars and breaking my milk teeth at the fair in that distant town where dad was earning money for us; while licking the ice cream bought by the 1 Mark given by Mr. Kindo, Heike's dad; while playing with the dolls given by the man who had rabbits, the school across our clovered house had already started a new educational season and my friends had learnt division and multiplication operations.

Only her dying energy could stop Nurgül's laughter. In the first seconds of this silence I started to beg Nurgül to write the same things in her notebook again on mine. "How can I write? The bells will ring soon," she said. "Please Nurgül, start at once! Write as much as you can!" I begged. On my insistence she couldn't refuse this. Making it clear that that she would write but it wouldn't look good because she would write quickly; she sank to her knees and started to write skipping two pages following my canvas embroidered page. When the first page was filled with the awkward and crooked numbers of Nurgül, we heard the bell rang. Nurgül could write her one page as two pages in my notebook. Some of the students were still out in the garden.

Nurgül finally said "it's over!" and the reason of my anxiety which had started yesterday changed suddenly. What if the teacher scolded me because of this ugly writing! What if she realized that I was not the one who wrote it! And what if she turned two pages back and saw my canvas embroidered page! Mingling with the students left behind we got through the school door crashing and squeezing each other. This year Hatice Teacher would teach us. Despite her straight lips, she would behave the children well and wouldn't light into anyone. This year I felt some kind of coldness and indifference towards me in her eyes. Maybe because of this, she just couldn't become my dear loving Hatice Teacher anymore.

My little heart would almost skip as a beat, it ached as if it bumped into a rock and then was pushed back; it grew bigger and bigger and it strained my little body. Until it was my turn no one was scolded. The pared stick hanging down in Hatice Teacher's hand hadn't done its work yet. I was cringed with fear at my desk, gazing directly at my notebook, I had prepared myself for the moment Hatice Teacher, who was getting closer to me as she walked through the desks, would come and stand in front of my desk. I wondered if we could break the ice between us if I had given Hatice Teacher the chiffon scarf my mother wrapped up for her. Then maybe she would remember how a successful student I had been last year. I had kept that scarf under the bed and lied to mum saying that I had given it to the teacher. I would secretly take this present out everyday then I would wrap it up again. I really felt under pressure as I couldn't give it to the teacher because of my shyness.

The only reason was not my shyness! My pride also prevented me. As I had started the school late, I was afraid the other children would think that I had done this with the fear of failing the class. The anxiety caused by the chiffon scarf, my old notebook with its dog-eared pages and the fact that I couldn't comprehend the lessons taught during my three months' absence had turned my life into hell.

In fact I should have got onto the train from Munich to Istanbul in September at the latest, not in December. During the three-day and night voyage my lemon yellowed haired, smiling doll was with me. At that time, I wasn't aware that difficult days were lying in front of me. Together with little Aysel, who was one year older than me, we would roam about from one compartment to another and whenever we found a compartment with people snacking something inside we would wait in front of it until they let us in. It wouldn't take much time before we achieved our aim, people would immediately realize us and share their food with us. Why did we do this, because of hunger or with the naughtiness of the childhood?

It was probably because of hunger: dad wasn't successful at feeding the children. He had become as forehanded as to cut down on food and he could easily take the gold medal in the miserliness race. On train, aunties and uncles, whose language we didn't understand, would crown the best parts of our childhood memories by giving us boiled egg, tangerine, chicken and little round breads. Everybody knew these two little hungry mice roaming about in the corridor. A Turkish uncle sitting on the stool near window with Aysel on his lap would call Aysel as "Taffy" and me as "Weedy". To him Aysel was a child as pretty as a picture and I was a bucktoothed, plucked haired, sallow girl. I was amused when he called me "Weedy", and Taffy was cringed with embarrassment when he kissed her on the cheek. Because Aysel had not grown used to such an affection. Dad would never kiss us and mum would only kiss me as I was the smallest child in the house.

The sound of the train sliding on the railway would never change; its beat would never increase or decrease. We could best hear the beat at the joints of the compartments while we were going to the toilet. Although the appearance of the rails made us a little scared, we would stay there for a while trying to memorize this rhythm. We would vamp the train: Ta ta tata, ta ta tata... Let alone three days, even if it took ten days, we would never get tired of or fed up with this voyage. New people would come to the empty cabins; in some compartments there would be drunken people dancing and we, the hungry mice, would find out new things to enjoy ourselves.

We arrived Sirkeci after a voyage like this, we didn't hastily get off the train like the other passengers did; we got up from our seats at a snail's pace and funereally left our cabin. I couldn't take my eyes from the mosaic decoration at the ceiling of Sirkeci Terminal. Such a big and different place it was. While waiting there, dad had bandy words with a short, beady eyed man clasping his hands behind his back. The man was gradually getting hot under the collar and it looked as if he would blow flames out of his nostrils like dragons did. Mum started to scare, I was shaking at the thought of dad being buttered and little Aysel was trying to calm him down. The man was sneakily getting closer to him, loosening his clasped hands. As dad girded at him, luckily the man didn't have to get his fists up for a blow because my aunt's husband came to take us from the station to his house at Fındıkzade.

What about Hatice Teacher? Would she raise her stick up and hit me on the head? Or would she flay my palms? Now she was standing next to me and checking my notebook. It didn't take long, no sooner did she say "Were you in a hurry?" then slapped me in the face and I broke down into tears. When this woman had drawn all her strength on the right hand and slapped her five fingers on my face, I thought half of my face had become paralyzed. It wouldn't hurt so much if I was hit with the stick.

I was sobbing; not to make it clear to anyone I was trying to bear against the tears and I was close to suffocation. This hand was the hand filleting red ribbon on me last year, wasn't it? The tears ran down on my notebook like big hail stones and I could feel my cheek tingling. There was no sound in the class; no moving pen, no swishing paper; only the deep sigh of a girl whose dull eyes were the clear evidence of the malnutrition was heard. My pride wasn't even worth the sponge eraser cleaning the chalk marks on the board. The hardworking child from our neighborhood, now sitting at the front desk, would certainly tell this event at home and my laziness would be heard among the whole neighborhood.

We had had a perfect holiday in the small town of that distant place. Our stomach would sometimes enjoy the creamy strawberry tart the maid of the homeowner gave us, sometimes the half bruised half edible seedless grape left at the bottom of the cases, the candies of Wolfgang and ice cream of Heikel; but it would most often grumble with hunger.

In the town called Aldingen by the Neckar River, we had learnt how to ride bicycles and a few words of German; we had taken the motherhood role when we found two black kittens, one white and one black, in the workplace of dad's chief, that old man with felt hat and cigar. The maid of the homeowner would not only feed us she would also give a feast to our kittens with broth. In this place where we could find many colorful childhood adventures; one event made us realize that the time was passing by: every morning Heike was sent off to school with a kiss from her grandma who had always been distant to us. The expression on Heike's face seemed to be saying "My school started, I don't have time to play with you." She wouldn't even condescend to look at our faces. We had also missed the school and with this secret desire we were watching our summer friend as she, with her reflector backpack, was going to learn new things step by step. Heike's grandmother would pass by shaking her head as she couldn't understand why the children at our age were not sent to school; and in a few minutes she would offer us Turkish delight we had given them as present.

They were so careful about the unfamiliar food! They would give our rice pudding back after sniffing; they wouldn't touch our cakes but they wouldn't toss it out either. Instead they would offer them to us again. Although I was about seven and Aysel was eight, in the registry we were twins at the age of four. As told, the reason behind dad's efforts to make us seem at a different age; to register his smallest two children as dead at first and then as twins, was related to coming to Germany. It wasn't easy to start school here with this registry problem. Anyway it wouldn't be worth it because we would arrive in Turkey in Christmas at the latest.

In the last few days of the school year which was like a nightmare because of the three months' of delay about which my family didn't really care, in the add-on clammy room of the clovered house, I took the chiffon scarf I had kept at the bottom of bed. How I wish I could give this wrapped up Germany gift to my teacher! In a quick moment when the students are going out for a break and when the teacher gets out of her chair to go to the teachers' room, I wish I could at one fell swoop say "Here you are, this is my mother's gift for you" and then get rid of this trouble! But it didn't' happen, didn't, didn't!

And the day for the distribution of the school reports finally came. The teacher gave me my report and I gave her the gift waiting at home for months. There was no need to look for a silent corner to cry, I had passed class with a *fair* degree. The last year's *excellent* grade remained as an issue of past.

This year the chickens of the house with the clover were again shared among the neighbors. Woods were nailed on the windows of the house and a big lock was hung on the door. The sons were entrusted to the uncle and big daughter to the grandparents. I was flying to that fabulous German town by the river with Aysel. I wondered instead of homework which handicraft I would bring to the third class, which I would start with three months' delay, this year. I'm welcomed to Aldingen again for a school year which will turn into hell and in the name of the children of the clovered house, some of whom drops out of school and some of whose school life becomes topsy-turvy, I'm welcomed!

Sabahattin Şen / Germany

He was born in Antakya in 1947. He had art training at İstanbul Teacher's College and İstanbul Educational Institute. He worked as an art teacher at several high schools, and at İstanbul Atatürk Educational Institute. He went to Germany in 1980, and studied Graphics and Printing Techniques at the Köln School for Art. He participated in many one-person and group exhibitions in Turkey and Germany since 1978. He painted six murals at Köln, Düsseldorf and Solingen. Some of his works were bought for the collections of German museums.

At present, he lives in Köln and continues to produce art. His most recent exhibition was at the İstanbul Atatürk Kultural Center on April 12, 2007, on the occasion of the 10th Anniversary of the "Brother City" agreement between Köln and İstanbul.

Look at the Moonlight

He had no idea what it was that had wrapped his head up against all influences from the outside. On his body, that seemed to know nothing better than resisting difficulties, there was a weight whose origin was unknown. Was it the weight of the melancholy filled to the brim, the joys of the past, the iceberg on which hopes glided away, or those dug out by the drill of evil that wanted to rid him all emotions? Perhaps he was like a small boat left on the shore after the tide. He was walking towards the Rein River, carrying on his subconscious struggle. If anyone were to ask him where he was going, he would have to stop and think before answering. He was aware that his steps were taking him towards a familiar direction, as though his feet knew the way. He wanted to sit down somewhere, to lean his elbows on his knees, and to take the weight of his head between his hands. He had not yet reached the light of consciousness. If only he could be freed of himself for a moment, the solution might appear before him.

It had been a while since the day had moved forward from the first light. The man didn't pay attention to the lights that seemed to cover the entire city with gauze. He was living the ebb and flow of short slices of time that joined each other. Perhaps there had been no morning and no evening. He was still far from the purity of the distinction between events. He was deeply engrossed in the confusion of the adornment of colour and colourlessness. At this place, life felt hemmed in, as though enclosed by a dome.

In his consciousness, his days since his arrival to this country were scattered like the snow on hills, scattered by the wind. Everything flew away to the point of illness, all become variegated and one. The roots of developments entangled with details, were being disentangled one by one as though they were giving new shoots in the midst of the murkiness, after all these decades. Despite all that time, he could now catch a clearer view of what he had lived. The lines of objects seemed to gain volume and substance as the darkness was wiped away. The tide had spread all over him. It was as if he was counting each step at points where he was stuck.

He had two bags. One of them was full of books because in his point of view, there was no life without books. He considered art and culture as superior expressions of human beings. In the second bag, he had put the rest of his books and his clothes. He also had a shoulder bag that he carried everywhere, all the time. He had the sudden impression of trying to squeeze in the books, notebooks and coloured pencils that he hadn't found space elsewhere. It was not easy to leave the past behind. Who knows, perhaps the past never leaves us behind. Is that so even if we don't want to leave it behind? He couldn't tell.

For decades he had studied. From all those years, the habits of teaching had left their traces. Who would want to leave everything behind and remain all alone? But the greatest support for life was in his books. In his papers on which he might be able to transfer the words in his head, his pens that challenged his destiny.

When he had arrived to join his uncle who had immigrated to Germany to turn the impoverishment of his village into prosperity, these were all his belongings. His uncle had frowned upon seeing the books. "With these, you cannot work in this country. You cannot earn money. You should be able to work. Here, you won't have time to read even one sheet of writing. It was for nothing that you carried all these things. This is a place to work like a donkey – you should know this..." He had said. His uncle was trying to convince him that the three or five years spent in Germany had taught him much. "... the sawdust that remains from a brain sawn up into debris..." thought the man.

His uncle could not see any meaning in any concept other than starting to work immediately and making money. He was explaining to his nephew what was what, with a pretentious language as if he were one of those who owned money and property. He seemed to learn no other way of expressing himself. He obviously wanted to spite the circumstances of his life that had prevented him from getting an education. He was now trying to cover up the sense of deprivation that he had expressed when he used to say: "No one was able to send us to school. My brother is sending you to school, but let's see what will become of you..." It was impossible not to sense the self-inflation in his manner as if he might have become someone important if only he had studied. That was why he was bristling before anyone who was educated. He wanted to believe that time had strengthened his own position in the face of a bag full of books. He was convinced that the material gains he had made until then were more valuable than anything else.

"Wherever you are, you are a human being first. You should know that. Don't forget me and others like me who have worked for so long to improve the lot of people. Sure, we have studies, we have learned many things and we are continuing to learn. We have to learn a great deal more. We have not forgotten your troubles or the pain of others. We have studied so people would be freed of working like donkeys," he answered to his uncle. These were words that poured out on their own. For someone who had worked for years to teach students, it was important not to compromise his principles, whatever the cost. He understood once again that he was not afraid of anything. Upon hearing his words, his uncle seemed to be frozen.

"I didn't mean you. You are an educated person. Of course you know what you want to do. I just meant that's how things are here. Don't misunderstand me from the first day. We don't understand books and things. Of course we are human, too. We have experienced many things. We have learned things. We are not donkeys," his uncle tried to save the situation.

He had stepped back so his nephew would not say "from day one, he refused to help." It was obvious that he was calculating how he would get even one day with his nephew who had forced him to take a step back.

Before this uncle had left the country for Germany, he used to come to town every summer to work, and stay at their house. He would eat with the family, get his clothes washed and ironed, without spending a cent of what he was earning. That's how his father had extended a hand to his brother. Perhaps it was in return for that kindness that he didn't mind letting his nephew stay at his home now. But whichever way you looked at it, the discord between uncle and nephew was opening up abyss after abyss between the two.

In an environment where the daily subject of conversation was the cost of fuel, time seemed to die away. You could stand only for so long the dead end conversations where nothing mattered other than how many pieces of real estate were bought, how many pieces of land were going to be bought, and how the most recent models of which cars would appear showier. Even a single day in such an environment, where endless ugliness would be displayed in a competition to impress and deceive, was a huge loss that could be equal to thousands of days.

Whoever had more money and more belongings, he was assumed to have the last say on anything, and he believed that he was able to defeat everyone else. The others, in the meanwhile, would swirl in the whirlwind of imagining how they would get even with him. Let someone catch a weak point! People were ready to call the police and experience the exalted victory of sending someone back home. Thus, they were shooting their own countrymen from behind. How could things deteriorate so fast? What was it that reduced these people, who had come so far away from their homelands to earn their bread, to a state of alienation from their own identities?

One day, his uncle said "Your father did not want to stay in the home of his closest friend in the village once. When I asked him why, he said 'the roof of his house is made of earth. When I lie down at night, earth drops down on my face. I can't sleep.' You father forgot his own village after moving to town. He began to look down on his village."

His answer was like a slap on his uncle's face: "And you, uncle, you left the village and came all the way to Germany. You are no longer sleeping in the earth-roofed house of your own village either. When you build a house at the village, you don't build it with a roof of earth. You had a bathroom built inside. You bought all your bedding here, in Germany, to take back. What is there to criticize about a person's wish to understand something that's better and more beautiful?" The uncle was speechless. He had blushed.

"Nephew, it's become impossible to tell you anything..."

As the days passed, the tension between them had increased. The uncle was not helping his defiant nephew in any way, to teach him a lesson. The nephew was not surprised at this – he knew it would be like this. He could see his uncle's resentment for having been deprived of an education and his need for revenge. The nephew needed to frustrate this need. He made this primitive weapon backfire, by not asking his uncle for anything.

This country had produced some very negative changes in the humane impulses of these people. They were no longer sure of their own identities, and the identities of others. They knew they were working like donkeys, and had become the slaves of a feeling that they had to take it out on other people. They seemed to be looking for someone to sink their teeth into, and to empty the poison that had collected in their fangs. Some of them had turned to alcohol.

In Germany, another world of prosperity and culture existed - but they were unaware of this. That world, which they did not know, consisted of the world of books, culture, arts and humanistic values. The nephew had quickly found a place for himself in that world, whose existence his uncle did not even know. The uncle was bewildered at the turn of events.

The man walking towards the Rhen extracted himself from the whirlpool of thousands of lost, unwritten stories of lost lives. The memories that surfaced by association, he had to abandon to their own waves.

He had witnessed an event that proved that despite all kinds of erosion, good hearts had not disappeared. Hope found the strength to show that it existed all the time and everywhere with human beings.

When he had left his uncle, a neighbor had said: "You have nothing now. I bought you some pots and pans. I also want to give you this bedding, just so that your early days will be more comfortable." He remembered her face now.

There are people among the lost souls, whose souls seem to be embroidered finely, like lace, and despite all, the pearl necklace of their humanness does not break.

His uncle did not offer him even a piece of straw. If he had, the nephew would have refused.

At this point, the thoughts of the man jumped forward, he thought of the days when he had brought his wife and children to this country.

After a short while, the state of his soul turned into the flow of a stream that's ashamed of its own winding path. That winding path represented the escapes and the inabilities to escape. When all his thoughts became entangled in the soup of memory, he realized that he was tired. At that moment, the sea had turned murky. He lifted his head to look ahead. The large river glistened as though it were coated with silver. He thought he was on a road lighted with silver. First, he understood that the past was far away. The weight of unattached thoughts continued to lie over his being. The waves of those thoughts seemed to carry him towards a shore. Then a crossing from one shore to another.

He had been forced to bring his wife here, at a time when difficulties were still unresolved.

Her father's oppression, beatings and put downs had turned her childhood into a black hell. She had attempted to free herself by fleeing to a residential school, and started a more regular life with a job and marriage.

He had heard her lament her bitter past so frequently that he avoided any word of behaviour that might hurt her anew. Since his own nature was the direct opposite of the father, he could not do her any harm even if he wanted to. No one could say that he expected a great deal from his wife. He did not force her to anything, and did not allow her to force him either. He never wanted her to get too tired at her job. She had worked half-time for half pay. He did not want her to feel like an outsider here. He did everything he could to provide living conditions that were no lower than those in Turkey.

One day, when he came home exhausted as usual after stopping at a bookstore to buy some books and magazines, his wife said:

"Oh yes. Once again, you've spent a lot of money on books. If you spend so much on books, you have to work like a donkey. Look at what everyone else has bought already! Look at all that they have accomplished. Even your uncle who is worth no more than a penny owns so much. And what about you? And what do you own? You're stuck on culture, books, art. To this day, you could not buy a single home or car with those things. With your few pennies of earnings, we're worse off than a shepherd on the hills somewhere. You keep saying we can't afford this, we can't afford that but you keep buying books. Do you want us to bring our cracked wheat and our dried beans from Turkey to economize? You think you're somebody because you got an education. Take a look at those labourers who come to Germany to earn a buck. They all have properties. And what have we got? They work like donkeys! What kind of a man are you? What kind of a husband are you?"

He suddenly thought "Look at this educated person. He shows off with his books but I guess I gave her a value she never deserved." He was re-living the anger he had felt on that day. It was as if a red hot iron was burning his nerve ends. He was furious with himself for having put up with her all that time. But how he hated this return to the memories of the past...

What had he done to deserve these words? He had studied, received his Ph.D., and was his wife whom he had supported through the years who had uttered those words. She had not even blinked throughout her speech. What a horrible moment it was! How could his uncle's words and the words of someone who had been educated overlap in that way?

When had all that happened? How many months, how many years had passed? Without measuring the time, he realized that those words were said on the day when he left his wife. It was such an iceberg that had confronted him after fifteen years in Germany. Now that mountain was far away.

His wife was someone who would emphasize the equality of men and women, at every opportunity. Especially when there were other people present, she loved to show her emancipation, but things were different when they were alone.

"You are a man and I'm a woman. You know I cannot do everything because my physical strength won't let me. I can't run in every direction. You are stronger in many ways. You like to sun in several directions at once. You are also thoughtful enough not to leave everything to me. I like that about you. I will try to do what I can. You know that you earn more than me. I would work more if I could but believe me; I would be exhausted if I did. I couldn't bear it. I would no longer have the strength to look after the children. No one but you can understand me. We are a couple that understands each other well. I know you are a good person who would never be unkind to me. Thank you. You do not wear me out."

After all those years, the man had turned to stone with the cruel words uttered after facing so many difficulties together. Nothing in his head could help him get over this crushing disappointment. Were there explosions in the universe that annihilated planets? The man could not even move.

It took all his strength to say: "What's important is not to feel like a horse or a donkey." He walked out without taking anything and never returned. He never walked back towards the past that remained on his back with all its weight.

At a moment when darkness seemed to fill him, he sat on a bank near the river. He placed his hands on both sides of his head, and wanted to remain in that position for a while. Suddenly he noticed the pizza in his hands. It was still warm. He realized that he was hungry and took a bite. Across from him a full moon was hanging in the sky as it had done for millions of years, transforming the river into a silver path. Suddenly he had such an appetite that the thought he would never get enough to eat. The light of the full moon was giving him strength, renewing the traces of his existence with its light.

"Thank you for existing," he whispered to the moonlight. "Thanks to this bright light, life will continue without erasing this day from my heart. Live starts anew everywhere, everyday, for those who recognize its value..."

Mehmet Bedri Kanok / Germany

He was born in Kapaklıkaya Village, Sivas in 1933. He worked at Turkish Sea Forces as non-commissioned officer for thirteen years. In 1965 when the compulsory service was over, he left the army and went to Germany. He had worked as a worker and got retired.

In 1984 his humor story book named *Memleket İpi;* in 1992 his satire book named *Köyün Delisi* were published. His play *Biz Almanya'dayken* was performed on Bursa State Theatre in 1985 and was published among the publications of Ministry of Culture and Tourism in 1997. He was awarded the championship award in play competition of Çaba Theatre in 1990 and in the composition competition on the topic of 75th Year of Our Republic organized by TRT and Association of Kemalist Thought in 1998. He also wrote articles in local newspapers and journals.

He stills lives in Elmshorn city.

Meister Pott

Arif Duman was dismissed from the job.

– How much compensation you received? I asked.

– None, he said.

– Why is it? I asked.

– I was dismissed due to insult, he said. No compensation is given when you are dismissed due to insult to The Chef.

– So couldn't you find anyone else to insult? I said.

– Don't say so, he said. You have found the very man to ask this!

"Now listen, he said. Do you remember the gossip that the companies would dismiss some of their workers? In our company, even the young Germans took some measures in their own way to save their own skins ... We, Turks in the company, are just four people. One of us hasn't been around for a few months as he had a serious operation. The other one has six children and his wife doesn't work; so leave him out... Only two of us, Cafer and I are left. He tried to hide it from me but I heard anyway... Cafer went to the office to butter-up them. He shifted the date of his annual leave from August to November saying he wants to make room for our German friends. What's more, he cancelled his unpaid-holiday. I had to do something different. I couldn't find anything else except trying to make them think that I love my job very much. So I started to be the last one to leave the workplace after the bells rang in the evenings and I arrived in the workplace, about half an hour before the start time in the mornings and waited at the gate of the company. While I was going back and forth with my hands in my pockets to warm up in the cold weather; I was also writing poems regarding our situation..."

Some tell their beads, and some others love cigarette,
Some play the saz(1) artily like a minstrel.

(1) A string musical instrument.

Gastarbeiter we are called, it is our destiny,
Some gab here and there, some known with their pedantry.
Some put all money in a small card table,
Immediately lose it all but anyway it doesn't matter.
Some just enjoy the day, trying to take some time off
Some refrain from their boss and pull string for a day-off.
Some have grandchildren, some are still all alone
Some came to retiring age; they don't really care eat all.
Ads are in the newspaper, some are looking for a spouse
Some are selling paste for all, serving for every purpose.
Some tell good fortune, spreading joy and delight,
Some prepare amulets to bring them all good luck.
Some worries himself to death what if I die here,
And immediately would add just bury me to my land.
Some are jobless though, some are workers here,
Some are doctors and dentists; some are sellers here.

Some spurted suddenly and became the employer
This is how they left behind the nickname Gastarbeiter.
Some sink his teeth in to trade,
No fellow or friend is left.
Different habits they each have,
Each one is on its own way.
How angry they become, time comes for the praise
Only common point is that: love for Turkey prevails...

"Soon their word came true. The alarm signs started to ring in the company. Two old German men at the charge of the warehouse were called from the office upstairs. Their checkout procedures were quickly completed in three hours and both of them were given the gate. When it was my turn, I went upstairs thinking that I should bargain well and mulct as much money as possible. I followed one of the girls in the office and she took me into the room of big chef and left the door open behind her. In fact she didn't need to close it, because there was nothing to hide now."

"Big Chef greeted me as if I was a guest. He stood up and shook hands with me. He even showed me a place to sit. And then,

– How many years have you been working with us Herr Duman? He asked.

– It's been three and a half years Herr Cheff, I said.

– I've always wanted to talk to you for these three and a half years, at last it's possible, he said.

– I wonder so much what kind of a country is yours. You know, everyone in your country is dying for coming to Germany; please don't take it personal, I'm just asking out of curiosity."

He was my chef, he was also older than me; maybe he could say such things. Even so, my left eye started to twitch upon these words.

– Our country is a good one, I said. Our people are coming here to work.

– And don't you have any big company in your country; why do you exert all your strength to come to Germany? Don't take it personal; I'm asking just out of curiosity, he repeated. "

Besides my left eye, the fingers of my left hand also started to twitch on my knees and I forgot all about the compensation or hard bargain;

– We have many big companies (like Moç-Holding, like Tabancı-Holding, and like Ahlaz–Holding…), it is as easy as duck soup for them to buy people as you and put them in their jacket pockets.

– Oh, really! I didn't know this, he said. People just mention corruption, drugs, traffic jam, pick pocketing while talking about your country. In short they say there's nothing there except these. No, mine is only out of curiosity; just don't take it personal!"

I wish it wouldn't be personal! But this man sitting on the cheff chair was not judging me, but my country. What can I do, I didn't create myself, did I? Against his judgement, a devil came and sat in my brain as an advocate. We were just trying to come to a decision about how to start. Should we start to with this man himself or with his family members? Then Big Chef said:

– Another thing is that... I just wonder why your women always walk behind their husbands.

– Because any woman who doesn't go behind her husband will follow another man, I said.

– Oh! Herr Duman, you are a bit offensive, aren't you? He said.

At that moment the devil advocate sent me a sign. I let all the good (!) words I learnt during my nine years in Germany go out of my mount one after another. I also remember banging my fists on the table two or three times. Things stirred up; there was some bustling. Four people dragged me out of the office; they took me in front of the company gate and left there. One of them also whispered in my ear: 'Go away from here or we will call the police.'"

"The following day a post was sent to the house. We saw that besides my check-out document there was also a letter enclosed. "If you make an objection to this check-out document, we will claim an action for damages against you with the charge of insult both to the company and the company owner," was written on it. I asked some people for advice, they said you had better not say anything, just sign it.

"Oh my dear Arif, they have obviously set a snare for you not to pay for the check-out compensation. So far you have boasted about being on the watch in vain! How I wish I were in your place at that time, your Chef would see who trapped whom! It is needless to get angry. When he mentions bribery you will say those accepting bribe today will certainly pay it tomorrow; justice will be served sooner or later. When he mentions poverty you will say a country without the poor won't house the rich either. When he ask you why your women walk behind their husbands, you will say they don't walk behind us, we, the men, walk in front of them.

In this way at least we learnt another trap of the employers. Maybe we will also come face to face with this fashion of dismissal some day. Just in case; I had better be prepared for it, I won't be late for work anymore, I won't eat anything with garlic at the lunch break, and I won't secretly smoke at work. Also I had better leave the habit of trolling.

Months passed by, nobody was dismissed in our company. Overtime work also started. But I didn't get this possibility out of my mind even for a single day. In the meantime, I ran into chef only for once. At that time he didn't talk about dismissal or anything of the kind. But he made a sore face and said:

– Did you smoke again by the machines?

– If I smoked, may I choke death on it! I said.

– So you didn't?

– May I have a hell of it, I didn't! I said.

– You did, you had certainly smoked, he murmured. Tell me about it! You smoke and say you didn't. The best thing to do is: from now on you won't work overtime. You can sit at home and smoke as much as you like during that two hours. Nobody can interrupt or disturb you. But if you quit smoking for good, then inform me and start working overtime again.

Look at this! What's he talking about? Even my father couldn't make me give up smoking. I won't quit smoking! Give that overtime work to your dad!

It is my habit, whenever I get the blues in Germany; I take the saz in my hand and play it in a silent place. Soon I feel as if I were reborn from my ashes.

The summer and the autumn,
Slopes, hills and mountains,
Eyes as black as coal and
Reproachers of the lovers.

My Turkey is like a song,
Hello to all, hello to all!
In the shape of a yearning,
Everywhere I go following.

Drums and the shrill pipe,
When they roll and blare,
Merry-making arrangements,
Everyone dancing halay(2).

My Turkey is like a song,
Hello to all, hello to all!
In the shape of a yearning,
Everywhere I go following.

(2) Anatolian folk dance.

Halva[3] and the date palm
And trays of burma[4]
Turkish bath and basin
Partridge and crane fly

My Turkey is like a song,
Hello to all, hello to all!
In the shape of a bird flapping
Everywhere I go following.

Bunches of red roses
Hands picking up flowers
Strings of the my bağlama[5]
Singing songs in circles

My Turkey is like a song,
Hello to all, hello to all!
In the shape of a yearning,
Everywhere I go following.

It was Monday. I placed an armful of cartoon into the machine. By the time, I bent over to open another package; Meister Pot came under my nose. "Chef wants to see you," he said. What the hell chef wanted to see me with no reason at all. For months, I neither finished up the work early, nor did I secretly smoke at work, or insult any German. Still the man wants to see me! It but me no buts meant check out. As I was passing by Mesiter Pott on my way to the office, I said "Did you also spy to the chef how many times I blew my nose in front of the machines?" I said so because I came down with the flu for a few days last month and I had no other guilt other than that.

I pulled my socks up in the elevator. I thought of the chef's probable words and sorted them in my mind. What could this man say frowning over his glasses?" He might say, your customs are like skimmers; it brings good profit for those with Mercedes and BMW"; or "those who have pulled with insurance institution can make themselves put on

---

(3) A sweetmeat like dessert mostly made with samolina or flour.

(4) Some kind of sweet.

(5) Some kind of stringed instrument.

salary"; or perhaps he might say "your government has changed 55 times in 75 years." There were lots of possibilities, he might say whatever he wanted. No matter what he would, I wasn't like Arif; every question had an answer!

When I knocked on the door and walked inside, the Chef left the newspaper aside and thrusted his hand out. "Please come here Herr Çelik," he said. "Oh, I'm so surprised! Yours is such a different country and we weren't even aware of it!" Aha! I thought inside, the game is starting; he thought he would heat me up not to pay compensation. You couldn't deceive me!

(Oh my dear; don't ever lose control of the event and be trapped like Arif! But no! With God's help, I didn't have any suspicion. As I said before, I had been already prepared. I was just like a student who had the exam questions in advance. Whichever side of Turkey the man would backbite, he would be snubbed immediately and would sit on his bottom.)

After he shook hands with me grabbed the newspaper left aside,

– Look Herr Çelik, he said, what the newspaper says."

("Look what the newspaper, he says!" Tell it to the marines!)

– Turkey is a country of heaven; Turks are very hardworking, creative and they are masters in trade.

(Hah ha! You can't deceive me this way; I'm not like Arif.)

– Each year the country achives a growth of seven per cent. The unemployment rate is almost half of that in Germany.

(Read, read... I'm not so fool as to believe in your stories.)

– Literacy rate is over eighty-two per cent and it has a dynamic population, the population is younger than that of any other country.

(Look at this! They don't implement family planning policy he means to say. Burst out with anger, we don't!)

– The country is like a beautiful bird confined in a cage.

(Talk properly. You're the bird-brained.)

– Development endeavours are breathtaking throughout the country.

(Okey, stop it, we know it anyway.)

– Turkey is on the verge of an economic burst.

(You burst up! I just won't get angry!)

Chef read me newspaper this way for about five-ten minutes. Of course I didn't sit there without doing anything. Although I looked as meek as a lamp, I answered back to every question inside in the way he deserved. At last he took off his glasses and left the newspaper aside.

– Herr Çelik, these are not my words but an economist's words, he said.

What could I say? I just stood there staring. Chef,

– And he is a universally known American professor of economics, he went on. Just for the sake of conversation, I said:

– So he is an American professor of economics.

But I was thinking to myself "Plague on it! He doesn't say Greece will burst up instead he says Turkey will burst up. It doesn't matter, we will build it up again but shame on America; we have regarded it as our friend so far.

At that moment Chef leaned back and said,

– Turkey is a perfect country. Here we wait for months so that the season will change from winter to summer. However in your country, it's not like that. When you are sick of snow and storm you can get on the bus and you'll be in Antalya in the twinkling of an eye! Then it is warm and sunny. Just think about it, we have to wait for six months before summer comes and in your country it's just six hours away!

– You're right, I said.

(Gosh! Now he plays other tricks on me. Do your damnedest! I'm not like Arif.)

– There was a family at the neighborhood, he said. "We were not very close but the previous day we had a couple of words. To my surprise, they told they were going to your country for holiday every year.

I quietly said:

– It's just normal. Everybody goes to our country!

– And they're not just going for holiday Herr Çelik; they said they'd buy a house there!

– They do the right thing. The houses are cheap there!

– Not only the houses, they say everything is cheap there; fruits, vegetables, flowers... People can go to swim during ten months; the sea is so clean and clear!

(Hey, that's true! Maybe the chef may also speak correctly at times. Well done!)

– Especially the neighbors! They said they were held in high esteem; the neighbors took them to everywhere they went, friendly conversations, nice presents, high respect... There's no other nation on earth like Turks, they said.

(Hey! Is it the normal way for someone wishing to annoy me to talk? Maybe we're a bit unfair!)

Chef pushed the button on the box at the table and said to the girls:

– Two coffee please, and I became all smiles.

– My chef, let's buy a house for you in Antalya, I said.

He leaned towards me and talked in whispers:

– I wouldn't stay here for a single day if I didn't have to deal with this company work Herr Çelik, he said.

I spontaneously said:

– I agree with you!

I said this; at the same time I was really moved. He had told his secret only to me putting his trust in me. And on the other hand I blamed him with no reason at all. And my face turned red with embarrassment. Arif's chef and my chef were as different as chalk and cheese. Mine was what I called chef! Just because I didn't smoke by the machines and never came to work late he would almost embrace me. People like him never hurt you, never!

Chef stayed thoughtful for a while. Then he said,

– I'll do that! I'll settle in Antalya. Wait until my son grows up a little, two years later maybe... You'll see I'll do that! I'll just leave the company to my son and go there. We'll find a place close to the sea in Antalya, maybe with a small garden... Plants, flowers, pruning and watering... We will spend all day in the garden this way and directly go to the sea in the afternoon. How amazing!

Chef told his future plans for so vividly that I escaped a good wish through my lips:

– Well! Enjoy your house! I said.

– Death is for people but leading a happy life is also for people. Earn little, spend little but live humanely.

– Of course, I said. Much money never brings happiness!

– That's right, he nodded. Where does the human being live well? He can lead a happy life in a place where water is good, weather is good, neighborhood is good, in a place where there are plenty of flowers and plants!.. A place like this is already created for us by God: This place is Turkey! He said.

Upon this, bending over the table towards me he said:

– Why does a person leave a place like Turkey and come here, Herr Çelik?

(Wov! You're the master Chef!)

What could I say,

– I made a mistake my Chef, I said.

– I mean, while there is such a beautiful country like heaven out there, anyone who spends his time here must be crazy... He said.

– Or he may be crack brained! I added.

– So why don't you put the signature on this! He said and put a paper in front of me.

I put the signature on it!

And I've been looking for a job since that day.

Wait until I get my hand on Arif! Although he said no compensation was paid to those dismissed with insult to Chef, he concealed from me that not even a single penny is paid to those leaving the job with their content. He says he is sharp witted in vain! If one day I run into him, you'll see how I'll make fun of him. Until that day I had better play my saz.

Hello to you my homeland your hills and mountains,
Roses on your soil and leaves on the flowers
Your urban citizens and the smiling faces,
Of course the good words of the welcoming citizens
Your spring and summer, autumn and the winter,

And nesting in my land, the western marsh harrier,
The chair of the officer and even his sullen face,
Who does his work not staring at our face.
Married or single; engaged or divorced
All God's creatures taking or refusing bribe.
    Hello to my hometown, my longing disappeared,
    Just got off the plane, your German Turk is coming!

They send us abroad saying 'go and work there'
And look forward to the money coming as exchange
The pilot's voice heard from the speaker,
And the hostess saying fasten your seatbelts here,
Your airfield is too small for the above floating planes,
Tourists come from Germany, Italia and Netherlands
Your women in chadors and some are in mini-skirts
Some still call German Turk instead of citizen,
The wanabe police writing fine even at the first second
Of my arrival unblushingly assuming cowboy posture
The urban tradesmen demanding ten instead of five
They are from abroad, they say, we don't mercy that's right!
Those abiding by the rules, stopping by the red light,
And those who just don't care and recklessly speed up,
The babies and the youth even the old men with stick
Both the smiling faces and the beetle browned ones,
    Gospel to you my homeland, my longing disappeared
    Just got off the plane, your German Turk is coming!

My renter in Turkey not paying for ten months,
Deepening my grief as I was living abroad.
Whoever hears and believes Germany is the heaven
And even assumes that it is paved with Euro.
The illegal workers deported at border
And returning back here their dreams disappeared.
Whoever comes to rant and rave, visiting us now and then
And forgets all about it after coming to homeland.
Who invests capital believing in the sweet words
Bankrupting all the money German Turk has ever earned
Spending all I earned trying hard with might and main
And then pertly saying "is it all that you can pay?"

Nylon shopping bags whether full or empty
Fresh vegetables and ripe fruits filling in them easily,
Those who pass Bosphorus twice a day for work
And whoever uses ten vehicles to arrive at work
Those who are tired of life whatever the reason is
And others full with joy, sparkling like angels, true it is.
Right wing or left wing, partial or impartial,
In short all creatures breathing in this air,
    Hello to my hometown, my longing disappeared,
    Just got off the plane, your German Turk is coming!

Esin Kutlu Demirlioğlu / USA

She was born in Bursa in 1955. She was graduated from İstanbul Erenköy Girls High School, and then from İstanbul Technical University Senior Electricity Engineering Department. She went to America for taking doctorate education in 1980. After completing the doctoral program in Stanford University; she acted as research engineer and specialist scientist within research and development departments of various organizations. She still lives in California and works as a manager in the R & D department of an electronic company. She is married and has two sons.

This story is translated by Duygu Demirlioğlu.

My Home

Among my siblings I am the one who resembles my father the most. Not only do my eyes and eyebrows and my hooked nose look like his, but I am like him in so many other ways, from my gestures and the shape my face takes when speaking to the way I step on the outside edge of my right foot when walking.

When I was six or seven, we were living in Bursa. My parents sent me to the convenience store to buy something, I cannot remember what. My mind was not on what I was sent to buy, but on the umbrella-shaped chocolate bars that hung from a string in the store. While I was drooling over the chocolates, a young man, much taller than I, approached me. He bent down and said, "Hello. Are you the daughter of Teacher Selim? You look very much like him!"

"Yes," I said.

"Can you take us to your house? We are his students. We have a few questions we need to ask him."

I became aware of four or five other young men waiting outside. "All right," I said, "our house is just up the street."

I led my father's students uphill along our narrow cobblestone street adorned on both sides with bay windows, and arrived at the house we rented just across from the school. My father welcomed the students into the house, and sent me to help my mother prepare something to offer them. I was very happy and very proud: I looked like my father, and I was grown up enough to guide visitors to our house.

Those days and our house are now in the distant past. It has already been over twenty years since I finished my university studies and settled in California. For twenty years I have been living in this land at the other corner of the world, in this land that is almost twenty-four hours away by plane, in this land where night and day are upside down from the way they are in Turkey. I am middle-aged now; I live with my husband

and two sons in a small city populated by many immigrants. Most of our neighbors and coworkers are Asians. At my age and among all these Asians, who can tell that I look like my father? And who cares? Perhaps this is why I have not embraced this place as my home for twenty years. Perhaps it is the lack of the cries of street vendors selling familiar snacks; perhaps it is the want of tea gardens around; I don't know. True, my sister and my brother, and their families, live close by us. True, I have a couple of very good Turkish friends. Sometimes when I am shopping I hear Turkish spoken; I walk over and exclaim, "Are you Turkish too?" and introduce myself. But we rarely get further; growing closer and becoming friends takes time and energy. Here no one has time for new friendships.

Today is one of those crazy days when I have to do ten things at once. My little son is sick, and my husband is teaching a night class on the other side of San Francisco Bay. I have left work early; I have taken my older son home and my younger son to the doctor. Now I am on my way to the pharmacy near our house. When I say near, I do not mean I can walk there in five minutes as I used to when I was growing up in Bursa; no, it takes seven or eight minutes to drive there. My son and I are in my large American car on a street that is about four times wider than the cobblestone pathway in Bursa. The street is empty and quiet. I turn on the radio. A woman commentator's voice fills the car.

"It is time to go back home," she says, " wherever you have come from, go home. It is getting so crowded here that we have to line up at checkout stands; the queues are too long; we have to wait a long time to pay. Whether you are from Iowa or India, it is time to go back home." I cannot believe my ears. I look out the car window. I only see two Asian people walking in the street. Perhaps it is crowded where this lady commentator lives; who knows? She says, " Our resources are getting scarce; we are running short of water and electricity." Curiosity overcomes me. Where does she live? She calls out to immigrants, "The East Bay used to be a pleasant and quiet place. There were not this many cars, such large houses and gigantic stores. Schools were not this crowded. Twenty years ago we used to walk to school. Now we cannot leave our children alone in the streets; our neighborhoods are no longer safe. Go back home, take your children, take your cars, and go home. Leave us in peace."

Do we belong in this group that she is trying to chase out? I find out she lives in the same town where my husband works everyday. Perhaps congestion is a relative concept; what seems thinly populated to me may seem overcrowded to her. But what about the shortages of water and electricity? I was here twenty years ago. My husband came to America when he was seventeen. Except just after the Loma Prieta earthquake of '89, we never totally ran out of water and electricity. I do not understand who this person is to chase out others, to send them home. Doesn't she realize that, even if all the people who immigrated in the last twenty years go back home, the past life that she is dreaming of will never return?

In daily life we do not notice that time and space change; we think that they are standing still, motionless and eternal. Both, however, keep spiraling in their orbits. Our memories are formed at the intersection points of these orbits; that is why they are unique. Sometimes space and time intersect so close to the location of a past event that we think we are re-living a particular memory; we reminisce. This happens so rarely that most people never get a chance to re-live the past in a lifetime. Of those individuals who do get this chance some feel the bliss of past days, some its fears, and some its sorrows. Perhaps the commentator does not know this. She wants us to go back – where, to what time? As time flies, not a single spot in this whirling world of ours remains untouched. Every time I visit Bursa on vacation, I think change comes there too often, dwells there too much, and touches far too many things, needlessly and carelessly. In Bursa, for example, an ugly automatic teller machine now sits where my little convenience store used to be. A little farther down, the corner once occupied by Orhan's toasted sandwich stand is now taken over by a luxury-clothing store. The street that winds up the hill is still the old narrow cobblestone pathway, but now cars pass constantly; one has to draw aside to the edges of the street or walk up leaning on the walls of houses. Time has forgotten to put in a one-way sign and to train people to heed this directive: if two cars come from opposite directions, one has to go backward into a side street to let the other pass. The bathhouse at the bottom of the hill has somehow been spared as a historic building, and my old school still stands. Time has seen fit to replace everything else, all the houses with bay windows that once decorated the sides of this street, with cold, high piles of concrete. Looking up from the street, the sky appears like a stream meandering between the tops of these concrete heaps. In the old days, houses had yards, gardens, balconies or terraces. Now these weirdly shaped structures called apartments, which look more like shelters or prisons, have small holes they call windows. Where do they hang out their laundry to dry? Perhaps Time was in a hurry, or forgot about this detail. Of course, the inhabitants of these cold concrete buildings generally own cars and are far more concerned about parking spaces for their cars. Time must have forgotten about this matter as well.

As children we used to skip rope, play hide-and-seek, hopscotch and soccer in the cul-de-sac behind our house. Sometimes we chiseled nine-stones or backgammon boards in the ground. Now cars reign supreme in this tiny cul-de-sac. I cannot tell where all the children have gone. From our old house I cannot hear children's voices; when I walk in the street I see no children. There is no longer any room for them here. If by chance they start a soccer game someone sticks his head out of a window and scolds them just in case they damage the cars. The children hang down their heads and shuffle homeward. Where do they play? Cars have also invaded the park behind the square where Atatürk's statue stands – the park with the little fishpond and benches. It appears that the adults' addiction to cars has overridden their dear children's need to play. The main street where horse carriages used to roam is now covered with columns of cars and buses, a flood of humans overflowing the sidewalks. I come here to visit my family; I live in the old Bursa of my memories. I have no way of catching Time and rebuking him, "Stop for a moment. Look at what you have wrought!" or asking him, "How can I bring my children back here?" I am still not at ease with calling our house in California our home, but my sons know it as their home, at least for now.

I arrive at the pharmacy and park my car in one of the many spaces in front. The radio and the commentator's voice shut off. Taking my son by the hand, I walk in the drugstore. My son has an ear infection, but his energy is undiminished. As we walk toward the back of the store to have the prescription filled he wants to stop and look at the toys and the candy on the shelves. "Not now, we don't have time, and we don't need anything from here," I say, and drag him along. There are few customers in the drugstore; I do not have to wait in line; I hand over the prescription. We have to wait for twenty minutes to pick up the medicine. My son has squatted down with his hands between his knees; he is either planning to do a headstand or jump like a frog. I scold him in Turkish: "Get your hands off the floor. Quick, stand up!" He doesn't listen to me or heed me, but starts leapfrogging. I walk toward him to get him to stand up. A balding man, a little taller and older than I, looks intently at me as if he is trying to identify me. I ignore him and concentrate on catching my son, who realizes I am moving toward him and hops away. The man who was gazing at me stops me, saying in Turkish, "Excuse me." I wait for him to follow with, "Are you Turkish?" Instead, he continues, "Are you the daughter of Teacher Selim?" I freeze. I am stunned. I stare blankly at his face, unsure about where I am in time and place. I don't remember saying yes. Perhaps the astonishment in my face gives him the answer. I am speechless. He goes on:

"I am one of your father's first students. He was my math teacher in the city of Malatya. When he taught us he wasn't even married yet. He got very angry with me because I wanted to be a pilot and went to the Air Force Academy. Is he alive? How is he? Does he ever come here? I would very much like to see my teacher again. Please let me know when he next comes. You will let me know, won't you? Here is my card; my address and my phone number are on it. My wife and I live very near here; if you have the time, we would very much like to have you visit us. When you talk to your father please give him my sincere regards. Good day to you." And he walks away.

I am still frozen in place. I cannot believe what I have just heard. A thought forms in my mind: "I still look like my father." A man who has never seen me before recognized me, in my middle age, because I resemble my father. Then it suddenly occurs to me: I am one of those rare people who are granted a chance to re-live the past. A short while ago I witnessed the intersection of time and space at a point very close to a memory in my past. I am so lucky to experience the joy of that past memory once again. Then my son awakens me from my reverie. Realizing that I am no longer chasing him, he has come back and is now tugging at my skirt. "Mom, they are calling you," he says. I remember that we are here to have his prescription filled.

I return home, impatiently waiting for the evening to arrive. First I call my sister and brother, and savor telling them what happened at the drugstore today. I want to call my father, but it is too early in the morning in Turkey now; I should not wake him up. I try to pass the time by preparing dinner for my sons and helping them with their homework, but the hours go by so slowly. My mind is not on what I am doing, but on the events of this afternoon. I wait with difficulty until it is seven in the morning in Bursa, and then press the keys on the phone. My mother comes on the line.

"I hope all is well, my dear," she says, "Is anything the matter? Nothing wrong, I trust?"

"No, mommy," I reply, "I just wanted to tell my father about something that happened today."

"All is well, my dear?" says my father.

"Daddy, guess whom I met today?"

"How shall I know if you don't tell me?"

"He was a student of yours in Malatya."

"I had so many students that it is hard to remember them all now."

"His name is Mehmet Gökçen."

"Oh, him? He lives there? He was a very bright and very obstinate student. He had a wonderful mind for mathematics, but was obsessed with going to the Air Force Academy and becoming a pilot. He became one, too. Is he still flying?"

"He is retired, Daddy; he is now a systems programmer for the municipal government."

"Well, it seems he is still working on things closely related to mathematics and logic."

"He sent you his regards."

"Very good. I am glad to hear that. If you see him again or call him give him my thanks and my greetings. Are all of you well?"

"Yes, Daddy, we are well. Little Selim is a little sick, but you can never tell by looking at him that anything is wrong. Very much like his grandpa, wouldn't you say?"

"Don't pay any attention to your aunt's tales; I was very well behaved as a child. Anyway, take good care of my little grandson; give him his medicines on time. Why haven't you put him to bed yet? It is very late where you live and I can still hear his voice in the background."

My father remembers not only his student, but also the argument between them. I have to force my son, who says, "I will wait for Dad," into bed. I hold his hand and sit beside his bed. I am not sleepy at all. Shadows cast by the dim light of the night lamp dance on the walls of the room. The silhouette of the little girl of six or seven that I left in Bursa takes shape among the shadowy figures. She is next to her father, who is sitting on the sofa, talking and smiling. She is smiling too. Then the father and the daughter hug each other tightly. The little girl, contented and at peace in her home full of love, is happy and proud that she resembles her father.

I hear the screen door opening and a key turning in the lock. It must be my husband coming home. The little girl walks toward me; draws closer. I know she has fused into me by the vibrant happiness and peace that envelops me. My husband embraces me wordlessly. Our hands caress our son's head and hands. Only our older son's clicking on his computer keyboard disrupts the silence. I remember the words of the commentator on the radio. "Never mind that woman," I tell myself. She is imprisoned in a narrow world of her own making. Regardless of what she says, when time and space came together today, they found me here in my home. Happy and at peace in my own home. This is my HOME; I am not going anywhere.

Ruhi Türkyılmaz / Germany

He was born in Sürmene, Trabzon in 1940. He was a student of Arif Nihat Asya and Cahit Külebi at the Ankara Gazi High School. He started to write during his school years. While he was a writer for the school newspaper, he worked as student press representative on the day when Atatürk's body was transferred to his Tomb in Ankara (Anıtkabir). He was graduated from the Faculty of Law in Ankara. He worked as a teacher and as a bank official. He has been living in Leverkusen since 1966, and is the president of an Association for Literature and Culture.

The Chestnut for Pain

A person can't see his own life. From time to time, he complained of a tasteless, monotonous life. To him, an uneventful life was equivalent to an unlived life. He longed for the fulfillment of his dreams in faraway lands, in geographic locations that were natural and colorful. He got tired of slowness. Those around him were astonished at his energy as a child. As he grew up, he made a habit of seeking adventure.

When he's a student, his collar and the tie, that he sometimes had to wear, restricted his freedom. He felt like a person who belonged to wild nature, and who could not accommodate himself to boundaries of cities. He was startled by dominance. He had an unpredictable, obstinate personality.

He sometimes found himself in birdsongs and sometimes in a head capable of thought. A bird meant flight. Rain clouds would pierce his eyes during long flights. A fast life meant becoming worn out early. He had chased his youth in trains and in air planes. In foreign lands, he was now loosing speed.

These days, his cap was always on his head, and his notepad was always in his hands. When he heard the call of his birthplace, he wished he could become a bird. Sometimes, his suitcase couldn't cover all of his clothes prepared for the month of vacation. When he found himself alone, he would take a stroll down his childhood lane. Sometimes, his eyes on the clouds, he shivered on the way back from these strolls.

His wings were worn out from flying towards the east and the west. In the air plane seat, working on a crossword puzzle, his eyes would close by themselves. The dreams above clouds of cotton would be as strong as the morning sleep, and the wings were not always soft. He wanted wings fast enough to catch up to the modern age. Those wings were also values that needed to grow freely from day to day as symbols of civilization, and they would pass across horizons of global geography...

He was anxious. According to his principles, a loss of speed meant a loss of blood for the age of enlightenment. Just when he needed wings, a weight would press down on his knees. When he heart was fast and the knees slow, disharmony might begin. He trusted his own ability to live at peace with what he had. He would resist as much as he could against the pressure to exchange the new with the old, the beautiful with the ugly, and youth with old age.

His home was at a place of natural beauty where the green gave pleasure and the flowers filled the world with colors; where birdsong was mixed with the song of flowing water. Almost everyday, he walked through a park filled with flowers to buy his newspaper. On his way back, he would settle on one of the banks placed at different spots in the park, to read his paper.

Could flowers hear good news? Why did their buds open slowly, and their colors get brighter? Or were all objects seen more beautiful, when looked through a kind heart? It is known that bad news and evil are against all loving hearts and the nature of beauty.

Whenever the Wild Blue read sad news, rain clouds moved in the sky and the wind folded up pages of his newspaper. Sometimes bad news darkened both his eyes and the sky, and a storm started, sending the person off to seek shelter. Then rain would begin to spill from the clouds.

In the park, Wild Blue usually sat under a horse chestnut. As the wind shook the branches, large ripe chestnuts would drop down. One day, he picked up the largest chestnut that had fallen down near him. Like a child, he caressed, mollycoddled and spoke to it: "Come my childhood friend. The remedy to my stomach pains. The hair color of lovely women comes from you; you would crown their beauty... You used to move from pocket to pocket in the village where Wild Blue was born. When people who had stomach pain would scratch you skin off with their teeth and licked your fruit, you would bring relief to their pain... No pain could withstand your poison. You were the medication available to people whose clothes were torn, whose pockets were empty, in villages where there were no doctors, my chestnut that cures pain..."

It was a September night... Strong winds had blown the ocean's anger towards the shores of the continent. Tiles had flown off from the roofs of houses, and trees had broken in parks and forests. That night, sirens had never stopped. The streets of the city were full of cleaners early in the morning. The road along the park through which Wild Blue went to buy his newspaper was closed off. He approached with curiosity and was saddened by what he saw.

The trunk of the giant horse chestnut that was the ancient tree in the park was split into two, the two halves collapsed on the lawn in death pangs. Only a natural disaster could tear down the powerful tree. A single trunk from the roots had grown on two large branches, almost like two trees joined together. It had branches parallel to the ground, and wide leaves. Carrying its majestic load, it had not been able to resist the storm that carried off everything in its way; the twin branches had split completely and fell on the ground to die...

That day, the road of park in front of the Doktorsburg villa was also closed. It was as if all the trees in the area, whether small or large, had forgotten their own wounds and pains, and were grieving for the giant chestnut. Some had branches that were peeled, some had their clothes torn off, some had broken arms, but they all seemed to accept their own pain, in the face of the great pain of their kindred.

The storm had ended but the sirens had not.

When business machines and construction cranes arrived at the park, their warning lights were blinking. The trees waved their leaves to greet them. Tree doctors and nature lovers, first prepared their reports. Although wounded tree was split in two, its roots were still adhered to each other. Rescuers started their urgent work, after marking the boundaries of the accident with red tape. First they cut the wounded and broken branches on the ground to reduce burden of the injured trunk. They smeared a healing cream of green color on the open wounds by using a special kind of brush. Cranes approached the split trunk gently. Connecting ropes shouldn't damage the bark. Trunks were wrapped with bandages made of sponge and covered the wounds with oval lids. Then the crane lifted the half of the giant tree, up to a standing position again.

The same process was repeated for the second half of the trunk. While the large ropes were being untied, construction cranes were replaced with other machines straightening the wounded tree up. They continued to serve the tree, like doctors who might hold the arms of a wounded person to keep him up, and to help him return to life.

Now, it was time for the life saving operation which was the most important stage. It was one life that had split into two. Returning to life would only be possible with joining tissues that had been torn apart. Tree doctors used their special instruments with great care. They brought together the tissues that were torn asunder, until the warmth of a kiss spread through the living cells of the tree. Tied by adjusted metal belts, it stood up in a way that made it look different from its earlier appearance. Its resurrection was a miracle, yet the pain of the giant tree had not ended yet.

It was time for fine tuning. If the wounds got wet, it would die. If they received air, they might rot. The wounded tissues of the tree that had suffered the wrath of storm were protected with medication and with bandages. The giant's loss of blood was prevented. A belt was tied around its waist. Water proof clothes were put on it, and suddenly, nature and the weather seemed to change. During surgery, white clouds had watched over the giant tree. After the procedure, the clouds parted and in the warmth of sunshine, pains abated.

Wild Blue was recording his observations in his memory, and was flying on the wings of his imagination. The wounds of the great tree, whose fruit was known to heal human pains at his homeland, were wrapped by people on this land to help the giant tree return to life.

Many years passed. The giant tree in the park returned to life without any trace of the wounds it had suffered.

It was a sunny spring day. Once again, Wild Blue sat under the wings of the magnificent giant. The trees and flowers in the park were full of blooms. Winged creatures drawn to the perfume in the air were visiting the flowers. They were alighting on some flowers long enough to smell them, and on others, they remained long enough for a kiss.

It was a day when nature had put all its beauty on display to win the admiration of all living things. The Green Wind who was sitting on another bank, and who was the Wild Blue's friend, was painting an image of the solidarity between nature and human beings. This time, it was the poetry of return that was passing through the Wild Blue's mind. He was embroidering flowers and weaving his designs with original symbols.

He was a yellowing branch broken from a tree across the border. Even if typhoons caused him to blow far away from home, he would not remain distant from himself for long. Sooner or later, he would fly back on white wings, to the place where chestnut for pain was passed from pocket to pocket. So, he would find comfort in the silence of his own return.

The chestnut that healed pain in his pocket should be his closest ally. He should be planted in deep ground with that chestnut... Maybe, near the house where he was born, a new shoot with broad leaves would grow one day. Those who had this chestnut in their pockets would never suffer. Perhaps they would not even die...

Filiz Dosdoğru / Austria

She was born in İstanbul in 1980. After completing the primary and secondary school education in İstanbul, she settled in Austria in 1997. After having a German course in Innsbruck University for two years, in 2001 she started her education in the same University in Pedagogy Department. Her studentship still continues and she is working in a store as a salesperson.

A Girl on the Butterfly Hill

No longer would stoves be lighted, and chimneys be cleaned. No longer would chestnuts be grilled, and corns be barbecued. Afrodit would not perform various tricks to attract attention. Hot soups would not be eaten; loud and jovial laughs would not be heard even from the edge of the street. Above all, the guests… They would not come anymore as well.

She would miss Sevim, her elder sister most. Who would tell her fortunes, who will teach her sewing? What about the husband of Sister Sevim, Uncle Sefa... While he was watching matches of Galatasaray or the national team, Ayşegül and she were watching him from a corner; they used to laugh giggly and imitate him stealthily. No longer would she see Uncle Sefa either…

They would not play card games with a feeling of drowsiness, after putting their cushions beside the stove. While her aunt was washing the dishes, Ayşegül and she would not go for drying the dishes together, and they would not infuriate her aunt by various devilments. They would not go to picnics or to seaside in the extremely hot days of summer all together, they would not fly kites in the wilderness, they would not build sand burgs on the coasts.

Ceren was alone in the house in a warm evening. One could feel spring thoroughly. She was thinking of that big eight years she stayed in her aunt's house and plenty of small and big memories awake in her mind. She had a bittersweet joy in her heart. She was broken off with her mom eight years ago. When her mom entrusted her to her aunt and went to Germany, her world turned black, she thought she was alone in life and she felt herself useless. But her aunt did not separate her from Ayşegül as far as she could go, growth her conscientiously and always behaved kindly and attentively to her. She didn't only love her, but also respected her. Her aunt was a self-denying, dignified and altruistic lady.

Above all Ayşegül... Ayşegül was more than her aunt's daughter, but she was as if her own sister. They would live in each other's pockets and they would not even know the meaning of resentment. Although they sometimes argued and be jealous about each other, feeling of sisterhood was always outweighed and they made it up easily. Their friends, tastes, the school they went, even the food they had were the same. Only their outlooks were not rather similar. Ceren's hair was very long and was in chestnut color. She had an athletic body and she was quite tall. That's why, she had always sat at the back desks during her primary school. In case, Ayşegül was a brownish and petit girl. She was always cheerful and tried to make the others laugh. She didn't have an attractive beauty, but she was really warmhearted. She was quite grouchy, so her mother especially took care of her nutrition and secretly she was feeling sorry about her daughter's being skinny. But she was in peace with herself and was an extremely self-satisfied girl. She wasn't eating unless she feels hungry, and made her mum exasperate.

Although Ceren had lost her real family, she felt the warmness of a family in her aunt's house. She felt the smelling of a mother when she hold her aunt, and felt the love to a sister with Ayşegül. Her uncle died many years ago. She never met him.

In addition, she had an elder brother, Murat. He was her aunt's son. His existence gave Ceren an invisible sense of trust. She was so inured to this feeling that she usually even didn't recognize it. Her brother, Murat was a gentleman who was always serious, and who never talked a lot, but always told the right things. He had a buffet in one of thoroughfares of the town. In the evening, with his arrival, a fresh breath had been felt in the house for hours.

She thought that, from now on, they would not be walking in the coolness of evening all together, they would not be buying cornets from the iceman at the seaside; they would not be melting their ice creams on their tongues at the beach park where gull pipes and human waves melded together.

Furthermore, could she ever forget Afrodit? Afrodit was the coquettish cat of the house. It had a so pretty look with its snow-white and cottony hair, and with its blue and shining eyes! It was a very funny pet. Ceren had many enjoyable memories about it. Afrodit was always riding herd on Ceren and Ayşegül in the house. While they were talking together, it was listening to them with full attention, and it was making its presence felt by meowing occasionally. When they concentrated on it, it was having the pleasure of being attractive by tricks it made, and it was climbing on the sofas and it was annoying at feet of them. Sometimes Ayşegül got angry with her as a joke, and she berated her for not letting them alone. Afrodit was usually taking defense with this, and was going to kitchen to look for the aunt. Two buds were getting sad at last for Afrodit, although they were enjoying this at the beginning. They were holding it again, and they were making peace with Afrodit by cuddling its hair.

Ever after, it was time for Ceren to go to Germany, to her family. Her mother said to her on the phone that she wanted her to go on her education in Germany, that she couldn't bear missing her and that she would take her soon as possible. The acerbity in her heart made her sober. She was sheltered in her memories and was removing the dust on every single piece of them.

Actually she missed her family a lot. Every year, they were coming on holidays even if it was for a few weeks. Although her parents were divorced when Ceren was a kid, they didn't have a known hostility. Ceren saw them in different times. She had a superficial relation with her mother and father. She never had a strong liking for them with whom she always had a limited relation. Did she feel resentful to them? She could not give a definite answer to this question. In some days, she become very sensitive, and withdrew behind her shelter. On those times, she felt so. She was silently rebelling against being abandoned by them. But this did not take so long, and she usually tried to understand them. Maybe, there was no other choice...

As Ceren fully adapted herself to the apartness and achieved to feel the warmness of a family with them, she kept down their yearning; and she got used to live in her aunt's house. Her mother's invitation to Germany, which was received when she didn't have any hope, was bowled Ceren over. It was really shocking for Ayşegül. She restrained herself for not crying and she had begged Ceren not to go for many days. But when Ceren had gone back of her emotions, and tried to think logically, she knew that on one side, she wanted to go. At least she had to go for a short time, she had to join her mother who was lost many years ago, and she had to follow the paths of her lost passions and her orphan aloneness. Of course, education was another important reason. May be she would have better advantages in Germany. She would go to the schools she'd like, and she might have the occupation she wanted. Moreover she loved adventures since she realized herself. A world of unknowns was waiting for her to get in, with wide open doors. She was curious about this new world, and she wants to get into it at all costs.

Although having an acerbity inside, because of the dilemma between going and staying, she should go. She was aware that new and bitter longings would surrender her heart. Maybe, new disappointments would break her heart, would make her depressed. But, in any case, life was pulling her in, and was blanketing her. Life was generous. Ceren should be learning to breathe in its goodness while being shaken in its narrow paths. She had to go…

•••

Pomegranate and peach trees in the garden had already started to indicate rising of spring. Sparrows had perched on willows, and were cheeping as if they were spiting each other. Ceren awoke early in the morning. It was Monday, so the garbage truck was arrived and it was crowded on the street. On Monday mornings, the street was always incredibly crowded, and all people were on a rush. Ceren, in front of window, with her hands on her face and her arms on table, was thinking. Her look was dead although she was looking at the street, because she was used to the view. She was at the bosom of utterly different ideas. This should have been a special day. She had a secret corner. She hadn't been there for a long time, and she had a desire to be there. She decided to go before Ayşegül's awakening. If she woke up, then she would definitely follow her, and hence the magic she could live in her secret corner wouldn't be experienced.

That was the year she just started school. She was separated from her mum a short while ago and being an orphan was burning her out. All children were going to school from the asphalt road and they were all hand in hand. In the beginning, Ceren also went after them. But then, she discovered an earth road. The road was narrow, because it was not used a lot. It was surrounded with wild pasture and weed, and it was not so pleasant to walk through. In such a day, Ceren went for scouting the rest of that road. She could find nothing but endless grass, a hill and several trees. She got so happy for finding such a forgotten hidden corner in the newly developing town. In time, she started to leave home early and went to her secret corner.

A day, she climbed up to the hill and she could not believe in her eyes. There were butterflies on that hill with many colorful and extraordinary figures. She was admired by the beauty of butterflies. Some of them were perching on a stone, and some on a flower. Ceren was running behind them, was catching them, was looking their beauty and then she was letting them go. How beautiful creatures were the butterflies, with their vivacious colors and varieties of figures on their wings. They were flying around Ceren, and this was as if they were spiting to her for their ability to fly. She found peace on that hill and wished to be a butterfly. If she had been a butterfly, she would have flied wherever she wished. No one could interlope to her. A butterfly, on her own and free... She opened her arms to both sides, and let herself run down the hill. While the intensity of running was increasing, she was feeling as if she was flying which made her cheery.

A day her teacher told about butterflies. She listened to her teacher with full attention, and she couldn't believe what she heard. Teacher told that butterflies lived only for a couple of days, and died afterwards. Ceren was shocked. How could those petit and innocent creatures die without having the pleasure of their freedom? She could not decide if she still wanted to be butterfly, or not. A couple of days wouldn't be satisfying for her. If she tried to fly to her mom, perhaps her life wouldn't be enough. Even if it was enough, her mom could only love her butterfly for a short time, and then she could lose her forever. Ceren was astonished with the nature. It was not as it should be... She was still going to the secret corner, and was climbing on the Butterfly Hill. But she was not satisfied as before, she did not run behind them for catching. She watched butterflies with a bittersweet sadness. They were happy with themselves. They were flying and resting themselves. Then, dying only hurt Ceren.

One day she decided to guide Ayşegül, Can who was Sevim sister's son and some friends from their neighborhood to there. She was walking in front of them as if she had a secret treasure to be shown, and the other children were following Ceren. What they saw at the end of the road was not so cheering. Although they might have deplored to Ceren, they tried to dissimulate this. But it was still a place they could go when they wanted to play far away from the crowd. Ceren led them till the top of the hill. With haughtiness as if saying "Here is my treasure." When they saw the butterflies, they all got very happy, started to run behind them with screams and started to catch them. Ceren was scared and got angry with them: "They will die in a short time in any case, why you are killing them even earlier" she shouted, and got sorry for bringing them here. Her eyes were full. Children were affected by the fact that butterflies would die soon. Ceren told them what she knew with a childish wisdom and they listened to her silently and with all their attention.

Sometimes they went to the secret corner, and played games only they knew. Ceren did never forget. She discovered a game. There was a short tree that she did not know its kind. She was climbing on it, was dropping her hair down the tree and was becoming Rapunzel. And Can was her lover, trying to climb on the tree through her hair. It was hurting her when Can pulling her hair. Their game turned to be a torture and they always fought with each other as a result. Then they found the easier way. Can was not pulling her hair, but was climbing on the tree. And when climbing, he was touching her hair to keep the real sense. Ayşegül was watching them from a distance, and was getting angry while watching. She started to grow her hair after that game, but until she could have long hair, they have grown up, and stopped playing the "Rapunzel Game".

One day, they were on the way back from Butterfly Hill after they had played there. There was a couple at an isolated corner of Butterfly Hill, they were quite older, and they were spooning and making jokes to each other. They watched the lovers for a while, and then they made fun of them, and laughed at them. Lovers ran after them. But when they arrived to the neighborhood, they didn't do anything but walked away after staring at them with menacing glances. How guilty Ceren felt, and how afraid she was for a while... In fact, probably the lovers couldn't manage to recognize Ceren.

Ceren climbed to the Butterfly Hill that day, and thought of the things she had exprienced. For some days, she was cleaning all the dust in her mind and reminding her memories for getting rid of her longing. Did the memories get old? Of course they did. She forced herself a lot, but did not remember some details. Some of her memories were like old pages which got blenched and lost their edges. She loved her blenched memories, and was enlightening them with a shadowy light. Butterfly Hill was a shelter for Ceren when she was a child. And butterflies were her beautiful friends who never made her sad or tired and who never questioned her. She was coveting them. She wished to have wings like them. It didn't matter if she was as beautiful as them, only the wings were enough. She could be to very close to her mom. Whenever she wanted, she could say "Mom, love me", and she could cuddle her mom, could hold her with full power. She couldn't say "Aunt, love me too" to her aunt. Ayşegül was her daughter. Of course, she loved her most! Every time her aunt caressed her, she had her mother's smell in her nose. She embraced her aunt more and more.

Whenever Ceren dreamed about being a butterfly, at first she got enthused in her dreams, and she was unable to contain herself. Then she got sad and gloomy. Because she felt that her wings were broken. She noted down to her diary that "When I was growing, my frustration was also growing with me. Whenever I see a butterfly, I feel a pang of sorrow in my heart; and looked for my mum."

Now, she had wings. She would fly to her mom. Maybe, it was too late. Maybe, she was not as young as to say "Mom, hold me." But she would fly... For the last time, she breathed the fresh air of Butterfly Hill. For the last time, she ran behind the butterflies with a childish acrimony. For the last time, she stared to every single part of her secret corner... She didn't fill her pockets with so many dreams; but she didn't burn them all either. She either did not get ashamed with her frustration which had many roots deep inside; she didn't push it back. Ceren wore her wings with self-confidence. She was ready to fly and felt semi-enthusiastic, semi-yearner and semi-depressed...

Sabriye Cemboluk / Germany

She was born in İstanbul in 1948. She was graduated from Bolu Teacher's College. She lived in several Anatolian cities with her husband. After spending a year in Switzerland in 1975, she settled in Germany in 1976. For twenty years, she had worked as a freelance journalist. One of her stories, was broadcasted on Deutsche Welle radio. She is the first Turkish writer whose story was included in the Luftküsse Anthology, in 2003.
She has a published collection of stories entitled *Kahraman ve Gölgesi (The Hero and His Shadow),* and two other collections entitled *Pompeii'de Hüzün (Melancholy in Pompeii)* and *Sınır Ötesi Öyküler (Stories from Across the Border).* Her piece of theatre entitled *Hayal Haritası (The Map of Dreams)* was staged at Theatre Dialogue in Karlsruhe. She lives in Karlsruhe, and is the mother of four children.

Angels Have Taken Her Away

– Look, I know you'll get angry. But there is a saying 'two naked people are suitable to a *hamam*(*)'. Obviously it wasn't said for nothing. We have hosted an engagement party and got into debt up to our necks. What have we got for the wedding? Let's give this up. Let's call off the engagement. My family cannot afford a wedding..."

The young girl looked at her fiancée with incredulous eyes. Was it herself who had been dreaming of marriage for three years, and who had defied everyone around her? An educated girl. An uneducated boy. What's more, he is quite short. She will not even be able to wear high-heeled shoes. No problem. Love is more important than everything else.

She is educated, but her family is poor. It was the neighbors and the relatives who paid for her schooling. So what if she has finished school? What has changed? She is still the daughter of woodcutter Osman. Which one of the wealthy families would want her? Is it a shame to be a car repairman? So what if I have not had an education? I did try high school. It was my luck to run into harsh teachers. They never gave me good grades! So I tried to earn a living. Like most boys who start to work early, I started to flirt early. I had a single hobby: to run after girls! I was not falling in love or anything. I was changing girlfriends like I might change socks. This continued even after I returned from doing my military service. Until about three years ago. Until the day, Gülnar, the daughter of woodcutter Osman brought a bowl of soup to my mother who was sick. It was as if I were seeing the girl for the first time. How had I not noticed such a beautiful girl right in front of my nose? While she stood before me, I had entertained my soul with all kinds of girls. What stupidity!

Gülnar had finished school and started working. She was supporting her family, and she was always dressed cleanly and well. Yes. This was

---

(*) Turkish bath.

the girl I had been looking for. My family was saying "It's time for you to get married." My future wife should be someone like this: well behaved, respectable, decent in a womanly way. What's more, no one would ask about the education level of the husband of a lady such as Gülnar. I'd make it! "If this is the realm, I'm the king…" I knew I would somehow make it one day.

Soon, I told Gülnar about my intentions. For a long time, she resisted. But in the end, she yielded to love or to an emotion she assumed as love. They would remain engaged for two years, until the boy returned from his military service. During that time, she could prepare her trousseau. The families were neighbors anyway. What's difficult in that? Of course the family of the girl would play hard to get. The family of the boy should lay down the line! But the girl deserves everything! Despite the fact that many people said "this bodes no well," they got engaged. The time flowed like water. The girl's brother returned from his military service and began to work. Well, it was time for the wedding celebrations.

Şakir was troubled. He was bored of this love. He no longer wished to remain in that small town. Many of his friends had married girls in families who worked in Germany and passed their vacations in Turkey, and were on their way to Europe. He was irritated with himself "Why did I not think about this sooner?" What do those young men have that he didn't have? It would be good to find a girl to marry from among those who worked in Germany. He didn't care whether she might be a virgin or a widow. He wondered if he should advertise somewhere. And this Gülnar… Why was she rushing to get her bridal gown, anyway? No, no. Before the bridal gown, the engagement should be broken. It was more important to find a woman from Germany. But where, and how?

While he was thinking like this, luck came to his doorstep. A family working in Germany had a road accident, and stopped in front of the repair shop where he worked. They had got over the accident with minor scratches. "We can fix the body, don't worry…" he said. "No one does this job better than Şakir." The owner of the van was pleased. "Get outside," he called to his family, "We'll stay here, at a hotel, for a couple of days. I can't go to the village with a smashed up car."

Şakir fixed the car with all the skill that he could muster. He also became friends with the rich client from Germany. The client had five daughters. The numbers two and three had many suitors but since no one was after the elder sister; the younger girls could not be married off as well. The elder girl was a little hard to control. She had had two abortions, but she was beautiful and willing to get married. Upon hearing these things, Şakir had a quick tryst with the girl and proposed to her in a hurry. The girl did not say "no." "It could work if you come to Germany," she said. Good God! What he had was even greater than his dreams. How could he not accept? "My family will come to your hotel this evening," he said, "to ask for your hand."

But first, he had to break it off with Gülnar. What if Gülnar were to now insist: I gave my virginity to you. I will not break it off! Well, his fears did not materialize. Gülnar was a girl of dignity. "If we cannot have a wedding celebration first, we can go for a honeymoon of a couple of days after the registration of the wedding," she said. But when she saw that he wasn't agreeing to anything, she took off her ring and placed it in his palm. "Goodbye! While I'm the inn-keeper and you are the traveler, it's sure that we'll meet again," she said. "Too bad! You were not worthy of me."

Şakir was free. Within a week, he got married to the girl who would be taking him to Germany. Now he was one of those in Germany! Even his way of striking his lighter had changed. "There is a lot of work," his father-in-law had said. "We can get you settled somewhere right away. Well, you can't expect better than that..." Everything had taken place suddenly. Within a week, he had left the town, as the groom of the family from Germany. His mother had understood what was going on. "I am not going to smell a rose after Gülnar," she had said. "I will not let that girl from Germany kiss my hand." He didn't care. If his mother didn't want to let her hand be kissed, that was her problem. The girl was not crazy about the mother-in-law either! His parents had not even attended the marriage registration. He had not set eyes on Gülnar after she took off the engagement ring.

He wondered what she was doing... She had not even uttered a reproach. An empty sentence. She had settled her glance, heavy as lead, on him and said "you were not worthy of me, after all." Had she not cried at all? Was she not disappointed? Who cared? Why did he want to know these things? He now had a passport. His dreams were coming true.

The gates of Europe were opening up before him. The woman sleeping beside him would take him into another world. When he put his hands in his pockets, he would always find money there. He was tired of the thriftiness of his former fiancée, who always tried to save pennies. He wanted to spend without counting. He wondered what kind of work his father-in-law might find for him. The man had lots of money. There! He was not educated either, but he had obviously made it. "You can take a plane to Germany," he had said. "We should not be too crowded in the van." Great guy! He was getting a plane ticket for his daughter's groom. "You should have a decent suitcase. Get decent clothes as well. In Germany, we have friends. You can tell everyone you fell in love with my daughter. You can say it was love that struck like lightning that led to a marriage as fast as lightning."

Actually, why had his wife accepted to marry him? He stroked his beard. I'm handsome! I'm also understanding, experienced... So many babes passed through my arms! I know how to handle women. But Gülnar... Gülnar was different. Her only fault was not having money. She was saying "We can earn money if we work hand-in-hand." But when? I want it now! While I'm alive. Is that too much to ask for? Why should I not have a sports car? My father-in-law said "that's easy. It costs about sixty thousand euro. We can get you one in a year." If he had married Gülnar, he would not see sixty thousand euro in sixty years. What colour should his car be? The roads in Germany are said to be good. I would press on the gas and drive at 200 or 240 km. an hour. Almost like an air plane. Hey mother! Take a look at Şakir! I should make an effort to remember my wife's name. What a weird name: Methiye. I can't get my tongue around it. Anyway, the Germans call her as 'Medi'. Maybe they should call her *kedi*(*).

Medi's boyfriends have been Germans. She also mentioned an Italian – that's also an infidel. She had said "This is the first time that I make love with a circumcised man." I told her "this is the first time you are being national..." What kind of a woman is that? She talks about her love without any embarrassment, as if I were not her husband. There is something strange here, but... I did not marry her because I was in love

(*) Cat in Turkish.

with her dark eyes. Once in Germany, I can get rid of her at an appropriate moment. But what if she gets rid of me first? What if she continues to meet her former boyfriends? At their village, her uncle had taken him aside to warn him "Look, my step-brother is a no good son of a .... Don't believe anything he says! His daughter has taken after him. They figure they cleared her honour by getting her to marry you. This girl has slept with everyone in this village. This year, the folks here were not going to let this family into this village. There are 45 houses in this village. One or two people in each house works in foreign countries. But not a single one among them, as bad as my step-brother. I'm telling you these things before it's too late. Don't go to Germany with them! It won't be good for you. That father-in-law you got for yourself sells his daughters. He wants to open a brothel. Your wife would work inside, while you give out tickets outside. They're into everything dirty like drugs and gambling. Who knows what dirty job he'll find for you. You should return to your town and get rid of this dirt. Once you fall into the hands of the German police, your life will be destroyed. It's not shameful to be poor. Listen to me. Don't go with them. You'll be miserable."

In the jail cell where he has spent eight years, Şakir frequently thought about these things, as the date of his release approached. The dream of Germany. That wealthy, generous father-in-law. The back streets of Hamburg, that port city. First, working at selling women at St. Pauli. Then as bouncer at bars and discos, and the last stop: drugs. His father-in-law had said "If you want a car worth sixty thousand euro, it's not enough for you to sell African women. If you attempt to sell white women, you'll find you don't have what it takes. You are new at this job. The best is to sell drugs. You don't have a record. You are married, with your wife. The police won't suspect you. It's a short distance. You'll pick it up here and deliver it there..." He had not thought much. He had started with ten grams, twenty grams, and after getting a taste of money, he had increased the amounts. When he got caught, he was carrying two and a half kilos of drugs. After that, his wife, his father-in-law and the entire family had disappeared from view. Only a lawyer had appeared, for the divorce. The marriage had ended soon after that. Germany is nothing more for him! A marriage of eight months. Running around like a dog. Experienced unbelievable troubles... And prison as the last stop.

The last stop… Was it really? What now? They would send him back to Turkey in three weeks. Almost forty-years-old, with a criminal record, and penniless. Plus the diseases he had acquired in prison. Where will I go? Gülnar has not answered any of my letters. My parents have never mentioned her.

He had asked people about her, but no one had given him any information. Oh, Gülnar, where are you? I am not worthy of you! You knew the truth. Why does no one speak about her? How I miss our neighborhood. The Samsun brand cigarettes from the corner grocery store… Lunches of bread and cheese. In summer, a tomato with it, and half a water melon… Ice cold water from the village fountain. You pour a bucketful down your head. Oh. The world is beautiful. What job am I going to find now? My father is ill and cannot work. It's my sister who is looking after my parents. My mother can no longer do cleaning for others. My poor mother… I've become rusty here. I wonder if my former boss would take me back. My hands have not touched car repairs and body work in nine years… It won't be easy to work for him at this age, anyway. That, if only I can find work. I have a criminal record now. I cannot even work as a bouncer anymore – I'm too old.

He got up, lit a cigarette, and blew the smoke towards the small, high, barred window of the cell. The window was open. The smoke rose in circles, and found its way towards the light and towards freedom. He followed the smoke with his eyes. How many thousands of times had he longed for freedom that the smoke had found? Cigarette smoke, rising slowly towards the window had become a symbol of freedom for him. He lay down on his cot, and began to hum an old village ballad.

Everywhere is covered by smoke
I wish to be your smoke
Your apple cheeks, cheery lips…
I wish to be admired by them, sacrificed for them…

A Turkish prisoner who was released five years ago had left his string instrument to him. "Here, my ram, this is best learned in prison. Don't be afraid, strum it. It's better than many unfaithful lovers," he had said. He was right. The instrument had become a faithful friend. He played and sang the ballads that he knew, invented new ballads in prison. But he had promised. When he was being released, he would leave the instrument to another Turkish prisoner. In Turkey, God help him, he would find something. He stood up and pulled out a cardboard box from under the bed. A whole bunch of letters – written but not sent. All of them written to Gülnar. All the pain and the poetry that was poured out into the ballads. Some old newspapers. They should be thrown away. Some pots and pans, some odds and ends to be given to a poor prisoner. What am I going to wear on my way out? They had taken away his clothes when he come inside. They would probably give them back. I would throw away the tie. If only I can button up the jacket and do up the zipper of the pants, no problem. He had worked in the workshop of the prison for many years, for one euro an hour, and had met his needs with that money. He had even saved a little. He must have spent most of his money on cigarettes. Half a day's work for a package of cigarettes... I wonder where that bastard of father-in-law might be. If I were to go to his village, I could trace him. So what? What next? Go shoot the man. Two bullets more for his daughter. Then? Get back inside, saying, "I've grown used to life in prison." No, I don't want that. May they become poles in hell, far away from me. I want my freedom.

It's too late to get married and have a family. Who would marry a man like me? But in freedom, I would want a woman... Well, we'll see. They say a blind seller will always find a blind buyer. Turkey is now full of Russian girls. The newspapers are all telling stories about those Natashas. Come on Şakir! You have not learned to run after silly dreams. Natasha, huh? Why don't you dream about Germany? Was it you who wanted a sports car for sixty thousand euro? Where was I when God was giving out intelligence to everyone?

Two German police officers handed him over to the Turkish police officers at the airport, without even untying his hands. Time seemed to have stopped. The paperwork did not take long. "You may leave", they said. Once the handcuffs were off, he offered police officers cigarettes from the package he had bought at the prison.

"Keep them. You'll smoke on the way."

"Never mind. I'll smoke Samsun. I've missed Turkish tobacco."

He went outside. He had forgotten how to walk in the streets, how to move his hands and arms. He was dizzy with the fresh air he inhaled into his lungs. It was as if he were walking on a soft surface instead of on the asphalt ground. His knees were shaking. Am I sick? No, just excited. I wish I had written to my mother to let her know the exact date when I would be arriving. She would have cooked dried beans and rice. How I miss that dish. Well, I should reach the bus station soon. The bus will stop somewhere for sure. I can find such dishes at roadside restaurants. Once I settle into the bus seat... I'll sleep for at least three hours. I have spent the last week almost entirely without sleep. I should get a ticket for a set in the front of the bus. I should be able to see the road when I'm not sleeping. I should see freedom. Perhaps on the way I'll meet someone I know. This is Turkey! I've even missed Kirpik Ali with whom I never got along. He would sniffle all the time. He doesn't take a bath very often so he smells. But that's O.K. I could embrace even him. How he used to cheat me at a game of billiards... I wonder what he is doing now. He never dreamt of getting rich. "A modest job would be enough for me," he used to say.

The bus was passing by the sea. The evening sun was hanging on the sky like a crimson tray. The water was still and glittering. Gulls bathing in the water and in the dying light of day. He felt like running to the sea. It would be cold at this time of year. In March, the sea would be too cold to swim, even in Antalya! Now, the surroundings were beginning to look familiar. About half an hour left to his town. How the place has changed... Large concrete blocks even in villages. Has Turkey got richer? I have two thousand and five hundred euro. It should be enough until I get a job. I should buy myself a suit and a pair of jeans. Absolutely essential. I should find myself a love. I've grown used to the string instrument – I can't do without it now. If you love something you should not leave it. I left Gülnar, and lost her. I will not leave my string instrument. I used to be a cruel, pitiless person. Even as a child, I used to throw stones at cats and dogs. Just to be cruel. I had blinded Gülnar's cat. She had cried. I made that poor girl cry a lot.

It's getting dark. That's better. I wouldn't want to pass through the neighborhood in daylight. "Yes, gentlemen. This is the last stop!."

He got up, picked up his handbag and entered the darkness. He wanted to embrace the familiar trees, streets, street lamps and walls. He wanted to kiss the cobble-stoned roads of the town. He began to whistle a tune. He felt good. He was getting used to walking, being free. He turned the last corner. Good God! Gülnar's family's house should have been there. What is this big apartment block doing here? The little corner grocery store has become a supermarket. A hamburger place has replaced the seller of meatballs. The coffee shop where my father used to go has become a gaming parlour. What's that? A disco across from our house! Is this Hamburg, or what? Let's see what has become of the car repair shop where I used to work... What? Lights are blinking. There's the sound of music. A night-club. Nightclub. Mondschein! That's German. All the stores have named in German or in English. Here we are. I'm at home.

"Mother, open up! It's Şakir..."

He heard slow footsteps. He mother was coming. She opened the door, embraced her son. Squeezed him on her breast. She cried, stroked his face. Then she led him into a room. His father was playing a card game with a small boy. He coughed for a long time, then he asked as though he were calling from two streets away. "Have you arrived? Come and sit down. We were expecting you. Your mother has cooked dried beans. She kept saying 'I sense that my son is coming today.'

"Who is this young man? My sister's son?"

The old man did not answer. He stroked the little boy's head.

"Haven't I told you that you have a dad? Go, embrace him!"

"Dad, who is this child?"

"Stop asking. Embrace the boy. You should know when you placed him inside his mother's womb."

"Gülnar... Was Gülnar pregnant? She never told me!"

"Dad. I've waited a long time for you. Can we go fishing together? Can we ride bikes together?"

"Of course. But where is your mother?"

The child looked up towards the sky.

"The angels have taken her," he said. "I can not see her, but she can see us."

His hands began to shake. He kneeled down to embrace the child. "Oh, Germany," he moaned...

Leyla Reis Öztekin / Holland

She was born in Maçka Köprüyanı Village, Trabzon in 1967. She received her primary and second education in Maçka and went to Holland in 1980. After she received the hairdresser training she worked here as a hairdresser. She has one novel which is soon to be completed. She lives in Roosendal. She is married and has two kids.

If Somebody Hurts Him A Little Bit...

It had been two years since they moved to the house numbered 22 in the street named Frans Halslaan, in Westrand district of the west Roosendaal. Both the mother and the father worked although it was a bit difficult for the children. They had to stand out against all the difficulties because of the mortgage on their house and to be able to achieve the life style they dreamed of. Their son was a plump, eight year old child whose blue eyes shone intelligently. His four year old sister was a quiet, clever child with sparkles in her brown eyes. Their father was a worker in a company and their mother worked under a farmer at the first presentation stage of products to the society.

Aysel hadn't been sent to the secondary school after primary school as her parents didn't find it necesary. Her husband Hasan was more educated than his wife, but he was far away from improving himself in many aspects. He was the kind of person who regarded the deficiencies resulting from the immaturity of his character as necessity of manhood, who believed that women were inferior to men just because of their gender, and who used this attitude as a way of proving and expressing his personality.

Ayşe worked in the farms on the basis of a system, in which working hours changed according to the product type. Sometimes she started to work very early in the morning, and worked until late in the evening. Hasan worked in four shifts. And this was a suitable way to be able to take care of the children.

After they moved to Frans Halslaan, the neighboring house was put up for sale. In this street where the row houses side by side; only a wall separated them from each other. Soon the neighboring house found its new owners. Ayşe and Hasan didn't feel the anxiety most people felt in Roosendaal, they didn't get upset as Turks were moving to the house next-door. Their new neigbours were the people they knew before. Both sides were delighted at this event in terms of helping each other.

Frans Halslaan was a street invaded by the people searching for a free place to park their cars while going to Roosendaal center. Sometimes even those living in the street couldn't find a place to park their cars. When the complaints of the community dwellers forced the municipality to handle the issue; letters were forwarded to people living around and it was announced that the right and left sides of the road would be turned into paid parking places. The community dwellers would obtain a parking card, paying a certain amount of fee annually. The protest of the people didn't deter the municipality from taking this decision. While the people kept their anger inside; the decision had already started to be implemented. This new rule prevented other people from parking here but it also restricted freedom of the people living in the street. This place was also put under the control of traffic officers like other paid parking lots and the problems started to occur.

It was mid February, a very special period for Muslims who wanted to fulfill their religious duties. It was Ramadan and devout people gave importance to fasting and living in the suitable way.

When Hasan returned home, it was ten fifteen in the evening. He left the work bag in the living room and ordered his wife to prepare a coffee for him. "Welcome" said Ayşe but she was not quite sure if her husband heard him. Some time later she came inside with the cup of coffee her husband desired and found him on the armchair in an a half lying and half sitting position. She left the coffee on the coffee table by his armchair and she herself perched on the edge of the bucket seat opposite him. Hasan, strengthening himself up, sipped his coffee. Putting it back on the table, he took a cigarette from the package he had thrown on the table a few minutes ago and took it to his lips. He searched his pockets trying to find the lighter. He was tired and nervous. "Where's this fucking lighter!" he growled. Ayşe silently got out of her place, went to the kitchen and came back with a lighter in her hand, reached it out to her husband in silence. Hasan, lighting his cigarette, didn't show any reaction. He lighted his cigarette, inhaled the smoke and blew it out of his nostrils and then started talking:

– Did children sleep?

– I could just put them to sleep.

– Will you work tomorrow?

– Yes, we will start working at six o'clock in the morning; don't you work?

– No. Don't you think I deserved a holiday after working for ten days without a rest?

– I didn't mean it; I meant it for the children. So you can take me to the work in the morning and don't ever forget to make weekly food shopping! Now I'm very tired, I'm going to sleep.

After his wife left the room, Hasan turned on the television and was immediately engrossed in a discussion talk. The cigarettes he smoked had polluted the air and smoke had fulfilled the room. He hadn't changed his half-sitting, half-lying position throughout the program and had never got out of his place. It was just after the midnight when he got strengthened up and turned off the television as the program was over.

At five in the morning Ayşe was busy with preparing the sahur(1) meal. Hasan, unwillingly, got up from the bed upon insistence of his wife. "Hurry up or I'll be late for work!" said Hatice over and over.

Hasan started the car. The streets were dark and quiet…

– Slow down by the street lamps ahead. Ayfer said she would be there; we will pick her up, said Ayşe.

– Why doesn't she go on her own, in her own car?

– Her car didn't work yesterday or something like that.

– You say she needs us! She has never asked to pick you up so far!

– Never mind. We should be kind anyway.

They eventually picked Ayfer up. Hasan dropped his wife off to work and came back home. He lighted his last cigarette quickly taking advantage of the last minutes of sahur. The children were still sleeping. With the relief of this thought he lied on the bed with his clothes on to have a nap. It wasn't even an hour before his daughter came and woke him up by touching various points of his body.

– Don't do that, Elif.

– I want to go downstairs dad.

– So, you can go downstairs honey; I'm sleeping!

---

(1) The meal eaten before fasting in Ramadan.

– Can I watch television?

– Of course you can, if you like.

After Elif left, Hasan fell into sleep again. When the child came back, he thought she had never left him.

– Dad, I'm hungry, said the child, tugging at his dad's arm.

This time he scolded her as he was still asleep.

– Didn't you go to watch television?

– I watched dad, said the child in her most petted manner.

Hasan sat up in his bed. What time is it, he thought. It was forty six past seven. Making a sour face he said:

– Ugh, my daughter. Why did you wake your dad up?

He got out of the bed with an apparent displeasure, and went down to the kitchen with his daughter. He prepared sandwich for her and put it on the table in the living room.

– Now, eat your sandwich calmly and quietly and don't ever come to wake dad up! he said; hoping that if he accentuated every word, it would be effective.

He went back to his bed. As he pulled the blanket over himself, he felt the imaginary pleasure of sleeping for another hour.

When Hasan woke up with the terrible clamor of the children it was still very early for him. Besides the stress caused by deprival from sleep, he was aware of the fact that he wouldn't be able to drink the cup of coffee he drank every morning. He thought it would be good to take a shower to facilitate awakening. When he got out of the bathroom the children were still struggling with each other. Quickly did he wear his clothes on, and hastily went to the living room.

– What's going on, he asked looking at his older child.

– Elif kicks up a row... I waited until her film was over. Now it's my turn. But she won't let me watch, said his son.

– My son, you're older. You must look after your sister, how many times I've told you not to make noise while dad was sleeping.

– You're always on her side, she was the one who disturbed you and who woke you up!

– You are required to take care of her. She is so young and it's beyond her ken. You are almost a young man.

– I don't care, said the child in his same tearful voice. You always listen to her! And he left the room running.

Hasan couldn't behave his daughter in the same rough manner as he treated his wife. This little girl managed to lead his dad in her own magical way she used to have anything she desired. With her petted manners and little girl speech, this little girl achieved to make his father draw in his horns. His father moved closer to her; trying to be serious he said:

– You'll watch television by turns. If you only watch the movies you like, then it's not fair. Now call your brother. It's his turn.

Elif's eyes were soon filled with tears. She threw herself into the armchair face down. Trying to be determined, her father repeated:

– Come on, just turn the television off.

Upon this the little girl started to cry loudly. Her father came closer and threw her up in his arms; the girl laughed and at the same time kicked his dad.

– What a shame honey! Now I'll let you go and you'll turn the television off, all right? Look we'll also go shopping soon. If you don't listen, I won't buy you the chocolate you like!

He set the child down. The little girl had probably understood what her father meant; she turned the television off and went upstairs running. Hasan took a deep breath, confident that the child would behave in the way he wanted.

They left the house around eleven o'clock. After walking over the pavements, they got into the car parked in its usual place, across their house. The children sat on the back seat. It was clear that their lack of the fastening seat belt habit had its roots in their father's behaviors.

Hasan had three destinations for weekly shopping. Firstly they went to the supermarket as usual, then they went to Muslim butcher to buy halal(2) meat and lastly they went to the bazaar set up on Saturdays to buy fruits and vegetables. Going to all these places and doing so much work were very tiring and time consuming. Hasan was really tired as he

---

(2) Religiously acceptable for Muslims.

was fasting and he had a strong desire to do shopping leisurely. So that he could easily kill time.

It was about mid afternoon when they came back from shopping. Hasan got nervous as he couldn't park his car in the same place. So he parked it on the pavement in front of his house as it would be difficult to carry the shopping bags. He helped the children get out of the car and then opened the baggage; took some of the shopping bags and headed for the house door. He especially wanted his daughter to get into the house at once as the street was really busy that day. He left the shopping bags in the kitchen; turned the television on for her daughter and took his son back to the car to help him with the bags. The father and the son were carrying the shopping bags to the house without hurry. By the time they got the last shopping bag out of the car and took it into the house; the phone rang. It was husband of Aysel, whom they had picked up by car. He said he would go to pick the ladies up by car in the afternoon and this pleased Hasan. As he got out of the house to take his car to the garage, he saw a scene which made his blood boil. Two parking officials were busy with writing a parking penalty notice. He got there in no time flat.

– God damn you! Don't I have the right to get my shopping bags out of my car!

He shouted.

The woman officer talked in a voice reflecting her dissatisfaction.

– It's forbidden to park the cars on the pavement! She said.

– Forbidden!? Piss off! Don't you have more important things to do?

While these words came out of his lips he also managed to pull the notice out of the woman's hand. He tore it into pieces and threw away. The other officer who wanted to interfere pushed Hasan back. Hasan who now spit feathers didn't fail to push the official back and things stirred up. The woman held the officer on the arm not to let him fall down and she scolded Hasan saying:

– It's a matter of our duty to implement the rules; if you have a problem you can make complaints to our institution!

– You, stupid bitch! said Hasan. You're all the same. To whom will I compain and about whom?

Stepping back, the woman attempted to write notice again but she couldn't succeed because of Hasan. The male officer came between his colleague and Hasan. The situation could not be worse. Hasan understood that they had no intention of leaving the place, he headed for his car and then came up to them with the stick he had taken from the baggage. The officials had to step back a little. While one of them tried to keep Hasan under control, the other one called the police.

The door of Hasan's house was wide open. His son sitting in the kitchen had realized the voice of his father among all other angry voices; he was standing at the doorstep; watching them with his eyes wide open and trying to fight against his fast –beating heart. Five minutes after the woman's phone talk, at both ends of the street two police cars appeared. Two angry police got out of each car. Another police car was also seen aproaching. While two polices from the first car blockaded Hasan; the other two went to talk with the control officers. One of the police by the car shouted:

– Put the stick on the ground!

Hasan, who already had a chip on his shoulder, was taken by surprise because of the police cars filling the street and was gradually getting angrier.

– Why did you also come running as if two bastards hadn't been enough?, he roared.

He wasn't aware that in the meanwhile the police getting out of the third car were silently getting closer to him behind his back. At the doorstep a couple of blue eyes were moving to the right and left in panic and his heart ached with great pain.

Hasan realized that two strong arms were trying to handcuff him behind and tried to get rid of them. But in a few seconds two more arms were added to them. Hasan tried to fight back with all his strentgh. Another police joined them and they didn't abstain from using force on Hasan. His arms were clasped behind and handcuffed in a position preventing him from moving, but he anyway tried to kick them.

The blue eyes were watching the event in great despair; and his father's desperate situation wrenched the little boy's heart so much that he ran out of his place and flew out at the police ahead. This beautiful child also had his share of the police's anger. He was pushed by one of the police and fell down on the floor on his bottom. In the meanwhile his father was tucked into the police car by force.

A Turkish man who was passing by in his car stopped there as he knew the person being forced into the police car. His six year old son was at the back seat of the car.

– Hey stop! What are you doing? He shouted at the police, pulling down the car window.

The police's answer was not kind:

– It's none of your business!

– I know him sir. Could you please explain what's going on here?

– I told you it's none of your business. Or do you want to be tucked in the car like him? Now shove off!

He was also wagging his fingers. The poor man was scared of this arrogant manner. While he had many questions inside; the responsibility of his child at the back seat overweighted. He stepped on the gas and slowly moved the car.

Another person who watched these last minutes of terror was the Turkish mother at the neighboring house. She was so shocked by the scene that she could only let out her breath when the cars left the street. She went out to the street from the doorstep where she stood and tried to catch sight of the blue eyes still staring dull at the empty street. The deep grief in these eyes made the old woman moved. Trying to cheer the small child up, she took him inside to his sister.

After Ali moved his car, he desperately tried to find a solution. And he headed for the house of Hasan's sister living in the same district. So he knocked at the door of Nazan who had taught his son Turkish. Ali's child hadn't been able to speak Turkish as he was married to a Dutch woman. He had asked Nazan to teach his son Turkish and she had accepted. They had some kind of friendship in this regard.

– Hello Mr. Ali, please come in.

– I can't, because the child is waiting for me in the car. As I was passing by your brother's house, I saw the police taking him by force.

– What are you saying Mr. Ali? Why?

– I also couldn't understand, I wanted to help him but they threatened me. I didn't know what to do. And then I decided to inform you.

– Thank you very much. You've really been of great help by coming here and informing me.

She took her bicyle from the storehouse and started to cycle with all her strentgh. She was immersed in deep thoughts; many different scenarios passed through her mind until she came to the door of her brother's house. She, with her hard beating heart, rang the bell of the door numbered twenty two. But noone answered the door. She rang the bell again and again. Sure that there was noone inside she came to ring the bell of their Turkish neighbors' house. Soon the door was opened by the aunty.

– Welcome, my girl. I'm glad that you came. I really didn't know what to do.

– What's going on, my dear aunty. Where are the children? Where's their mum?

– They are here and their mother is at work, my girl.

They went into the living room where the children were sitting in silence. The young woman immediately ran up to the older child and caressed his hair. The hope glimmer in his blue eyes didn't slip his aunt's notice. She bent over and kissed him and then she took the little one on her lap.

– What happened here honey?

When his eyes met with his aunt's, he couldn't choke back his tears, clenching his fists, he said:

– Those bad police took my dad!

– I know my dear, don't worry. Your aunt will go and talk to the police and your dad will be home at this evening.

– Ih, my girl! I was cut to the heart as those monsters dragged him into the car by force. How I wish my son were at home. If only I knew how to phone them I'd call all of my sons. Then the police would see if they could take him so easily. His desperate situation touched my heart so deeply. But anyway he struggled against them, he let fly at them any curse you could think of! What about leaving these children there all alone and unprotected? They even pushed back this very small child. They left the door of the house open and shoved off ignoring these children. This poor child saw the entire event. If only you saw how he floundered to help his dad! You wouldn't have been able to bear it. What would happen to them if I weren't there?

– You're right, my dear aunty. May god be pleased with you. Now, I'll go to the police office and demand an explanation.

After trying to relax the children with her kisses, she went out of the house still feeling the eyes on herself; eyes which couldn't realize what was going on and had put all their hope in her. She took her bicycle again. Nazan was shaking when she came in front of the police office in Nieuw Street. She took a deep breath in front of the door and walked inside. It was unpleasantly crowded. She walked to the counseling trying to stay calm, she told them the event and said that she wanted to see an official. Soon a woman police came through the dark glassed door.

– Ms. Nazan!

– It's me, madam.

– We don't have any suitable room so I can't take you inside, but I can talk to you here if you don't mind?

Nazan thought that was a tactic of them. Probably the officer thought she would shy away from the crown and go.

– Okey, we can talk here, she said in a calm voice.

– Your brother threatened the control officers! He stood up to the police and used brute force.

– I don't know what happened. I just want to highlight one point: my brother was taken by force; and the entire event took place before the eyes of his eight year old child. If you see the event through the eyes of an eight year old child; I think you'll understand how important it is. There was also another child at the age of four in the house and these children were left there in confusion while the door of the house was wide open. I wouldn't expect this from the police; I'd expect them to behave in a more responsible way!

– You're right, lady. I didn't know this! I apologize.

– Fortunately the neighbors were at home; otherwise what would happen to those kids?

– Your brother insulted a lot. Especially to the woman officer!

– As I said before I don't know what happened. If he behaved as you told, of course it's a shame. Generally he is not a bad-tempered person. I'm not sure if you know, but it is Ramadan now and we're fasting. My brother smokes a lot; maybe he lost his temper because of it.

– Does everybody become so furious while fasting? Said the officer with a meaningful expression on her face.

– No, it's just the opposite. In fact it's supposed to be the opposite! While fasting, we should internalize the good human being concept in all meanings and we should see its effects on our lives in the aftermath of fastening. Or else it doesn't have any meaning if we stay hungry until the evening. You see I'm also fastening but I'm quite calm. It seems my brother couldn't achieve this. When will you let him out?

– There are procedures. It depends!

– Will you please give him this phone number? It is mine. He may have forgotten it as he was quite confused. And as I've told you before, he is fastening. I hope the procedures can be completed before iftar(3) hour in the evening. I'd also like to thank you for the information you gave. I'll call you half an hour later. I hope I can get more useful information then.

– You can call any time you like, said the woman police and went behind the dark door.

Nazan persisted in calling the police every thirty minutes. She was worried about their treatment to her brother and she wanted them to see that her brother was not all alone. Upon hearing the desired response she called his brother's neighbor's house and told them the good news. In the meanwhile her brother's wife had also come to the house.

The phone rang at the house of Nazan about half an hour after iftar dinner. Nazan ran to lift the receiver. It was her brother who called. He said he was in front of their house and wanted her to come out. Nazan sneakily went out of the house, went towards the car and holding the car's door opened since his brother sat at the front seat.

– Hello, brother.

– Hello, Nazan.

---

(3) Fasting breaking dinner in Ramadan.

They looked at each other for a while; there was a short silence.

– I could never imagine you'd do such things for me, as you did today!

– You would do the same thing for me if you were in my place, said Nazan looking in her brother's eyes.

– No... I wouldn't!

Tears run into Hasan's eyes and how hard he tried he couldn't prevent some tears from falling down his cheeks.

– I believe that you'd do the same thing for me!, said Nazan emphasizing the words.

– You are my brother. The same blood runs through our veins! I'll never let anyone hurt you. That's right, we don't see each other. But for me it doesn't mean that our bonds of love will be overcome with it.

– Thank you for everything you've done. And also for distracting the police by calling again and again. They told me I was very lucky to have a sister like you!

Nazan smiled. She was glad that her plan had succeeded.

– I didn't tell Ali to go and ask you for help! said Hasan in his old rough manner.

– As a matter of fact Ali didn't tell me anything like that.

– I just wanted you to make you sure!

Nazan didn't like his behavior, just to change the issue she asked:

– Will you tell me what happened today?

– You know the event in front of the house, anyway it wasn't easy to take me, I let fly at them all the curses.

– They say you talked very offensive!

– They deserved it!

– I wish none of these had happened. It is not nice, especially while fastening.

Nazan said these words with great care and quite calmly.

– Yes but they drove me crazy! Anyway we managed to settle the matter with one thousand euro.

– What a pity, said Nazan, thoughtfully.

– Otherwise I'd have to face court. The event would be registered. I accepted it for the sake of my clean registry.

– You did the right thing, said Nazan, watching a woman passing by the street.

– Today after this event I thought that...

Hasan didn't complete the sentence; his voice was very sensitive.

– We can see each other! We didn't experience anything to be regarded as resentment!

– You know brother... You can visit me whenever you want and it will be so forever! You can knock on my door anytime you like...

– What about dad?

– He also wants to see you; although he won't leave his pride aside and admit it, I'm sure he wants!

– I'll come and he will make a face again. Can you be sure that he won't sulk?

– Look, brother... For many years I've been torn between you two and I don't want to bear it anymore! He is your dad and you have to handle your problems with him by yourself! You also experienced fatherhood. You two, father and son, should solve your own problems like two adults.

– I'll come but I just can not be sure.

– He is your dad; you'll see he'll be happy.

Saying these word Nazan opened the door of the car.

– Give your wife and the children my best regards and wishes. I'll wait for you! she said

Hasan waved at his sister as she was moving the car, and Nazan also waved at him in deep feelings until the car disappeared in the street.

APPENDICES

JURY

Prof. Dr. Şükrü Haluk AKALIN
President of Turkish Language Agency

He was born in 1956 in Adana. He was graduated from Istanbul University Faculty of Litrature, Turkish Language and Literature Department in 1979. He was assigned as an assistant professor to Çukurova University, Science and Literature Faculty, Turkish Language and Literature Department; he was assigned as an associated professor in New Turkish Language Dicipline in 1990. In 1995, he was appointed for the Science Comission of Turkish Language Council. In 1996, he was promoted to professorship. He was assigned as the President of Turkish Language Agency by the ordinance declared in Official Gazette in April 15, 2001.

Conserning the effects of foreign languages on Turkish and spreading of foreign words especially in the field of informatic technologies; he performed studies on translation of computer terms into Turkish and, developing and spreading Turkish contexts on internet. In February 1997, he created the website, Türkoloji Dünyası (World of Turcology) in Novemer 1998, and further he formed the Turcology Communication Group. In 1999, he started to publish the Journal of Virtual Turcology Researches which is the first example in internet. Besides, he has 10 books and 112 articles and papers on the field of Turkish language.

Being employed in Hacettepe University, he is also performing the Presidency of Turkish Language Agency.

Lütfiye AYDIN
Author

She was born in 1949 in Gaziantep. She completed her primary and secondary education in Gaziantep. She graduated from Izmir Buca Education Institute Turkish Department in 1972. She worked as a Turkish Language and Literature teacher until 1982. In 1982, she took office in the Center of Education Through Film Radio and Television, which was organized under Ministry of National Education. While writing screenplays for the educational films, she also started to right stories here.

In 1985, she went to Germany for the tranlation of her first book *İkili Yalnızlık (Double Loneliness).* She participated in the tranlation studies in Essen University Turcology Department. She wrote more than 20 drama programmes for TRT Ankara Radio. She wrote documentaries and many radio plays. She was retired from Ministry of National Education FRTEM, where she had worked as a dramaturgist, in 2000. She is still living in Ankara.

Works:

İkili Yalnızlık (Story, 1985)
Cemre (Story, 1991)
Sengin Semai Bir Ölüm (Story, 1992)
Ölüm Erken Bir Akşamdır (Story, 1993)
Kül Tablet (Narrative, 1997)
Tsunami (1998, Story Award of Ministry of Culture).
Gri Gül (Story, 2005 Rıfat Ilgaz Story Award)

Some of the Radio Serials Written by Her:

Bin Yıllık Beste (Life of tamboura artist Mr. Cemil)
Gizli Bir Kadın Ozan (Life of Nezihe Yaşar Bükülmez who was the first Turkish women worker poet according to Asım Bezirci)
Güneşin Çocukları (A scene from the defence of Gaziantep. Awarded the First Rank in the Competition of TRT Radio Serials)
Ah O Yemen'dir (Withdrawal of Ottomans from Yemen)

Ass. Prof. Dr. Fahri TEMİZYÜREK

Deputy Chairman of Gazi Education Faculty Turkish Education Department

He was born in 1965 in Kayseri. He completed his primary, secondary and high school education in Ankara. He was graduated from Hacettepe University Literature Faculty Turkish Language and Literature Department in 1988. In 1994, he completed his post graduate by his study named "State Policies Developed About Education of Turkish during the Period of Atatürk"; in 1999, he completed his doctorate by his study named "Selim Sabit Efendi and His Role in the New Method Movement".

He took charge in the establishment of Kabil University Language and Literature Faculty Turkish department in 2003; and Gagauz Auronomous Region Komrat University Turcology Department in 2004. He worked in Kişinev State University Turkish – English Translation Department; he made researches in Macedonia within the scope of Turkish Education in the Balkans. He studied for renewal of the programme of Tiran University Philology Faculty Turcology Department together with Prof. Dr. Ramazan Kaplan. He is still working as the Depute Head of Gazi University Education Faculty Turkish Education Department.

Kemal ATEŞ
Author

He was born in Kaman in Kırşehir in 1947. He completed Ankara Atatürk High School. He was graduated from Ankara University Faculty of Language History and Geography, Department of Turkish Philology in 1970. In the same department he had a master's degree on "Tendency towards local language in Turkish Literature". He had Doctor's degree in Ankara University in the department of Turkish Language Education.

His articles were published in the journals *Varlık, Türk Dili, Yansıma, Hürriyet Gösteri, E, Virgül, Öğretmen Dünyası;* and the newspapers *Milliyet* ve *Cumhuriyet*. In the literary environment he was known with his novels and short stories which depicted shantutown. He is still in charge as the head of the department of Turkish Philology.

Works:

Çürük Kapı (Short Story, 1979, Lions Jury Prize)
Toprak Kovgunları (Novel, 1991 Mehmet Ali Yalçın Novel Prize)
Yitik Kuzular (Theatre play, 1992 Sıtkı Dost Children Literature Prize, published under the name *Çıngırak* in 2000)
Geç de Olsa (Novel, 1989)
Bir Şarkıyı Dinlerken (Short story, 1995 PEN Orhan Kemal Short Story, Award of Merit)
Gülten Dayıoğlu'nun Çocuk Romanları (Research, review, 1998)
Öğretemediğimiz Türkçe (Research, review, 1999)
Küskün Fotoğraflar (Short story 2005)
Türkçem Mahzun Ben Mahzun (Assay, 2005

Pınar ŞENEL
TRT Producer

She was born in 1970 in Konya. She graduated from Hacettepe University Department of Public Administration in 1992 and Ankara University DTCF Theatre Department, Deparment of Dramatic Writing in 1996. She had her Master's degree in Theatre Department with his thesis on *Hamlet* play of W. Shakespeare with semiotics method and its comparison with cinema adaptations in 2000.

She taught the courses Drama Theory, Dramaturgi, and Semiotics in Department of Theatre in Bilkent University and Ankara University. She has been a member of International Theatre Critics Union. From 1999 on she has been working in TRT Radio, Voice of Turkey as producer. Her name was in the USA based list *The Women Making Difference (Fark Yaratan Kadınlar)* of 2006 in the *Daughters of Atatürk (Atatürk'ün Kızları)* Prizes.

Some of the Published Works:

Laleli Konak (The prize winner in TRT Radio Play Competition, 2000).

Theatre critics and interviews in the journal Theatre Theatre (1999-2001)

Articles on Ankara (Milliyet, 2004)

Adalet Ağaoğlu Tiyatrosu (Kitap-lık, 1997)

Şairin İkmal Topları (Radikal, 2001)

"Bütün Huzursuzluğumuz Bundan" - Inteview with Yücel Balku (The journal E, 2004)

Radio Programs

Posta Güvercini (an anthology of the published letters of the artists)

Pop Müziğimizden Renkler (The history of Turkish pop music)

Kanadalı Türkler (a documentary on immigration experience)

Odama Girmeyin and *Uzakta Yükselen Nesil* (Youth programs)

Sizin Öyküleriniz (Contestan stories for the Short Story Competition)

Almanya'daki Türkiye'nin Müziği (Regarding musics produced and listened by immigrant Turks in Germany)

Türk Tiyatro Tarihinden Notlar (The history of Turkish theatre)

TRT VOICE OF TURKEY
SHORT STORY COMPETITION
2006

STATISTICS

According to gender: Of the 118 participants in our contest, %56 were men and %45 were women. (65 men, 53 women).

According to age groups:

The highest participation came from the 25-35 year-olds (those born between 1970 and 1980). This group represented 25% of the participants (37 people).

The participation of those between the ages of 45 to 55 and 55 to 65, (born between 1950 and 1960 and between1940 and 1950) were in equal numbers, with 15 persons from each group. 15%

11 persons whose date of birth was between 1980 and 1990 participated, making up 9% of the total participants.

Participation of the 65 – 75 age group, whose birth dates were between 1930 and 1940 remained at 4 % with 5 people.

Themes that Were Used in the Stories

The issues faced by the Turkish immigrant community	(23)	% 28
The Loneliness of Immigrants and pains of Belonging	(18)	
The Issues faced by 3rd Generation Immigrants	(8)	
Marriage and Immigration	(10)	%13
Immigration from villages to other countries	(7)	
Educational needs, criticism of traditions, immigration	(5)	
Viewing the foreign community	(5)	% 6
Discrimination	(2)	
Marriage to a foreigner	(3)	
Longing for home	(4)	% 5
Those who are far away	(2)	
Family (return to childhood, longing for the past, inter-generational conflict.	(39)	%22
Fantastic and experimental stories	(25)	% 14
Vacation in Turkey	(2)	% 1
Texts with a moral and other genres of texts	(10)	% 6
War and terror	(8)	% 5
Refugees	(2)	% 1
	(173) story	

TRT VOICE OF TURKEY
SHORT STORY COMPETITION
2006

Distribution According to Participating Countries

	Participants	Stories
GERMANY	51	83
HOLLAND	16	21
BELGIUM	2	5
AUSTRIA	6	7
SWITZERLAND	6	6
CANADA	7	9
USA	5	5
AUSTRALIA	7	8
JAPAN	1	1
ENGLAND	4	7
FRANCE	5	8
ISRAEL	2	3
DENMARK	1	3
IRAN	1	1
VIETNAM	1	1
UNITED ARAB EMIRATES	1	1
TURKISH REPUBLIC OF NORTHERN CYPRUS (TRNC)	1	3
RUSSIA	1	1
	118	**173**

70 YEARS in EXTERNAL BROADCASTING

1937-2007

TRT